ANDREW COMEAU

MySQL
EXPLAINED

Your step-by-step guide
to database design

OSTraining

(Notes)

(Notes)

Table of Contents

Introduction

If you're looking at this book then you've probably been faced with the challenge of managing or storing a collection of data and need to know how to do it with MySQL, the open source database software from Oracle. Maybe you're designing a new web application and need to learn how to use MySQL to store its data. An understanding of how to organize data is essential to anyone who needs to understand how software works or design a new application.

It actually might surprise you to know that the people who understand database principles and use them regularly such as database administrators, software programmers and developers make up less than 2% of the U.S. population and a similar percentage worldwide. I decided to write this book in order to help bring this information to the other 98% and to help people such as yourself get a better handle on the valuable data you need to store.

While there are many database software titles available, this book focuses on MySQL to demonstrate the principles you need. Much of the information that you learn here is applicable to other database software and it's a great idea to compare different titles to get a perspective. As a introductory database, however, MySQL will enable you to gain experience with all the aspects of database operations on a system that's widely used in real life. The variety of tools available for managing your MySQL databases are user-friendly enough to make that experience a good one.

Who should read this book?

Personally, I would say *everyone* but then, I'm a little biased. Still, I've written this book with everyone in mind in hopes that it will benefit the most people. Ideally, you should read this book if you can say "Yes" to any of the following:

- *You are new to MySQL and perhaps database design in general and need to learn how to work with the tools.* MySQL is one of the most widely used database systems and a common choice for storing data behind websites and online applications. If you're involved in designing or managing a website, it's good to know how the data is moved back and forth and organized within the database.

- *You work with database designers regularly and need to do so more effectively.* Even if you never design a database yourself, knowing the principles involved goes a long way toward understanding the abilities and limitations of the software you work with. This will save you a lot of misunderstandings when asking for new reports or system enhancements.

- *You want to enhance your career and need a better understanding of software.* A promising career can start simply by being the person in the office who can produce results nobody else can. Database design is a valuable skill that will continue to be relevant for many years to come. While reading this book won't add it to your resume immediately, knowing the basics can put you in the position to volunteer for that project that will get you noticed later.

- *You work with large amounts of information on a regular basis and would like to know how to organize and understand it better.* This can be true even if you don't work in the technology field. Maybe you're an accounting professional trying to make sense of expense data or an administrative assistant putting together a database for payroll or inventory information. Regardless of your job, an understanding of how databases work will enable you to produce better results and save you work in the long-term.

- *Finally, you're an I.T. professional,* maybe even a programmer or software developer, who is still not sure of the details of database design or MySQL. Maybe you're just coming back to it after years of doing other work and need a refresher course. Having a reference by your side can be very helpful when working on your latest project.

That's still not quite everyone but it's a lot more than the 2% I mentioned above. Chances are, if you're reading this introduction, then you can benefit from the knowledge of database design you'll find in this book.

Why *this* book?

Right now, you're probably comparing this book to others on database design and trying to decide which one to buy, so what makes this one different?

First, this book is written for *you*. No matter who you are or how little experience you have with database and technology concepts, this book is written so that you will understand the ideas presented here. Clear explanations of ideas come first; technical terms and jargon, second. The multiple examples used here are based on everyday situations that the average person can relate to.

Also, while this is a book about MySQL, much of the focus here is on the overall concepts that will help you understand database design regardless of which software you're using. This book is an adaptation of my previous book, *Your First Guide to Database Design*, which covered multiple software titles. Software and programming languages come and go and new ones can be learned by experienced people in a short time. It's more important to know the concepts behind software so that when a new system comes along, you will know what to expect from it and be able to evaluate and learn it that much faster.

A final reason to select this book is for the author's experience. I have been working with databases since the 1990s when I started designing database programs for the company I was working for. Some of the examples in this book are based on actual systems I've designed, such as the Job Search Plus application. While I eventually ended up as a programmer rather than a database administrator, I have maintained a special focus on database design and it's a part of software development that I enjoy. Now, with the renewed interest I'm seeing in the field of software design, I've decided to share my experience with you through this book.

Chapter Guide

This book is written as a tutorial that you can work your way through from start to finish. It's possible, however, that you just need to focus on certain areas of MySQL operation and would prefer to go directly to the appropriate chapters. The following summary should help you to decide which chapters will be most helpful for your situation.

- If you are completely new to database technology, start out with **Chapter I: Databases - In Theory and Everyday Life**. This chapter explains the basics of data storage and compares the different types of database systems. This will give you the basic information and perspective you need to understand the benefits of working with a software like MySQL.

- If you have previous database experience and are new to MySQL, you can skip to **Chapter II: Choosing and Installing MySQL**. This chapter explains the benefits of MySQL, the various ways to install it on Windows, Mac and Linux machines and introduces some of the design tools available for MySQL.

- **Chapters III and IV** explain the process of data modeling and database normalization. This is the process of organizing data into specific tables and relating them so as to eliminate duplication and inconsistencies in the data. It's an important aspect of database design and if you need an introduction or a refresher on the rules of normalization, these chapters will help.

- **Chapters V and VI** explain the actual process of building a MySQL database, from gaining access to the server and managing database users to the options involved in table design. Once you have all the tools installed, these chapters are a good practical guide to the process of creating the database, tables and other objects.

- **Chapter VII: Reading and Writing the Data** is an introduction to Structured Query Language (SQL) as it's implemented in MySQL. If you've never written queries before or you're coming to MySQL from another database, this chapter will get you started writing queries and commands on your new database.

- **Chapters VIII and IX** are case studies that review everything you've learned about data modeling and database design. The Human Resources and Training database in Chapter VIII and the Recipe database in Chapter IX further explain how the rules of database normalization can be applied to real world situations and some of the challenges that result.

- Finally, **Chapter X** presents some options for designing a user interface that will enable others to easily and effectively use your MySQL database.

Again, this book is written as a tutorial and most of the chapters include questions and exercises at the end which I encourage you to work through. This will help you review the material and ensure that you understand and retain it.

This book occasionally references the **MySQL Reference Manual** which is available from the official MySQL site at http://dev.mysql.com/doc. The manual is available in many searchable formats including EPUB, Adobe PDF and HTML At over 4900 pages, the manual is also an exhaustive and invaluable reference that will provide every detail you could need for working with MySQL.

Supplemental Files & Errata

Throughout this book, you'll see a lot of SQL examples and references to database scripts. If you'd like to download the scripts and see any corrections that are made after the book goes to press, please visit the official page at https://ostraining.com/books/mysql. You can also find updates on my sites at ComeauSoftware.com and Drewslair.com.

Formatting Notes

This book features code examples and screenshots as part of the material. If you're reading this book on a handheld device, you might need to occasionally adjust the orientation of your screen for the best reading experience. I've made every effort to present the material in a clear, readable manner but if you have any issues, please contact me at the e-mail address shown below.

I want to hear from YOU!

If you have purchased this book or if you've even downloaded a sample and have more questions, I'd like to hear from you. I've always enjoyed corresponding with the visitors to my websites and the readers of my previous books. If you would like to contact me, you're welcome to do so by e-mail at **acomeau@comeausoftware.com**.

Andrew Comeau
Ocala, Florida
August 2015

Chapter I

Databases - In Theory and Everyday Life

What is a Database?

The word *database* is not one that you hear in everyday conversation. It's one of those technical terms that's used by business and I.T. people that might evoke images of computers and long reports of names and numbers or indecipherable data. Some people might think of marketing or mailing lists. In fact, *a database is simply any collection of data that's organized so that it can be retrieved and used as needed*. Usually, it refers specifically to data that has been stored within a computer system so that it can be quickly manipulated into reports. Databases take many forms but any time a computer needs to present information of any kind, whether it be a store's customer data or patient data at your doctor's office, there's usually a database involved.

Everyday Database Examples

Our everyday lives are constantly influenced by electronic data from the web pages and e-mails on our computers to the uplink at a credit card terminal. In June 2011, the EMC corporation, a worldwide I.T. consulting firm, stated that the world's collection of electronic data was doubling every two years. They also forecasted that during 2011, 1.8 zettabytes of data would be created or copied. A zettabyte is 1 *billion* gigabytes of information. To show you what that figure means, the average new home computer in 2012 might have included 500 gigabytes of storage on the hard drive. That means the amount of data estimated to be generated in 2011 would fill 3.6 million home computers or more than 212 million DVDs. That's a lot of data to store and the amount of data being generated is increasing every year.

A large portion of this data is stored in separate files such as Microsoft Word documents and image files but much of it needs to be stored in a way that can be quickly accessed and searched by record. For some examples of this, let's look at the different ways you might access databases throughout the day.

- You get up in the morning and, if you're like me, you check your e-mail. That means your computer or phone connects to whatever service you use and requests a list of new e-mails that have come in since you checked last. Your program retrieves at least the essential parts of the e-mail including the sender's address and subject line. All of this information is stored within a database on your e-mail service.

- Many of your morning e-mails are probably junk mail which means that your e-mail address is stored in the database of an online advertiser somewhere, probably several.

- After you get the incoming e-mail, you decide to send an e-mail to your friend, Bob, asking if he wants to get together after work for a movie. In the "Send To" field, you type in the first characters of Bob's name and the program accesses your electronic address book to get Bob's e-mail address. Address books and Rolodexes have always been a type of database with fields for the name, phone number, address, etc.. Now they're often *electronic* databases that can be quickly searched and updated.

- On your way into work, you stop at the local coffee shop to get your coffee and danish. When the cashier swipes your card, the software requests your record from the credit card company's database to verify that the card number you just provided is valid. If you stop for gas, the pump might verify your ZIP code when you swipe your card. The

ZIP code that it verifies against is also part of the database record from your credit card company.

- If the building you work in has a moderate amount of security, you might have to punch in a code, swipe a security badge or even scan your fingerprint to get in the door before you can get to your desk or work site. The system then consults a security database in which you are, hopefully, listed as a current and authorized employee and decides whether to admit you or make your morning more challenging. Depending on your company's policies, the card swipe and its result might be recorded back to the security database for reference.

- If you use a computer at work, the programs you work with access data from company databases to provide the customer, order, shipping, employee or financial information that you use in your job. The computer itself, your printer and the phone you use might be listed in one or more inventory and administrative databases on your company's network.

- One or several times that day, you probably read and post comments to Facebook, Twitter and other social networks. All of these comments and their attachments such as photos and videos are stored in databases that power the various websites.

- Finally, on your way home for the night, you stop by the pharmacy and the grocery store. The pharmacist uses a database, likely more than one, to verify the details of your prescription order and check for any interactions or side effects you need to know about. The clerk at the store scans the barcodes on your items which are simply numbers that the register uses to look up your items in a database to get the right price and adjust inventory.

- You probably used your credit card again at the grocery and pharmacy. These transactions are stored in a database on your credit card company's system along with the ones for the the morning coffee, your lunch that day at a restaurant, the tank of gas and the movie tickets. All the items can then be included on your statement at the end of the month.

In most of these examples, I talked about single databases being used to store data but since companies and government agencies love to keep information, the data can be linked to, duplicated, manipulated and transferred into other databases many times over. As I've *repeatedly* warned people on a certain social network, once you put your information online, you lose all control of where it will go and who might use it. Essentially, you pay for the convenience of having your data available to the services you use by potentially sharing it with anyone else who might find it useful.

My real point here is that, in this electronic age, more and more of your daily activities generate or rely on information stored in databases of one kind or another. Unless you are completely off the grid, your daily life follows and leaves an electronic trail. It is in your best interests to learn how databases work so that you will be aware of how information is stored and shared between systems.

Types of Databases

As I mentioned earlier, even your address book qualifies as a database. It's a list of records with a set of fields for names, addresses and other bits of contact information. It has a structure which you can use to quickly record and retrieve the information you need. Electronic databases can be as simple as a text file on a local computer where the information is stored in rows of text. They can also be extremely complex and hosted on servers where they're accessed by multiple programs from around the world. It all depends on the requirements of the people using the data. The following are a few types of databases that you might see in everyday life.

Text files - Data Exchange and Basic Storage

The simplest form of electronic database can be stored on a local computer or network in a plain text file. While providing the fewest features in terms of sorting and indexing, plain text formats are the most compatible with different software systems and are also readable by humans. Three prominent formats of text-based databases right now are CSV, XML and JSON as I'll explain below.

CSV

CSV stands for *Comma Separated Values*. It's the simplest database format in which the data is stored in a consistent set of fields and separated by commas or other separators such as spaces and tabs. If you were to store a book collection in this format with the title, author, release year and pages, it might look like this:

```
"Stormy Weather","Carl Hiassen",1995,335
"Dune","Frank Herbert",1965,528
"The Stand","Stephen King",1978,1200
```

Other names for this format include *comma delimited data* and *tabular data*. It's a format that goes back decades to a time before the personal computer. CSV can still be used to transfer data between programs. For example, you could save the data from your favorite spreadsheet program to CSV and import it into another analysis program that did not read the original format but could import CSV data.

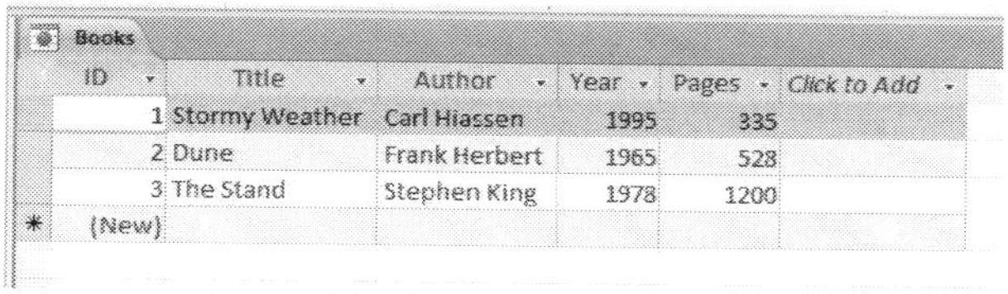

Books

ID	Title	Author	Year	Pages	Click to Add
1	Stormy Weather	Carl Hiassen	1995	335	
2	Dune	Frank Herbert	1965	528	
3	The Stand	Stephen King	1978	1200	
(New)					

Figure 1.1 - CSV is commonly used for the transfer of data between programs but can also be used to store and work with small amounts of data.

XML

A newer standard of text data is the *XML* format. XML stands for *Extensible Markup Language* and was developed in the 1990s mainly for data exchange over the Internet. Figure 1.2 shows a sample of XML based on the book list in Figure 1.1.

XML gets its name from the fact that the various fields are marked with the tags that you see indicating the field names such as Title and

Author. The word "extensible" means that there is no limitation on what tags can be used.

Figure 1.2 - XML can be used to store and transfer data in a structured format.

Unlike HTML, the markup language used to create web pages, the tags in an XML file are determined by the user based on the needs of the data. Extra documentation might be included in an accompanying XSD file to provide more information on the structure of the data.

XML has a couple of advantages over CSV. First, it can handle more complex data such as categories and sub-categories of report data. For example, if you had a list of employees and each employee had a list of absentee days, that data could be exported to one XML file and then imported to another program. The link between each employee and his or her specific absences would remain intact. Unlike some other data formats, XML is also readable by both human and machine although it can look a little confusing to a person who is not familiar with the initial data. The final advantage is that when transmitting data over the Internet, XML can go through security precautions such as firewalls and e-mail filters without posing any risk to the system receiving it because it's simply a text file. Other *binary* formats like spreadsheet and word processing files can carry viruses and are often blocked by filtering systems.

XML really shines when it comes to transmitting continuous record-based data that needs to be regularly updated and synchronized.

Years ago, I worked with an automated system that maintained an inventory of the computer workstations in the company. Every time a user turned on their computer, an XML file would be generated by a small client program on their machine with their computer name and current specifications. The file would be sent to the main program on the network and the program would update its database of workstations with this record. When we found that the program wasn't doing such a great job of updating the inventory, it was easy for me to design another database program that would import the XML files and maintain a better inventory.

JSON

The *JSON* format is the newest of the three text formats, having been developed starting in 2001 by Douglas Crockford at his company, State Software, Inc.. It was developed as a data interchange format which would be easily readable and writable by both humans and computers and is used by some applications as an alternative to XML. The name stands for *JavaScript Object Notation* as the format is based on the JavaScript web programming language. Unlike XML, JSON recognizes actual data types such as numbers, strings and True / False values. The format can specify individual named values as well as arrays of values and it enables highly structured data to be written to a plain text format. Figure 1.3 shows a sample of JSON based on the previous list of books.

```
[
    {
        "Title": "Stormy Weather",
        "Author": "Carl Hiassen",
        "Year": "1995",
        "Pages": "335"
    },
    {
        "Title": "Dune",
        "Author": "Frank Herbert",
        "Year": "1965",
        "Pages": "528"
    },
    {
        "Title": "The Stand",
        "Author": "Stephen King",
        "Year": "1978",
        "Pages": "1200"
    }
]
```

Figure 1.3 - A sample of JSON used to store book information

As database formats, all three of the above text formats are limited by the fact that they are stored within text files. The program generally has to import the entire file to work with the data. There is no security on a text file meaning that it can be read by anyone and if it's deleted or corrupted, the data is lost. For these reasons, most programs that work with more than small amounts of data use other formats.

Mobile Databases - Smartphones, Tablets and the Web

Most sophisticated computer programs, including those on your smartphone or tablet, need something more than a text file to store their data. At a certain point, the data needs to conform to a structure and a set of rules. Relationships between different categories of data must be enforced, the data must be easily searched and the program must be able to access the right information without having to sift through an entire collection. These requirements are common enough to different programs that they can be delegated to a separate software which will manage the database and provide access to the data. This software is often written independently from the programs that you use on a daily basis. If the program you're using is well designed, you should never even be aware of the existence of the database manager itself.

There are many database software titles available. Here are just a couple with examples of where they're being used. See the links section at the end of the chapter for the websites associated with the software titles listed here.

SQLite

SQLite (pronounced SEE-kwel LITE) is a public domain database software promoted for its small size, speed and reliability. These are definitely considerations for programmers who want to design small, efficient programs and make their users happy. Since it's public domain, programmers can design their programs around an SQLite database without having to pay any licensing fees. It's used by such well known programs as Mozilla Firefox and McAfee anti-virus.

Microsoft SQL Server Compact and Express Editions

Microsoft's SQL Server is one of the big names in the database world with various editions of the software being used for everything from small mobile apps to giant business systems. The Compact and Express editions of the software are designed specifically for smaller applications. The Compact edition focuses on mobile apps and the Express edition is used for desktop and website applications. These editions of the software are also free for programmers to use and are sometimes bundled with other programming tools. If you are developing websites on a hosting service or network powered by Microsoft Windows, there's a good chance that you're also using SQL Server Express for your data needs.

Oracle Database Express Edition

Oracle is another heavyweight in the database field. The Express edition of their self-titled database software can be used to create software and for software testing by programmers. Oracle Express also has limitations on the amount of data it can store and the amount of computer memory it can access but, for the average developer or user with a single machine installation, it's enough to work with.

MySQL

MySQL is one of the most popular software titles for use with web applications. It's an *open source* software which means that the source code is available for independent programmers to modify as needed and also very often means that the software is free. MySQL is cross-platform meaning that it runs on different operating systems including Windows, Linux and OS X. In my experience, MySQL and Microsoft's SQL Server Express are the two primary database systems for use with web applications. If you build your own website and sign up for a website hosting account, you'll often see one or both of these offered for use in storing whatever data your site needs to access. WordPress, the popular blogging tool and content management system, uses a MySQL database in order to store the data for the site including posts and other content. MySQL also does not have the limitations on database size that SQL Server Express and Oracle Express do and the databases can run into the terabytes (*trillions* of bytes).

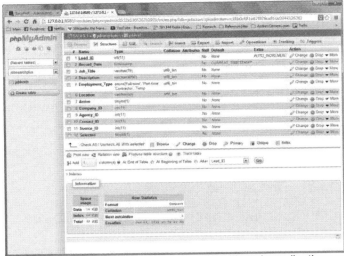

Figure 1.4 - MySQL is a popular database for use with web applications and is often administered in a web browser with the phpMyAdmin web application.

Desktop Database Software - Local Analysis

Another type of database software enables individual, non-technical users to create databases and analyze data. Several software titles offer powerful data analysis and reporting features that can be run straight from the desktop. MySQL, SQL Server Express and Oracle Express might be suitable for the advanced user as they can be installed locally and used to create databases but others are designed for the average business user or even the home user and are often packaged as part of a larger suite of applications. This includes programs like Microsoft Access and OpenOffice Base.

These programs enable the user to create databases in one or more files on the user's computer, analyze the data in various ways and create reports. The software can even link to other spreadsheet and analysis programs to pull additional data into the analysis. Some desktop databases include advanced features such as embedded programming languages and the ability to package user-designed databases to be run on remote machines and in Web applications.

Early in my programming experience, I used desktop database software including Borland Paradox and Microsoft Access to design database applications for the company where I was working. These applications worked with a variety of data including manufacturing statistics, employee and payroll information and customer communications. By using these software tools, I was able to save the company hundreds and maybe even thousands of dollars in software purchases and training hours while providing the other employees with quick access to the information they needed.

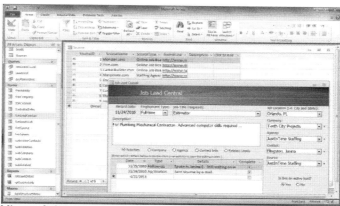

Figure 1.5 - Microsoft Access and other desktop database software can be used to create sophisticated applications for analyzing data.

Desktop databases often represent a *single-tier* design. This means that whatever forms, reports and other interface features the user creates around the database are stored within the same database file or files as the data itself. An installation of the management software is usually required in order to work with the database. Some desktop database systems can allow for a basic *multi-tier* arrangement by splitting the forms and reports into a separate file called a *front-end* that is linked to the tables in another file called the *back-end*. This way, the design of the presentation and business programming is separated from the data and changes can be made to one without affecting the other. Multiple copies of the front-end which link to the same set of database tables can also be distributed to users to enable the database to be more efficiently accessed by multiple people.

Most of the databases I've mentioned so far are great for moderate amounts of data, even up to a few gigabytes. They provide a structure for the data and maybe even security to determine who can access it.

In the right hands, they can be used to produce very sophisticated applications. At a certain point, however, it's time to go to the next level. Mobile and desktop databases typically support a limited number of users and are also limited in the amount of data that can be stored, the security features available and other management tools that help to maintain the kind of data collections you find in companies, universities and other organizations.

Server Databases - Organizational Data and Enterprise Applications

Just like the other types of database software, server database software can be used for small databases but is actually designed to support immense database systems containing up to hundreds of *petabytes* of data (1 petabyte = 1,000,000 gigabytes). These systems can contain multiple databases on powerful networked machines and provide data access to thousands of users. These massive systems can be worlds unto themselves that even contain sizeable amounts of programming code used to run automatic operations on the data within the tables and provide data to the reports. Server databases represent *multi-tier* systems and are accessed by multiple pieces of software, websites and devices by users across an organization or university campus. Very often, the databases themselves will be maintained by one or more full-time database administrators (DBAs) who will monitor the security and performance of the systems, respond to any access problems and either design new databases as needed or provide expertise for the software designers.

At the server level, the database software is no longer just a standalone program or a series of files but might actually be integrated into the operating system of the network machine on which it runs. It could also be running as a collection of services that can be started, stopped and managed by the administrator. For example, Microsoft SQL Server can use Windows security to verify that a user is authorized to access specific databases. When a user logs into their Windows desktop machine and runs any program that accesses the database server, SQL Server will permit them access only to the databases for which their user account has been authorized by the administrator. This means that the user only has to enter a password once, at Windows startup, and the DBA can grant or revoke their access to specific resources with a couple clicks of the mouse. Another benefit is that database servers are often listed as network resources so that a person with enough knowledge can find the right database no matter which machine they're using on the network and without needing to know what machine it's stored on. Programmers can design applications to call a database over a company network or even the Internet so the average user can continue to be completely unaware of the database itself so long as everything is working correctly.

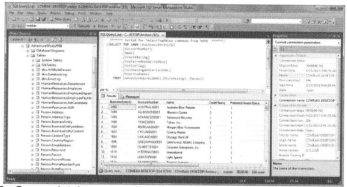

Figure 1.6 - Server databases can host immense database systems that serve many hundreds or even thousands of users. This screenshot shows a view of a database maintained in SQL Server 2012.

The two big players in the server database market are Oracle and Microsoft. As I've mentioned, Oracle has both their self-named Oracle database and MySQL while Microsoft has Microsoft SQL Server. IBM has its own database titles, DB2 and Informix. Organizations might use more than one title depending on their needs. I personally have Microsoft SQL Server Developer Edition and MySQL installed on my local machines for development and testing while the hosting services that I use for my websites offer access to both SQL Server Express and MySQL for the creation of databases to support the sites. Sometimes, tools like WordPress use specific database titles but it can also come down to the preference of the individual database developer or programmer. Cost can also be a factor. Depending on the needs of the organization and the applications being developed, database software might be a free download or it might cost an organization thousands of dollars in license and support fees.

Cloud Databases - Outsourced Data Storage

The newest category of database seeing wide use is the Cloud Database. Cloud computing is a computing model which enables companies and individuals to lease computing, data storage and database services from outside providers, paying only for the services they use. Applications and databases are stored and run on the provider's servers and accessed over the Internet from any computer in the world with an Internet connection. It's similar to the way in which a website designer leases space and resources from a web hosting company but with more types of services available and more flexibility in configuring them. Cloud computing enables an organization to add resources for a project and obtain the resources as a paid service rather than a large equipment investment and the service can be easily managed, increasing or decreasing the CPU, memory and other resources as the needs of the project change. Software licensing costs are included as part of the service which further reduces the cost for the subscriber. Cloud computing providers might also offer service and security guarantees which can lift some of the burdens from local I.T. departments.

Cloud databases are one of the many services offered by a cloud computing service provider. A subscriber creates an account with the provider and would then have access to a web-based control panel, much like the one on a web hosting account. This control panel enables the user to create as many computing environments, databases and other remote resources as are needed. The user specifies the resources needed for the database, often including the CPU, server memory (RAM), hard disk space as well as the database and operating system software to be used.

Cloud computing services might offer both Windows and Linux configurations with both MySQL and SQL Server available. These resources are then allocated to the database project by the service, the database is created and the subscriber is provided with the information needed to manage the database over the Internet. The subscriber would then connect to the database as needed through the database management program of their choice or through a custom application that they or their company designs to use the data. The resources such as bandwidth or operational hours used by the project are billed to the subscriber monthly. If the application is not performing well because it lacks the necessary resources such as CPU or memory, the subscriber can login to the service's control panel and request that additional resources be allocated.

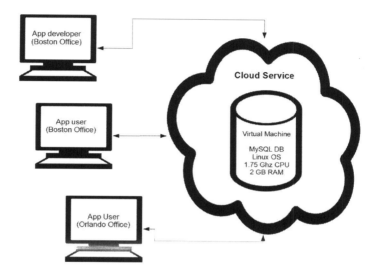

Figure 1.7 - Cloud databases are run remotely through a cloud computing service and accessed through any computer or device.

With this type of model, a single subscriber can create and run as many different applications and databases in different operating systems and configurations as their budget will allow. An application developer can quickly create test applications and environments and then dispose of them when they're no longer needed. A company can lease database resources on a monthly basis and treat it as an operating expense rather than buying and maintaining the actual servers. From a security standpoint, there is the issue that the subscriber's data is being stored on another company's servers and this might be a concern depending on the application but this is just one of the questions to consider when designing any application.

Currently, a number of large and well-known companies including Google, Amazon, Microsoft and Oracle are offering various selections of cloud services and provide free trials of the services for potential subscribers to try. There are also smaller cloud computing companies offering specific services such as ClearDB.com, a cloud database provider used by Microsoft's Azure service to provide support for MySQL databases. You might see a service like this referred to as 'Database as a Service' (DaaS) with other types of software delivered in this way being referred to as 'Software as a Service' (SaaS).

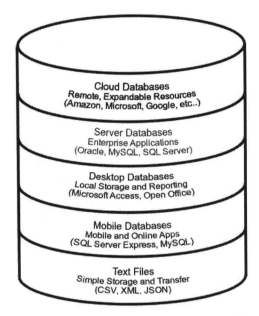

Figure 1.8 - There are many types of databases to suit the need of any application. The type of technology needed is one of the first considerations when designing a new application.

Figure 1.8 shows a summary of the database types that we've looked at in this chapter. Each level of technology has its advantages and appropriate uses and it's important to have a basic understanding of these technologies in order to make the best decisions when organizing a collection of data or building an application. A sophisticated database solution that uses too many resources for the environment where it will be used causes just as many problems as a solution that is not adequate to the needs of the data being stored.

Chapter Summary

The flow of information has always been important. In today's electronic world, it's easier to store and manage than ever. Our everyday activities including purchases, communications, work and entertainment leave a trail of electronic data that is stored in various types of computerized databases. These databases can take many forms depending on the needs of the data and the organization managing it and might range from small databases on personal smartphones to massive networked databases owned by corporations and government agencies. Many software titles and services are available to assist in the cataloging of data, each having their own features, limitations and appropriate use. Understanding how databases work can provide you with a better perspective of how information is stored and used and is essential in the pursuit of both technical and non-technical careers.

For Further Study

Review Questions

1. What is the basic definition of a database?
2. How does information stored in a Microsoft Word file or JPG image file differ from information stored in a database?
3. Other than data storage, what is a popular use for CSV and XML data?
4. What is an advantage of the XML format over the CSV format?
5. If you were transmitting continuous information over the Internet that needed to be collected and stored on the other end, what data format would you use?
6. How does a desktop database like OpenOffice Base differ from a server database like Oracle's MySQL.

7. If you are designing a website, which two database software titles are you likely to be using?

8. What are the advantages of a multi-tier design in a database application?

9. What are some of the advantages of cloud computing for a business over the traditional purchase of equipment? What is one potential concern?

10. Name three resources that can be specified and allocated for a database on a cloud computing platform?

Exercises

1. Examine your own daily routine for examples of information that needs to be stored somewhere and ask yourself how this might be done. How long does the data need to be kept? How much data actually needs to be stored and how might the collection of data grow over time? How confidential is the data? What would the consequences be if the data is lost or mishandled? Consider the examples of databases in everyday life from the first part of this chapter as well.

2. Using some of the links provided, check out the websites for some of the software titles mentioned in this chapter. Search for information on the abilities and limitations of each software.

3. Review the cloud computing services mentioned and compare the services they offer and costs involved.

Terms to Remember

Back-end - In software development, the database is often referred to as the back-end. The use of this term implies that the business and presentation programming is designed separately from the database and the design of each can be changed without necessarily affecting the other. See *Multi-tier Design*.

Cloud Computing - A computing model in which computer and data services are leased by an individual or organization from a remote service provider. This enables computing resources to be purchased on an as-needed basis rather than as an large equipment investment. Many services including document storage, software and database resources can be purchased under this model.

CSV - Comma Separated Values, a plain-text file format in which information is broken down into fields and stored in order to transfer the data between programs or simply store small to moderate amounts of information on disk. Also known as delimited or tabular data.

Database - A collection of information, usually in electronic form, stored in a specific format for easy retrieval and use in reports and other applications.

Database-as-a-Service (DaaS) - A service under the cloud computing model in which subscribers can design databases on the server of a remote service provider, often specifying the database software to be used along with the server space, CPU speed and server memory. The subscriber can then use local software to access the database over the Internet from any computer in the world and pay only for the server resources that they actually use. The amount of resources allocated to a database application can be changed as needed.

Front-end - In software development, the front-end represents any logic and presentation code such as user forms and interfaces, reports and business logic that exists separately from the database. See *Multi-tier Design*.

Gigabyte (GB) - One billion characters of information. More precisely, 1024^3 bytes (1024 x 1024 x 1024 or 1,073,741,824 bytes).

JSON - JavaScript Object Notation, a text file format that uses a format based on the JavaScript language to store complex data.

Multi-tier Design - Software design in which the program code is developed and exists independently from the database and the two communicate with each other, enabling multiple users at different locations to use the same application to access the same data.

Open Source - A software distribution model under which source code is made freely available for study and modification by independent developers. This means that the software is often free as well although more advanced versions and product support might be provided as a commercial product.

Petabyte (PB) - One million gigabytes of information (1024^5 bytes).

XML - Extensible Markup Language, a plain-text format which uses user-defined markup tags to store structured data for transfer between systems or over the Internet.

Zettabyte (ZB) - One billion gigabytes of information (1024^6 bytes).

Links

- JSON text format official site - http://www.json.org
- MySQL Database official site - http://www.mysql.com

Chapter II

Choosing and Installing MySQL

Why Choose MySQL?

Someone once asked me "So what made you choose the Microsoft road?" and he was referring to the fact that I was then focusing on Microsoft products such as SQL Server. My answer was that those were the products that were immediately available when I got serious about learning programming. That was in the 1990s and Microsoft did a great job of promoting their products while alternatives like Linux weren't as visible. Languages such as PHP and JavaScript that are popular today didn't appear until the mid-'90s and it was easy to use the products that were immediately available from what was then the giant of personal computing.

Now there are plenty of alternatives within easy reach over the Internet with answers to any question just a few clicks away. Some of these products that were just getting a foothold in the 90s are now fully developed, valuable tools for the person who wants to add new career skills or find technologies to aid with their latest projects. Best of all, many of them are still free for most users along with all the documentation you could ask for. Companies have worked out the business models that enable them to continue offering these valuable tools for download. This has, in turn, saved consumers huge amounts of money and opened up more access to technology than we've ever seen before.

Oracle's MySQL database software is one of these tools. MySQL was initially released in 1995, having been developed primarily by an independent developer named Michael Widenius at his company,

MySQL AB. It was eventually acquired by Oracle Corporation and remains available as an open source solution. According to <u>DB-Engines.com</u>, MySQL was the second most widely-used relational database management system as of March 2015, following Oracle's database itself. MySQL is used by a variety of organizations including universities, government institutions and online services such as Twitter, Wikipedia, Sony and WhiteHouse.gov. It's also used as the database for content management systems such as WordPress and Joomla.

There are a lot of opinions on both sides between MySQL and other database systems. While some of them are quite adamant, there are definitely benefits to using MySQL for your database needs.

- MySQL is a cross-platform software with versions for Linux, Windows and other popular operating systems.

- MySQL is a free database solution for the many developers now producing open source applications.

- MySQL offers multiple storage engines within its product with the engine being the actual software that manages the database. This can provide options for different types of data with different storage and retrieval requirements.

- MySQL has a rich selection of data types to accommodate the needs of any application.

- While MySQL does not include graphical interface tools as part of it's main installation, there are several tools that are available to create and manage MySQL databases. These tools provide a variety of interfaces according to the user's preference and are generally free to download and install.

- MySQL can be used with Microsoft tools such as Visual Studio by installing the correct software libraries in the project.

Notable Features of MySQL

As a *relational database management system (RDBMS)*, MySQL shares a number of features with other network database systems.

It's a good idea to have a basic familiarity with these features so that you can evaluate different database systems against each other.

- Stored Procedures - MySQL is able to store and run subroutines known as stored procedures which allow for sophisticated processing of data. These routines are stored directly on the database server so that business logic and the necessary data transactions are run there rather than on a remote machine. This can reduce network traffic and speed up operations.

- Views - Views are a bit like query definitions that are stored on the server. They can be used to limit the columns returned from a table for a report or provide a specific selection of columns that are returned to whatever program accessing the data. They can even be referenced like tables themselves.

- User Authentication and Privileges - Users are required to login with a username, domain (at least 'localhost') and password. Users then receive privileges to perform specific operations on various database objects. This provides administrators with the flexibility to grant users the access they need while providing the necessary protection to resources.

- ACID-compliance - ACID stands for *Atomicity, Consistency, Isolation and Durability* and it's a standard by which to ensure that database software processes data transactions reliably. MySQL meets this standard in its operations which means that each transaction within the database, such as the copying of data from one table to another, passes the following tests:

  - *Atomicity* requires that a data transaction is either completely successful or is reversed and does not change the database at all. If you're deleting a set of records according to specific criteria and the system crashes before the operation can be completed, atomicity requires that the transaction be completed or rolled back.

- ○ *Consistency* means that all data transactions must abide by all rules programmed into the database including data constraints.
- ○ The level of *isolation* determines whether the changes made by data transactions are visible and accessible to the rest of the users and processes running on the system before the transaction is finished. This could affect the reliability of the data if a program accesses data being written during a transaction that's later rolled back as unsuccessful.
- ○ *Durability* means that once a data transaction is successful and committed to the database, the changes are permanent, even if power is lost or the system fails for some reason. Mainly, it means that the changes are written to the appropriate tables and those tables are stored on non-volatile media.

GNU General Public License and Open Source Software

MySQL is an open source database software distributed under the *GNU General Public License* (version 2). The term *open source* simply means that the source code for the software is freely available to the public for study and modification. Independent developers can modify the code and create their own version of the software or contribute to the original version.

The GNU GPL is a free software license that enables users to use, share and modify the software as needed, provided that any modifications and derived works are distributed under the same license. This requirement is known as *Copyleft* and actually makes use of existing copyright law to ensure that users of the software adhere to it by licensing the users to make certain use of the software.

The GPL was first written in 1989 by Richard Stallman, founder of the Free Software Foundation and last modified in June 2007 when GPLv3 was released. The GPL actually does *not* require software to be distributed for free although that is the case with much of the software licensed under the GPL. The GPL *does* require that users not be prevented from sharing the software with others and that the software follow the open source model.

MySQL is dual-licensed. Developers who wish to include MySQL in their own open source applications may use the free version while those developing proprietary and commercial software for distribution require a paid license from Oracle.

Installing MySQL in an AMP Environment

Even though MySQL is a server database, there are many options for running it from your desktop, regardless of what operating system you're running. We'll be looking at a number of those options in this chapter.

Installing and getting hands-on experience with MySQL and other databases is vital if you're really interested in learning about database technology. It costs nothing more than the time it takes to download, install and play around with some free software. MySQL itself doesn't even require an installation program if you're comfortable working from the command line and making some configuration changes on your own. You can simply download the files, store them in your preferred location and create the shortcuts that you need to quickly start the server and the command window as needed. Installing MySQL this way will enable you to create and manage databases and user accounts through the command line.

If you would prefer some graphical utilities to make things easier and want to explore a few more uses of MySQL, you can also install it as part of an AMP environment or stack. A software *stack* is a collection of software that's designed to work together in order to run different parts of a process.

Traditionally, AMP stacks are referred to as LAMP (Linux), WAMP (Windows) or MAMP (Mac OS X) stacks. AMP stands for Apache / MySQL / PHP (or Python). Apache is a web server software that will enable you to run web applications on your computer that can read and write to the MySQL databases that you create. PHP and Python are programming languages that are used to create the web pages and add extra functionality to them. Once you have all of these components installed, you can create databases along with the applications to go with them. You can locally run applications such as WordPress or Joomla, content management systems that use MySQL to store website content. You can also install phpMyAdmin, a MySQL management tool written in PHP which will make it a lot easier to work with MySQL.

A Word on Virtual Machines

Before we get into the actual installation options, it's a good idea to get familiar with the concept of *virtualization* since it's something you might very well encounter if you're working with network databases such as MySQL or even installing it at home.

Virtualization software enables a single computer to act as a host for multiple computer sessions with different operating systems or different software installed on each. These sessions are actually *virtual machines* that can be accessed remotely and used just like a normal computer. Virtualization can help to get the maximum return from a company's investment in network hardware. Virtual machines can also be used on individual desktop computers for testing software, isolating specific programs from the rest of the host system or maintaining older operating systems for use by specific programs after an upgrade.

In addition to MySQL, Oracle offers a free virtualization software called Oracle *VirtualBox* which supports many operating systems including Windows, various flavors of Linux, Solaris and OS/2. VirtualBox is a free download from VirtualBox.org and is licensed under the GPL so it doesn't cost anything to try. The installation is very straightforward although it might include some extra Oracle networking components to support the virtual machines.

Once you have VirtualBox or another virtualization software installed, creating a virtual machine is really no different than setting up a new computer. You need a licensed copy of the operating system you plan to use. If you have it on CD or DVD, you can even boot the virtual machine directly from the disc since virtual machines can access the host system's drives and other resources.

Each virtual machine has a settings panel through which you can allocate memory and hard drive space from the host system. Figure 2.2 shows a VirtualBox control panel where I've setup virtual machines with various versions of Windows and Linux in order to work with them. When you're running a particular OS in a virtual machine, it requires just as many resources as it does on a physical machine. Since the virtual machines have resources allocated to them through a settings panel, it's much easier to adjust the memory and other resources allocated to the machine. It's also possible to duplicate virtual machines to make variations on the same machine setup or to save time by creating a base system and then using it for different projects.

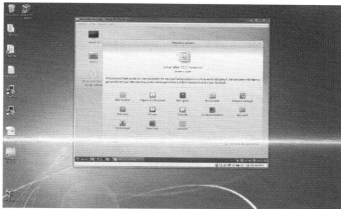

Figure 2.1 - A Linux Mint session running in Oracle VirtualBox on a Windows 7 host computer.

You could use virtualization on your computer if you have a version of Windows installed such as Windows 10 but you have software or maybe a peripheral such as a scanner that no longer works under that version of Windows. A virtual machine running an earlier version of Windows will enable you to continue using that resource. You could have another machine which holds software that you don't use as often in order to keep your host system from becoming cluttered. You might need to maintain multiple versions of a particular software that don't play well together on the same system and a virtual machine can house one version while the other version goes on another virtual machine or the host system itself.

Figure 2.2 - Oracle VirtualBox Manager with multiple virtual machines created

In addition to local software like VirtualBox, it's also possible to create and access virtual machines over the Internet through services such as *Microsoft Azure* and *HostMyApple.com*. This can free up demand on your local hardware and provide a solution that you can use from anywhere that you create a remote desktop or VNC connection.

As I show you the various MySQL installation options for both Linux and Windows, primarily in combination with the Apache web server and PHP language, it's possible that you might be running Windows but would like to try working with MySQL in a Linux system or vice-versa. As many people don't have an extra computer lying around that can be easily reformatted to another OS, a virtual machine can come in very handy for trying out different configurations without committing your hardware.

Installing MySQL on Linux

Installing Linux Mint

During the writing of this book, I have been using Linux Mint which is a great entry-level version of Linux for Windows users who want to transition over. It has an installation routine and user interface that's very familiar to anyone who's been using Windows for awhile. If you're installing it for the first time, it's now as simple as installing Windows on a computer.

Figure 2.3 - Linux Mint is a good version of Linux for beginners. The installation and user interface should be very familiar to anyone experienced with Microsoft Windows.

1. You can find the downloads on the official Linux Mint site at http://www.linuxmint.com/download.php. The installation packages are provided for download in the form of ISO files which contain disc *images* - compressed files that contain all the necessary files and programs that are needed to create an installation disc.

2. Choose the 32-bit or 64-bit download depending on the type of machine on which you will be installing Linux. There are also multiple packages featuring various desktop configurations and interfaces.

3. You can choose the site or *mirror* from which you want to download the Linux distribution file. Select whichever one you're most comfortable with. Some might feature better download speeds than others, especially if they're closer to you. The 64-bit version of Linux Mint 17.1 is 1.4 GB in size so it's going to take a little while to download.

4. After you've downloaded the ISO, you can use it to create an installation disc. For this, you need a DVD writer and a blank DVD-R disc. In Windows, this can be as simple as inserting the disc into the DVD writer and double-clicking on the ISO file. The native disc burning utility in Windows will prompt you from there. Some pre-installed CD / DVD writing packages will also handle ISO files. Use the best options available on your system.

5. After you've created the disc, use it to boot your computer and it will load a disc-based version of Linux Mint for you to try out. By default, the startup routine does *not* show all of the messages detailing the various processes being executed in the background. If the startup routine freezes for any reason, you can retry it and press the TAB key at the screen shown in Figure 2.3. This will bring up the boot options command line. Remove the words "quiet splash" from the line and press ENTER to allow the boot process to proceed while displaying *all* messages and any errors. This should give you enough information to resolve the issue or seek extra help online.

6. Once Linux Mint loads, you will be running it from the DVD. On the Linux Mint desktop, there is an icon titled **Install Linux Mint**. If you decide that you want to install Linux to your computer's hard drive, you can double-click this icon to begin the actual installation routine. Be careful not to do this on any computer without backing up all of your data first.

Once you have Linux installed, additional software can be installed from the Linux Software Manager or from within the Linux shell program which is the equivalent of the Windows command line. Using the Linux shell isn't difficult and provides you with a lot more detail about the installation process and a sense of how much work Linux is actually doing in the background. It's also more consistent between various types of Linux which is why I detail it here.

There are a few programs available to access the shell but you can use the default Terminal program in Linux for any of the following commands. If you're running Linux Mint, it's available from the UI's taskbar or menu. If you're running Ubuntu or another version of Linux, you might need to search for it. Creating a shortcut for the program on whatever desktop is available to you is a time saver.

Installing MySQL

The first step is to install MySQL itself and to verify it's working. When you open the Terminal program, you should see a blank command prompt with the dollar sign at the end, similar to the one in Figure 2.4. Simply type in the following line and press Enter:

```
sudo apt-get install mysql-server
```

It's a good idea to understand any commands that you type into the Terminal so here's a brief explanation of what this command is doing. *Sudo* is a Linux program that enables you to run single commands with the privileges assigned to the default administrator account. Sudo actually stands for "**su**peruser **do**". Linux maintains a file indicating which users are authorized to use this command. User access to administrative functions can be controlled in this way. Since you're installing software, you need access to these administrative permissions. Sudo will ask you for your password when you run the command.

An alternative to using sudo for each command is to simply type `su` at the shell prompt. Linux will ask for your password and you will be placed in superuser mode so that every command you type will use the administrative privileges. Typing `exit` will take you out of superuser mode.

Apt stands for *Advanced Packaging Tool*. This is another program which simplifies the management of software installations and updates within Linux. The `apt-get` command with the install option instructs the program to download the specified Linux package and to install it. This command will include whatever other software is required to support the requested package, also known as the *dependencies*. The `mysql-server` package is actually a pointer within the software repository which will determine the most updated package available at the time of installation.

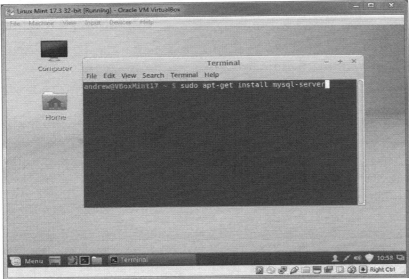

Figure 2.4 - The Advanced Packaging Tool can be used within the Linux Terminal to install and manage software packages and their dependencies. It actually does most of the work with just a few commands by the user.

If you get a message for any package that reads "Cannot locate package ...", check the spelling of the package name and try again. If that doesn't work or you see other errors, try running the following command to update all of your machine's references to the software repositories:

```
sudo apt-get update
```

During the installation, you will be asked to create a password for the MySQL root user. This is the default administrative user with complete privileges to the system so you should create a password at this time, make it a strong password and keep it someplace safe because retrieving a lost root password is very difficult, if not impossible. Once the installation is finished, you can test your new database server by logging in as the root user with the following command:

```
mysql -u root -p
```

The -u switch instructs MySQL to start for the root user and request a password. Enter the password you supplied during the installation and you should see the welcome message and further instructions. When you're finished, simply type exit to leave the MySQL program and go back to the main terminal command mode.

If you are satisfied with this and don't want an AMP environment, you can stop here. Otherwise, we can move on to installing Apache.

Apache

The Apache web server enables your machine to process requests for web pages. When you have Apache installed as part of an AMP stack, you can locally develop and run web applications that you would normally access over the Internet. You can also run web applications like phpMyAdmin and other tools that help you manage your MySQL installation. The Apache installation is pretty simple compared to MySQL and just requires one line typed into the Terminal:

```
sudo apt-get install apache2
```

During the installation, you might see messages like "Could not reliably determine the server's fully qualified domain name ...". That's okay since your "server" probably doesn't have a domain name. Once the installation is finished, it should start your new Apache server. You can verify that everything is working simply by opening up your web browser and typing localhost or 127.0.0.1 as the web address. This tells your web browser to point itself to your machine's local network address which should take you to the Apache default page with the heading of "It works!" as shown in Figure 2.5.

PHP

PHP is the scripting language used in many web applications. It enables web designers to pull information from a MySQL database, process it as needed, display the results on the page and save user input back to the database. You've probably seen web pages with the extension '.php' which signals to the network server that there is PHP code within the page and it needs to call the PHP interpreter on the server to process that code appropriately. In this way, PHP differs from a web design language like JavaScript which runs on the user's local machine. In order to design and process PHP web pages on your local machine, you will need to install the PHP interpreter.

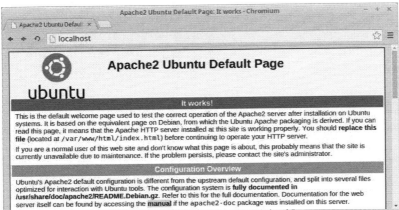

Figure 2.5 - If the Apache web server is correctly installed, then opening the web browser and pointing it to 'localhost' or '127.0.0.1' should load the Apache default page shown above.

You will get some experience with the Terminal in this step since it's the easiest way to do certain things in Linux. From the Terminal, type the following command:

```
sudo apt-get install php5 libapache2-mod-php5
```

This actually installs two packages, the main PHP interpreter and a module that will allow PHP to work with the Apache server you installed previously. Once the installation is finished, you will need to restart the Apache web server in order to ensure that it works with PHP. Open the Terminal and type the following command:

```
sudo /etc/init.d/apache2 restart
```

When you restart the Apache server, you might get a message that starts with "Could not reliably determine the server's fully qualified domain name, using 127.0.0.1 ... ". As long as you are doing the installation on a local machine without a domain name, this is fine.

To test that PHP is working, you can create a simple PHP file. Open the Terminal and type the following command:

```
sudo gedit /var/www/html/testphp.php
```

This command will open the *gedit* text editor program outside of the Terminal window. The Terminal will show as busy until you close the gedit program. The `/var/www/html` directory in this command is the primary location in Linux where the files served up by Apache are stored.

Add the following line of PHP code to the new file:

```
<?php phpinfo(); ?>
```

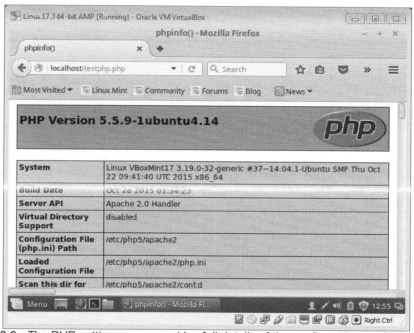

Figure 2.6 - The PHP settings page provides full details of the configuration settings and can also be used to verify the installation.

Click on **Save** and then close the gedit program and the Terminal. In the web browser, open the page `http://localhost/testphp.php`. If everything is working right, you should see a PHP settings page like the one in Figure 2.6 indicating that PHP has been successfully installed and is working.

Installing MySQL on Windows

When installing MySQL or an AMP system in Windows, you could go through the separate installations just like in Linux but there are a couple of easier options I recommend if you want to do minimal setup and changes to your existing system. For Windows, there are pre-packaged WAMP servers (*Windows*, Apache, MySQL, PHP) that contain all the components and configuration tools that you need.

EasyPHP, available at EasyPHP.org, is a popular software bundle or *stack* that includes all the software that you need for a WAMP along with an administration program that will be available from your Windows system tray and provide menu access to all the components. EasyPHP also includes phpMyAdmin for administration of your MySQL server.

One the advantages of using EasyPHP is that the installation is simple and the components are self-contained within the program's directory which can be installed on a flash drive if you want a portable system to run on multiple computers. The subdirectory `EasyPHP/data/localweb/projects/` serves as the storage for localhost web files. The EasyPHP installation automatically detects and adjusts a number of settings so that everything works together and you can focus on working. EasyPHP is also not attached to a specific drive letter as other AMP stacks are so you can easily use it on a portable drive which might receive a different drive letter on different systems.

The EasyPHP Development Server edition is a free download from EasyPHP.org or Sourceforge.net which sets up a local WAMP environment. Installation is as simple as running the installation program and choosing the right options. The installation will handle the rest and create shortcuts in your Windows start menu.

You can also start EasyPHP by running the executable file in the main EasyPHP directory. It does not immediately open an interface but instead loads in the background and shows an icon in your system tray which you can right-click to access the various features as shown in Figure 2.7.

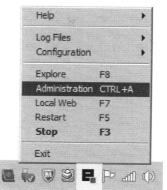

Figure 2.7 - EasyPHP runs in the background and is accessed through a system tray icon.

Selecting Administration from the EasyPHP menu will bring up the main interface shown in Figure 2.8. This is really just a web page that opens the address http://127.0.0.1/home/ to point back to the Apache web server on your own system. Depending on your system, it might also reference a port number (http://127.0.0.1:8080/home). The page points to the home directory, looks for the *index.php* default web page there and loads the page in your browser.

About halfway down this page, you'll see the Modules section with an item called *MySQL Administration* under it. Click the **Open** button on the right of this item and phpMyAdmin will load in the browser. This page once again points to http://127.0.0.1 but, this time, it points to the folder which holds an instance of phpMyAdmin. You can actually have multiple instances of MySQL on the same machine if you install EasyPHP multiple times and each will show up as a separate item under the Modules section. EasyPHP also has extensive support online through FAQs and user forums.

WampServer, available from WampServer.com, is another installable WAMP stack available in both 32-bit and 64-bit editions and is also portable although it does need a consistent drive letter. There might be a little bit more configuration involved and a few more options available. Otherwise, it's similar to EasyPHP in operation. Later on in the chapter, I'll also talk about an AMP packaged called *MAMP* which is available for OS X and also has a Windows edition.

Figure 2.8 - The EasyPHP Web Interface

MySQL Community Server

If you want to focus on the MySQL experience rather than a WAMP server, there's *MySQL Community Server* which is the full installation of a MySQL server along with MySQL Workbench. Workbench is a complete administration utility with which you can create data models and administer both individual databases and entire instances of MySQL.

In addition to Workbench, the MySQL Community Edition includes multiple storage engines for MySQL and connectors for using different languages such as the .NET languages with MySQL. The installation is also pretty straightforward and you can download the installation package from the Downloads page on MySQL.com at http://www.mysql.com/downloads/.

Be sure to select the correct operating system and system type for your download. The Windows package is available for both 32-bit and 64-bit systems and multiple platforms including Windows, Linux and Mac OS X. There are a couple of downloads for Windows that give you very different installation packages so be sure you get the right one.

- The package with an MSI installer which will take you through the complete installation of the MySQL Community Edition is found at http://dev.mysql.com/downloads/windows/installer.

- The ZIP archives, downloadable from the main page at http://dev.mysql.com/downloads/mysql/, contain a simple MySQL installation *without* graphical tools. These files can be stored in the directory of your choosing and the program can be run from there. This page also has a link to the MSI installer package which I recommend.

When using the MSI installer file, you have the option of downloading a small installer file that will download the rest of the necessary files from the web or downloading the full installation file which you can use if your connection to the Internet during the installation is not guaranteed. If you've previously installed components such as MySQL Workbench, this installer will also upgrade them to their latest versions.

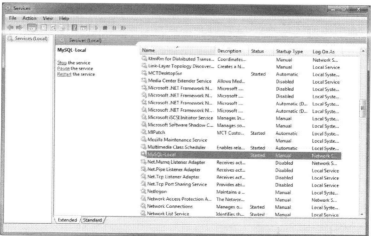

Figure 2.9 - MySQL can be installed as a Windows service so that the server is automatically started with Windows or it can be set for manual startup as needed.

MySQL typically uses port 3306 to listen for network connections to the server but this can be changed to 3300 during the installation if

3306 is already in use by another instance of MySQL or another program. The MSI installer will offer the option of configuring MySQL to run as a Windows service rather than from the command line. This enables MySQL to be started and stopped automatically when Windows starts and shuts down. The service can also be configured to be started manually by the user when needed. MySQL Workbench offers this option and the WampServer package mentioned earlier appears to do it by default.

MySQL Community Server includes a number of utilities and features which are provided as options during the installation process.

- MySQL Workbench - The main program in the package. This graphical tool makes it easy for the user to manage MySQL instances and administer databases. It has data modeling tools including diagramming and forward / reverse engineering of databases and diagrams.

- MySQL Notifier - This is a tool that resides in the system tray as an icon through which the user can manage and configure multiple instances of MySQL on the machine. This includes starting, stopping and restarting the services as needed.

- MySQL for Excel - This is an Excel add-on that enables easy access to MySQL data from within Microsoft Excel as well as transfer of data between Excel and MySQL. It manages the connections to the instances and integrates with MySQL Workbench if it's installed.

- MySQL for Visual Studio - Like the Excel add-on, this simplifies the connection to MySQL from Microsoft Visual Studio. The developer does not need to leave Visual Studio in order to connect to a specific database and access the tables within it. The connection can be easily created and opened from within the Server Explorer.

- MySQL Fabric - For administrators, Fabric helps to manage MySQL server farms.

- MySQL Connectors (ODBC / .NET / Python) - These are additionally available connectors that enable developers to access MySQL data within their projects.

Installing MySQL on Mac OS X

Configuring Apache and PHP

Unlike Windows, OS X already includes the Apache web server and PHP language pre-installed so it's a much simpler process to ensure that everything is working together. For simplicity, I'll be providing the instructions for installing everything through the OS X Terminal program.

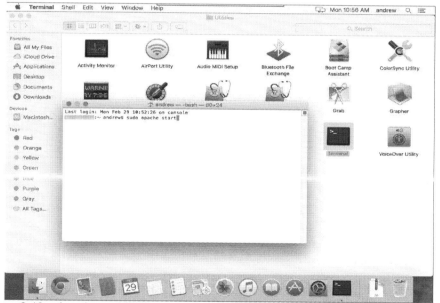

Figure 2.10 – Apache and PHP are pre-installed on OS X so an AMP environment can be created with fewer installs and a little bit of configuration.

You will need root access in order to install and configure the components. Open the Terminal environment from the Utilities (**Go >> Utilities** from OS X main menu and then select **Terminal**). While it is possible to get root access by activating the root user account with dsenableroot, improper use of this command can cause security issues in your system so it's better to use sudo ("**su**peruser **do**")

before each command or temporarily switch to root access with the
`sudo su -` command.

You can activate Apache simply by issuing *either* of the the following
commands in the Terminal. See Figure 2.10 for an example.

```
sudo apachectl start
```

```
sudo apachectl restart
```

The restart command will start Apache even if it's stopped. There
won't be any notification on the command line as to the change in
status so you will need to verify that Apache is working by opening a
web browser window and navigating to `http://localhost`. If
everything is working, you should get a simple white screen with the
heading "It works!" indicating that the web server is up and running.

In order to configure PHP, the Apache configuration file (httpd.conf)
must be changed to load the necessary software module so that PHP
pages can be served up. This is easily done from the Terminal. First,
you will need to change to the Apache directory and you should make
a backup of the file.

```
cd /etc/apache2/
```

```
cp httpd.conf httpd.conf.bak
```

To edit the file, you can use the Unix command line editor *vi* or the
Mac *TextEdit* program, either of which can be opened from the
Terminal with *one* of the following commands:

```
vi httpd.conf
```

```
open -a TextEdit httpd.conf
```

If you choose the TextEdit command from above, the TextEdit
program will open *outside* the Terminal and will load the configuration
file for you to edit.

In either editor, you'll need to find the following line within the
httpd.conf file:

```
#LoadModule php5_module libexec/apache2/libphp5.so
```

Remove the hashtag (#) from the beginning of the line to un-comment it and then save the file. You will then need to restart Apache with the following command in the Terminal.

```
sudo apachectl restart
```

To verify that PHP is working with Apache, you can create a *phpinfo.php* file in the web document root folder where the localhost files reside. On OS X, this folder is generally located at `\Library\WebServer\Documents`. Create a simple text file in that folder with the following text on the first line:

```
<?php phpinfo(); ?>
```

Save the file with the name 'phpinfo.php' and then load the file in your web browser.

```
http://localhost/phpinfo.php
```

If everything is working, you should then get a PHP settings screen similar to the one in Figure 2.6.

Installing MySQL

The latest versions of *MySQL Community Server* are available from the MySQL downloads page at dev.mysql.com in both TAR and DMG format. I recommend the DMG format which is a disk image that can be mounted as a drive accessible from the OS X Desktop.

The image file contains a single PKG file which you can double-click to run the installation wizard. As of this writing, the latest version, 5.7.11, is labeled for OS X 10.10 but I was able to install it with no problems on El Capitan (10.11). During the installation, you will be asked to create a password for the root MySQL user – make sure to write this password down somewhere safe!

After the installation is finished, it's a good idea to add the MySQL program directory to your PATH statement so you can run it from any directory. Add the following line to the file at `~\.bash_profile` using your favorite text editor.

```
export PATH=/usr/local/mysql/bin:$PATH
```

Then, try logging in to your new MySQL server as the root user.

```
mysql -u root -p
```

It's also a good idea to run `mysql_secure_installation` from the Terminal. This program takes you through the following steps to secure your database server:

1. Changing the root password that was chosen during installation if necessary

2. Removing the anonymous MySQL user

3. Disabling remote logins

4. Removing the test database and access to it

5. Reloading the privilege tables

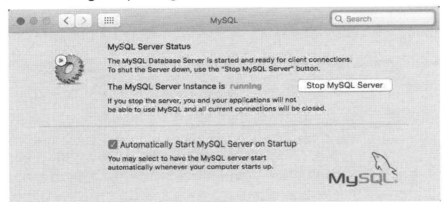

Figure 2.11 – After MySQL is installed, its settings pane is available through the System Preferences panel.

Once MySQL is working, it needs to be able to work with PHP. This is done by creating a link to the MySQL socket file which will allow PHP to communicate with the server. Entering the following commands in the Terminal will create a new MySQL directory in the system VAR directory and a symbolic link (similar to a shortcut in Windows) in that directory to the socket file.

```
cd /var

mkdir mysql

cd mysql

ln -s /tmp/mysql.sock mysql.sock
```

To quit the Terminal program, select **Terminal >> Quit Terminal** from the top menu or use the **Command-Q** key combination.

When the MySQL installation is finished, you should be able to Access the MySQL preference pane shown in Figure 2.11 from the System Preferences panel. This pane enables you to start and stop your MySQL server and set it to start when the OS starts up.

Installing a Pre-configured MAMP

While the manual configuration of the AMP components is relatively easy in OS X, there's also the option to download a ready-made AMP stack that you can install in about five minutes. *MAMP* is a free AMP stack from appsolute GmbH with editions for both OS X and Windows. You can download it from the official site at Mamp.info.

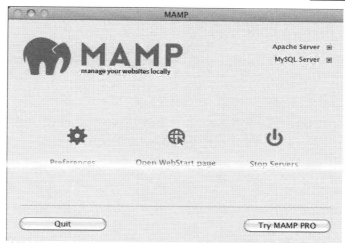

Figure 2.12 – MAMP provides a quick installation of an AMP stack on OS X and Windows.

In addition to running its own copies of Apache, MySQL and PHP, MAMP includes the Perl and Python languages. It also includes management tools such as phpMyAdmin. On OS X, its installation is self-contained within the MAMP folder which is created under the Applications directory. In Windows, the location defaults to `C:\MAMP` but the package also installs a few extra components on the system including Visual C++ redistributable packages.

As with other pre-configured AMP packages, MAMP uses its own folder, `MAMP\htdocs`, to hold the files to be served up at http://localhost. This can be easily changed through the Preferences settings along with the ports it uses for Apache and MySQL.

Additional Resources

MySQL Workbench

MySQL Workbench has the advantage of being able to easily access *multiple* MySQL instances, including remote instances over the Internet or a company network. So if you've signed up with a web hosting service and have access to a MySQL database behind a website, all you need is the server database address along with your user name and password and MySQL Workbench can log into that instance. If you are using a pre-configured AMP stack like EasyPHP, Workbench can also connect to that MySQL instance while it's running and then you can switch to another instance if you need to.

MySQL Workbench is essentially the MySQL counterpart of SQL Server Management Studio. Figure 2.14 shows the WordPress database from my website being accessed by Workbench.

Another advantage of Workbench is that, even as a standalone program, it's available for multiple operating systems.

- In **Linux**, the following line will install Workbench from the Terminal.
  ```
  sudo apt-get install mysql-workbench
  ```

- In **Windows**, Workbench comes with the MySQL Community Server package but can also be downloaded and installed separately from http://dev.mysql.com/downloads.

- Both MySQL Community Server and MySQL Workbench are available for **Mac OS X** and can be downloaded and installed separately as DMG image files.

When you first run MySQL Workbench, you will need to connect to the MySQL server you just installed. You can do this by selecting the **Database >> Connect to Database** menu and using the following settings:

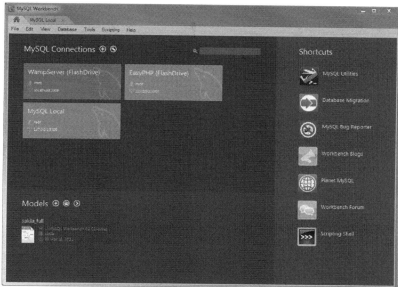

Figure 2.13 - MySQL Workbench provides a graphical environment in which you can manage multiple MySQL instances and create and administer databases.

```
Hostname: 127.0.0.1 (localhost)
Port: 3306
Username: root
Enter the password you set when you installed MySQL
```

The port setting is the machine communication port that MySQL will use. This is not an actual hardware port but a software address that enables the database to communicate with other programs as necessary. If you're running another database software such as SQL Server or are trying to run multiple instances of MySQL, you might be notified that the port is already in use. In this case, you will either need to disable the software or change the port number that MySQL is using which can be done through the configuration files. This is also detailed in the *MySQL Reference Manual*.

PHPMyAdmin

PHPMyAdmin is a MySQL interface written in PHP and designed to run in a web browser which means you can run it from an online source or locally. As a browser application, it also works on all platforms.

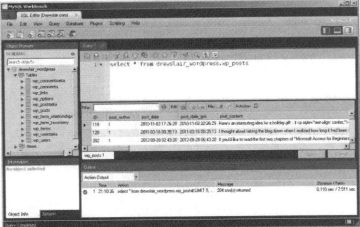

Figure 2.14 - With the MySQL Workbench that's included as part of the full MySQL installation, you can access local and remote instances of MySQL.

In **Linux**, you can download and install the files through the Terminal.

```
sudo apt-get install libapache2-mod-auth-mysql php5-mysql phpmyadmin
```

This command might result in the removal and replacement of a couple of items previously installed which is okay. The installation might also prompt you for the type of web server to be automatically configured to work with phpMyAdmin. There should be an option for 'apache2' and this is the one you should select using the keyboard.

The installation might also ask for the MySQL root user password and ask you to set another password for the PHP application user. Make sure to set strong passwords and store them in a safe place. After the installation is finished, type the following address into the web browser and phpMyAdmin should load.

```
http://localhost/phpMyAdmin
```

If you are asked to login, you can do so with the root user account.

If you get a 404 (Page Not Found) error when loading phpMyAdmin after installing it in Linux, you will need to edit the Apache configuration file in order to point it to the phpMyAdmin installation folder. This is how Apache knows where web applications are stored when they're not located in the /www/html directory. Type the following in the Terminal.

```
sudo gedit /etc/apache2/apache2.conf
```

This will open the necessary file in the *gedit* text editor. Add the following line at the very end of the file.

```
Include /etc/phpmyadmin/apache.conf
```

Then save the file, close the editor and issue the Terminal command to restart the Apache server.

```
sudo /etc/init.d/apache2 restart
```

Once the restart is complete, you should be able to load phpMyAdmin in your browser. Type `exit` to leave the Terminal program and you're done!

For both **Windows** and **Mac OS X**, you can download the files from the official site at PHPMyAdmin.net, unZIP them to a folder under your localhost files directory, name that folder PHPMyAdmin and perform a small amount of configuration detailed below. In Windows, PHPMyAdmin is also available as part of the EasyPHP WAMP stack and will be installed automatically and made accessible from the administration page.

To configure phpMyAdmin,

- Copy `config.sample.inc.php` from the downloaded files to a new file named `config.inc.php` in the same folder and open the new file for editing with your preferred text editor.

- Look for the line that starts with `$cfg['blowfish_secret'] =` and add an encryption value of your choice. This value can be a series of random letters and numbers if you like.

- If you would like to have a default user and password for phpMyAdmin, you can add the following lines to the `$cfg['Servers']` section of the file, substituting your own values for the user name and password.

```
$cfg['Servers'][$i]['user']      = '<username>';
$cfg['Servers'][$i]['password']  = '<password>';
```

- Once this is done, you should be able to run PHPMyAdmin simply by navigating to `http://localhost/PHPMyAdmin`.

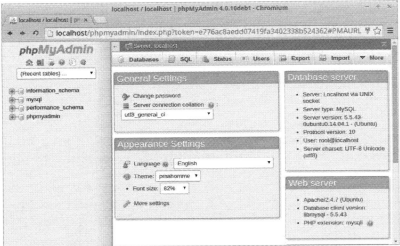

Figure 2.15 - phpMyAdmin is a web interface which provides many of the same management and administration features as MySQL Workbench. It is commonly found on web hosting services that feature MySQL database management.

If phpMyAdmin runs successfully, this actually demonstrates that all of the components in your AMP system are working. Failure of any of the components would not allow it to run.

- Apache is required to serve up the pages from localhost. Without it, you would get a 404 error when pointing your browser to the address.

- Without MySQL, the program would have nothing to access and could not complete a login.

- The user interface in phpMyAdmin is designed with PHP and, if that was not working, you would get pages full of raw PHP code.

SQLBuddy

SQL Buddy is another free web utility that you can use to manage a MySQL database as part of an AMP environment. It's biggest advantage is its simplicity in comparison to other programs like phpMyAdmin and MySQL Workbench. SQL Buddy performs the basic tasks including management and design of databases and tables, user management, running queries on the data and import and export of data. There are none of the advanced features that you'll find in phpMyAdmin or data modeling features from Workbench. For quick and common operations, however, it offers a clean interface that can reduce the learning curve for new users. See Figure 2.16.

Another feature is that there is no installation routine and, since the program is written in PHP, one version works on all operating systems. After downloading the ZIP file from SQLBuddy.com, just unpack it to the localhost folder on your machine and then access the program in your browser at `http://localhost/sqlbuddy/`. The login screen asks for your host name, MySQL username and password (you can use the root account) and you're all set. The program also has a timeout so sessions will automatically be logged out after a certain amount of inactivity.

Documentation

In addition to the instruction you'll receive in this book, there is no shortage of documentation available over the Internet and elsewhere for any aspect of MySQL. Here are a few other sources of information that are worth getting familiar with:

- The *MySQL Reference Manual* is exhaustive, covering over 4900 pages in PDF format and available in a number of other searchable formats as well as online. It covers all aspects of working with MySQL from security to the MySQL implementation of SQL which does have some minor differences from other database systems. You can view the documentation or download it in your preferred format at http://dev.mysql.com/doc/.

- PHP.net is the official site for the PHP language and covers both basic and advanced features of the language. I thoroughly recommend being familiar with at least the basics of PHP as it's one of the most common languages for working with MySQL. This is true whether you're programming on your own, using a content management system like WordPress or running some of the server utilities mentioned in this chapter.

- While EasyPHP and other WAMP software includes the Apache web server, you might never have to play around with it if you've just installed them to experiment with MySQL. The documentation is available on the Apache site at http://httpd.apache.org/ and it's a good thing to bookmark in case you run into problems.

Figure 2.16 - SQLBuddy provides a simplified cross-platform web-based interface for MySQL administration.

For Further Study

Review Questions

1. What are two of the benefits of using MySQL as the database behind a website?

2. What are the advantages of running MySQL in Windows as a service?

3. What are some of the uses for virtualization software and virtual machines?

4. What is the difference between a LAMP and a WAMP system?

5. Other than PHP, what programming languages can be used as part of an AMP system?

6. What would happen if you tried to run phpMyAdmin in your browser with the Apache web server stopped or uninstalled?

7. What are some advantages of running MySQL as part of an AMP system and in what situations would these be most useful?

8. What components are available in MySQL Community Edition that enable connections from other programs?

Exercises

1. Go back to the first two sections of this chapter ("Why Choose MySQL" and "Notable Features of MySQL") and review the benefits and features attributed to MySQL. Take some time to compare them to the corresponding features of competing database software such as Microsoft SQL Server, IBM's DB2 and SQLite. The specifications for these packages can be easily found with a few Internet searches. Here are a few links to start with.

- Microsoft SQL Server - http://www.microsoft.com/en-us/server-cloud/products/sql-server-editions/

- SQLite - https://www.sqlite.org/features.html
- IBM DB2 - http://www-01.ibm.com/software/data/db2/linux-unix-windows/features.html

Terms to Remember

Apache - A web server software that processes requests for web pages. Apache can be used on a web server that serves pages over the Internet or on a local machine in order to run web applications and projects.

ACID compliance - A four-part standard against which database software can be measured in its ability to process data transactions. 'ACID' stands for

- *Atomicity* - Data transactions are either completely successful or rolled back so as to leave no effect on the database.
- *Consistency* - All data transactions must abide by all the rules applied within the database, either through settings or programming.
- *Isolation* - The level of isolation determines how changes are visible between users before they're finally written to the database.
- *Durability* - Once changes are finally written to the database, they are permanent even in the event of software failure or power outage.

AMP stack - A software collection that includes the Apache web server, the MySQL database software and either PHP, Python or Perl as a programming language.

Copyleft - A variation on the copyright system that's applied to open source software to allow the software to be freely copied while ensuring that the open source standards are maintained by all distributors and resulting projects.

Cross-platform - A software that can operate on multiple operating systems, either through multiple editions or an online application that works through a web browser.

Database engine - The portion of a database software that carries out all data operations and applies the necessary rules to ensure that the operations are carried out correctly.

Dependencies - Components in any system that are required for the operation of other parts of the system. With a software package, dependencies might be other programs, database connections or hardware resources.

Disc Image (ISO) - A compressed, downloadable package which contains all of the files necessary to create an installation disc on CD or DVD.

GPL - General Public License. A licensing arrangement under which software can be freely used, copied, distributed and modified.

GUI - Graphical User Interface. Software which provides menus and other tools with which the user can visually access and work with various software functions without having to go through a command line interface and memorize commands.

Hostname - The name assigned to a computer or other device on a computer network for reference and identification. On the Internet, a domain name such as MySQL.com is used as the host name.

Localhost - The name that a computer or server uses to refer to itself in relation to the rest of the network, regardless of what type of network it's connected to or how many other machines are connected.

Open Source - A software distribution model in which the source code for a program is freely available for copying and modification by other developers. In many cases, compiled open source software is also free for end users although separate licenses might be required for use of the programs in business or other proprietary settings.

Port Number - A software address on a computer that is used for communication over a network. This number can be combined with a hostname or IP address in order to access networked software such as a database system. Various port numbers are commonly associated and registered with specific applications and the standard port number for MySQL and other database software is 3306.

Root user - In MySQL and on some operating systems, this is the primary administrator account that has complete access to the system. In addition to referring to a specific user, it can also refer to the permissions associated with that user which can be granted or revoked as needed on other user accounts.

Virtual machine - A separate computing session that is defined by and contained within software on a host computer and can be isolated from the host's operations. Virtual machines are often viewed within a separate window on the host system and can perform all the actions of a separate computer with its own software and resources. Given enough host resources, multiple virtual machines can be run on one physical host machine simultaneously.

Links

- EasyPHP - http://www.easyphp.org
- Linux Mint - http://www.linuxmint.com
- MAMP - https://www.mamp.info
- MySQL Home Page - http://www.mysql.com/
  - Documentation - http://dev.mysql.com/doc/
  - Downloads - http://www.mysql.com/downloads/
- Windows Installer - http://dev.mysql.com/downloads/windows/installer/
- Oracle VirtualBox - http://www.oracle.com/technetwork/server-storage/virtualbox/overview/index.html
- PHP official site - http://php.net
- WampServer - http://www.wampserver.com

Chapter III

Database Design - The First Steps

Creating a Model

In Chapter I, I listed a number of software titles and services that are used to organize information for analysis and reporting, each one with its own place in the database market. Although it's important to understand the software involved, database design starts independently of any software and involves principles which I'll be writing about in the next couple of chapters. If you understand these ideas, you will have a solid foundation in your study of database concepts. After that, learning to use a specific database software such as MySQL is much easier.

The first step is to organize the data into subjects and create a structure it will follow when stored in the database. This is part of the practice known as *data modeling* and is often done on paper or in a flowchart program rather than the database program itself. During this important planning phase, you can start from a blank page, determine what data needs to be stored, how it breaks down into tables and how it will fit into the final database structure. The practice of data modeling is often applied to large business systems and can cover many databases and networked systems but for the purpose of this book, I will describe how it applies to the creation of a single program.

Formal vs. Informal Data Modeling

The *formal* practice of data modeling is a process in and of itself that uses a language and set of symbols to document the process in three separate phases - conceptual, logical and physical. These phases can build on each other or even overlap as they add more detail about the structure of the database that will house the data. Entire books have been written just on the theories of data modeling.

In *practice*, data modeling is often done on an informal basis as organizations operate under deadlines and priorities that often discourage an abundance of documentation. Designers also often prefer to get down to the process of physical design rather than spending time creating a large collection of meticulously drawn flowcharts. Regardless of the style used, data modeling is an important part of design. Among the reasons for this:

- Often, when designing a database, beginning users are in a hurry to start entering data and don't think through the types of data that might be needed or where it will come from. This means going back later and redoing some or all of the design.

- A data model needs to be designed with the understanding that it might need to expand or change as new data and reporting requirements are discovered. This can happen either during the initial project or months later when business needs change. A clear data model, regardless of the process steps and symbols used, helps designers plan out the system in advance and anticipate changes that might be needed.

- Sometimes, databases are designed by one or more groups of people. It might be a designer from one department working with data owners and managers from other departments. Taking the time to model the data, preferably in a written specification, assists in communication between members of the team and helps to ensure that the right questions are asked to gather *all* of the requirements.

I am more interested in showing you how to organize data than detailing symbolism which is highly varied in practice and which you might never see again. The first part of the data modeling process that I describe in this chapter is an *informal* one that is meant to show the process of organizing the data without spending time on flowchart language that could distract from the principles involved. In the next chapter, I'll get a little more formal as I talk about the final step of mapping out the actual database tables.

Example Database - Job Search Plus

A few years ago, I designed a professional application with the current version of Microsoft Access to test the software's abilities at that time. My database experience started in earnest with Access in the late '90s and I later moved on to more advanced tools but I wanted to go back to Access for one project and see what could be done with it. I decided a program to assist people in managing a job search was timely and useful and I also wanted to take the application development process from start to finish. I wrote up a specification for a program called JobSearch 2010 and detailed what this application would do and the features it would contain. I designed the database structure in Access, created a program around it and even had someone test it for me and went through some formal revisions before making it available for download.

Now called Job Search Plus, this database serves as the first example in this book because of its moderate size; there's enough detail there to demonstrate the principles but not enough to get lost in. In addition to organizing a number of topics related to a job search, it shows how a database can be used to track activities as opposed to physical items and financial transactions.

Throughout this chapter, this example will demonstrate how real world requirements affect the structure of a database and the design of an application. Often, these requirements are referred to as *business rules* when they reflect the conditions of the business or process for which the system is designed. In Job Search Plus, for example, the possibility of multiple job leads at the same company and the need to allow for their entry is a business rule that dictates the relationships between different types of data. The possibility of more than one contact person at the same company requires that the database enable multiple contacts to be stored per company while defining one as the current contact on a particular job lead.

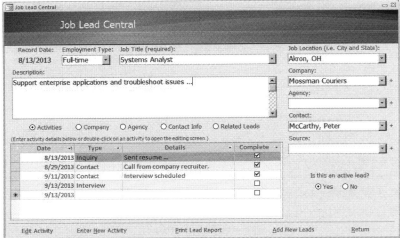

Figure 3.1 - Job Search Plus and its main data collection screen, shown here, demonstrates how a database program can pull together multiple types of information in one application.

The gathering of business rules might be performed by business analysts whose job it is to act as a liaison between the business and I.T. or it might be done by the programmers and developers themselves. Either way, the ability to ask the right questions for as long as necessary to get the required answers can determine the success or failure of a project.

Data Concepts and Relationships

The first step in creating a data model is to map out the concepts involved in the database and the relationships between them. This is a very important step, especially if you've been asked to build a database around a process where you don't fully *understand* all the relationships between the different types of data to be stored. Defining a central theme for the database can help you to get a clear picture of what the system needs to look like.

Job Search Plus is built around the process of an employment search where a job seeker is following up on a continuously growing collection of opportunities. Therefore, the central concept in the database is the *job lead*; an opportunity of one kind or another with information the user needs in order to follow up with the employer. The presence of a job lead implies another concept - the lead *source* that supplies the details of the opportunity. This could be an online job board, an employment agency or any other resource that provides the user with the initial notification of the job lead. There was the question of how much information I wanted to maintain on job lead resources. In the end, I decided not much was necessary but it needed to be more than just a list of names. Many of the resources might be online so I wanted the user to be able to keep a web link if there was one along with a description or notes about the resource. Therefore, the resource qualifies as one of the concepts in the database.

Looking at the job lead itself, each lead is going to have a company associated with it and a contact person, maybe more than one, and contact management is certainly part of the scope of a job search. At this point, we don't need to decide exactly what information will be stored but when it comes to contact management, the more information that can be stored, the better, so it definitely earns a place in the design.

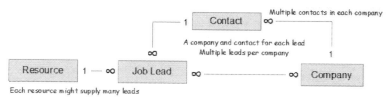

Figure 3.2 - The beginning data model shows the relationship between the job lead, resource and contacts.

In addition to listing the concepts, the model establishes the relationships between them. Figure 3.2 shows a basic conceptual model of the system at this point. Again, the symbols and style of notation used are my own but they present a clear picture of the objects and relationships involved. The job lead itself maintains one-to-many relationships with the resources and contacts as shown by the 1 and ∞ symbols on each end of the relationship lines while maintaining a many-to-many relationship with the Company object.

- Each resource that the job seeker uses, such as a website or newspaper, is able to supply more than one job lead and will therefore be referenced by each of those leads

- A recruiter or human resources person might serve as the contact for more than one opportunity over the course of a search. Therefore, each contact in the database can correspond to more than one job lead.

- While there is usually only a single employer for most jobs, many job seekers might go through recruiting agencies or temporary services for opportunities. Sometimes they might be employed by the agency while actually performing work for the agency's client company. While I've never seen more than two companies associated with a job lead, this still represents a many-to-many relationship between the concepts in the model; there might be multiple companies for each job lead and multiple job leads for each company. This requires special arrangements within a relational database as many-to-many relationships cannot be directly defined and I'll go into more detail about this in the next chapter.

The Contact object in the model maintains a relationship with both the Company and the Job Lead objects as it has a clear association with both. Each contact person might represent more than one job lead and each company might have more than one person on staff who is functioning as a contact person for job openings.

Moving forward, each job lead implies a decision on the job seeker's part about whether or not to follow up on it. If the job seeker does pursue the lead, he or she will need to record and document one or more activities such as applications, interviews and phone calls. I also wanted the user to be able to record reminders for future activities. I eventually decided to store these simply as activities with future dates and let the application display the necessary reminders based on them.

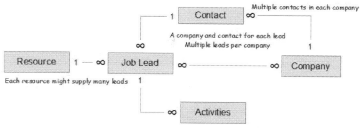

Figure 3.3 - Addition of job lead activities to the model with its relationship to the job lead

Figure 3.3 shows an informal conceptual model for the Job Search Plus database. It also might be referred to as an *Entity-Relationship Model* (ER Model or ER Diagram). It doesn't go into exhaustive detail but shows all the important concepts in the database and establishes the relationships between them along with some of the process details.

Filling in the Details

The concepts shown in Figure 3.3 are sometimes referred to as data *entities* by database professionals and there will usually be one or more items that describe each entity such as the job title or the company name. These are called *attributes*. Sometimes, they are defined as part of the conceptual model shown in the previous step and other times, they're saved for the next part of the process. In practice, it really depends on the preferences of the designers.

The next step in the modeling process goes into more detail about the data that needs to be stored and the relationships between categories of data. To understand this a little better, let's continue with the data model for Job Search Plus. As I stated in the last section, the central part of the data model is the job lead itself, the information that the average job seeker needs in order to pursue an opportunity. If you were recording a job lead, you would probably want the following information:

- Date Received / Recorded
- Job Title
- Description

- Full or Part Time
- Job Location
- Company Name
- Contact Name
- Phone Number

Each one of these items is an *attribute* of the job lead *entity* within the data model. Each item describes an aspect of the job lead that is required in order to completely describe the opportunity when it's stored. Just like with the previous step, it doesn't have to represent exhaustive detail or even the final list, just a list of items that could be generated within one or two planning meetings so the designer has a good idea of what is needed.

Now let's look at the Activities entity in the model which addresses the job seeker's activities on each job lead. If you're following up on an opportunity, there are a few things that you might want to record when documenting your search.

- Activity Date
- Activity Type (Sent Resume, Scheduled Interview, Follow-up call, etc..)
- Detail / Comments
- Complete

I included the last item since, as I mentioned before, this application will allow for future activities to be scheduled so that the program can show reminders. This is the kind of detail that I might not have included in the original version of the model as I hadn't realized the need for it yet. That's okay because, in systems of any great size, the data model can be a continuously evolving (or *living*) document that can grow and change along with the needs of the project.

Now we have a data model with entities described for job leads and activities. Notice that the Activities entity contains an attribute called 'Job Lead ID' which is used to refer back to the Job Lead entity. This is an example of how entities in a relational database (which will later become tables) are able to reference and relate to each other. You'll see more about this in the next chapter.

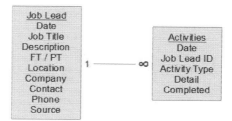

Figure 3.4 - The next step in the model is to show the entities and relationships as well as the basic attributes.

To complete the data model, we need to include the company, contact and resource entities from the conceptual model in Figure 3.3. When you're going after a job opportunity, it's a good idea to get as much information on the prospective employer as you can. Some of the information you might find helpful would be:

- Company Name
- Address
- City, State, Postal (ZIP) Code
- Phone / Fax
- Email
- Website
- Business Category (Technology, Pharmaceutical, Finance, etc..)
- Contact name and information

Again, this is not necessarily a complete list but adding the company and the contact entities to the model provides a place to put additional details as they're established. I've also added the Resource entity and a short list of attributes for it.

Many of the contact attributes are the same as the company attributes to allow for the possibility of multiple locations for the same employer. Again, notice the ID fields that allow some of the entities to reference each other. The job lead, in particular, references a job lead resource, a company and a contact. Adding these reference attributes is part of the process of deriving a working model from your data collection.

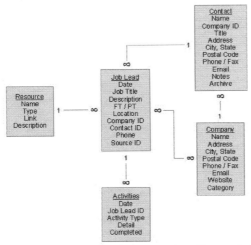

Figure 3.5 - Updated data model with all entities and attributes

While the data models in Figures 3.3 and 3.5 have the same set of entities, this doesn't always need to be the case. One concept in the first model could translate to two items in the next step and require other supporting objects. The two models represent different parts of the process and express the required information differently. The most important thing to focus on is understanding how the system is to work and what information is needed.

Another difference between this approach and the formal documentation you might see elsewhere is that the entities in the above diagrams do not include details such as whether the fields contain numeric, date or text values or how many characters are allowed in each field. You'll learn more about data types and field sizes in the following chapters. Sometimes, a logical data model will have the attributes translated into table fields along with the types and sizes for the fields themselves and sometimes this is left for the next phase of design.

Figure 3.6 shows a portion of an Enhanced Entity-Relationship diagram (EER diagram) prepared in MySQL Workbench, one of the free tools available for MySQL. Earlier in the chapter, Figure 3.3

showed a simplified ER diagram with the basic concepts and relationships.

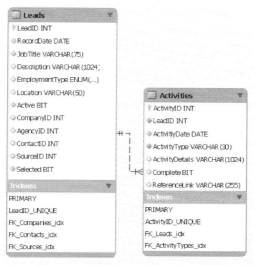

Figure 3.6 - A portion of an EER diagram for Job Search Plus prepared in MySQL Workbench showing the Leads and Activities table linked by the LeadID field

The *EER* diagram, which has a greater resemblance to a formal logical data model diagram, shows the fields in detail with data types such as INT (a numeric integer) and VARCHAR (for text and other alphanumeric data) along with the number of characters allowed for fields where relevant. Also notice the different way of representing the relationship between the tables.

This diagramming tool assists in the modeling process in MySQL Workbench and the diagram in Figure 3.6 is part of a larger one that I created in that software. After defining the tables and fields, I added the relationships and was then able to drag the table definitions onto the diagram area and the software generated the nice, neat representations of them that you see above. This diagram then serves as a blueprint which MySQL can use to generate the physical tables and other database objects. Comparing this model diagram to my earlier diagram demonstrates a few things that you'll encounter while working with databases.

- It's best not to get too attached to one set of symbols or type of representation. The point of documentation is to communicate the necessary facts about the system to whomever might need them, not to demonstrate a mastery of documentation techniques themselves. An allowance for different methods of expression is as important here as it is in other types of communication.

- Documentation is as important *during* and *after* design as it is *before* and is often left for that point in the process anyway. Designers might find it easier to design within the database software than on paper as the software includes all the necessary tools. It's also possible to create design areas that are separate from the live data. Once the prototype has been designed and tested, the software often provides tools which make documentation easier and less time-consuming.

- There is a difference between attributes and table fields. You'll notice more items in the Leads table in Figure 3.6 than in the Job Lead entity from Figure 3.5. This is because the basic descriptions of the data required have been broken down into the actual fields required to store it and relate the tables. A more graphic example would be in the Company and Contact entities where attributes like 'City, State' and 'Phone / Fax' would be broken down into multiple fields as needed. You'll see the reason for this in the next chapter. A practiced designer can often predict the actual fields needed as part of the logical model. If you're just starting out in design, however, it doesn't hurt to start with the descriptive attributes shown in my earlier example.

Defining the Tables

The final phase of modeling the data is a *physical data model*, also referred to as a *schema*. In the case of designing a database like Job Search Plus, this means organizing the required information from the existing data model into a set of tables and fields within a particular database software. The entities from the logical model each become one or more tables and the attributes are the basis for fields within those tables that can hold the data entered by the users. Just as the entities in the logical model are related, the tables can be linked to each other so that, for example, a specific job lead can be retrieved along with all of the activity records for that lead. In addition to tables, the physical model might include queries that will retrieve data from one or more tables and lists of procedures for manipulating data within the database.

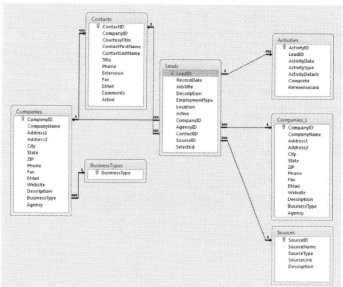

Figure 3.7 - The Microsoft Access relationships diagram for Job Search Plus

A lot more detail is added in this phase if it hasn't been already. In addition to the field sizes and data types mentioned earlier, these table definitions also include indexes to speed up searches and fields that will identify specific records. This is so the relationships can be maintained between tables. How long this step takes depends on the thoroughness of the information already gathered and the experience of the database designer. If I have complete information on the database I want to design, I can put several related tables together in an hour or two although there will probably be some tweaking here and there as the system is tested. I usually develop the queries and procedures based on the needs of whatever application is accessing the database.

Although this final phase can be done relatively fast, there are some rules to follow that require a fair amount of explanation and I'll be doing this in the next chapter as I show you how to design the physical model for Job Search Plus. While I will ultimately be demonstrating this in MySQL, Figure 3.7 shows the working model of the database as it was represented in Microsoft Access.

The relationships diagram in Figure 3.7 would more closely represent a logical data model as it includes all of the tables, fields and relationships but it does not show the field types or sizes. I've arranged the tables within the diagram for clarity but as you can see by the relationships, the Leads table is at the center of things with other tables for activities, company and contact information and lead sources. (The 'Companies' and 'Companies_1' tables are actually the same table referred to twice for different purposes.) The tables are laid out according to the rules of a process called *database normalization* which you will learn about in the next chapter. While the model might look a little complex, you will see the advantages to categorizing data into separate physical tables and how easy it is to pull the data back together with queries and reports.

Chapter Summary

As you saw throughout this chapter, real world requirements affect the structure of a database and the design of an application. Often, these requirements are referred to as *business rules* when they reflect the conditions of the business or process for which the system is designed. Business rules are a very important part of program specifications as software must serve the needs of the businesses and individuals who are expected to use it. The gathering of business rules might be performed by business analysts whose job it is to act as a liaison between the business and I.T. or it might be done by the programmers and developers themselves. Either way, the ability to ask the right questions for as long as necessary to get the required answers can determine the success or failure of a project.

Once the business rules are defined, data modeling is a necessary step in database design and can be done independently of specific database software. This process creates a logical structure for the data and helps the designer to better define the information that needs to be included in the design. A data model is a living document that enables the design of a robust database that can more easily change and grow with the needs of the organization.

The three phases of data modeling can build upon each other, starting with the conceptual model. This phase expresses the structure in terms of the real-world concepts or objects described by the data and how those concepts relate to each other. The logical model then defines the attributes that will be used to describe these objects and further defines the relationships. Finally, in a relational database, the physical model defines the data structure in terms of a set of related tables, indexes and other objects that enable the data to be stored in a physical database.

For Further Study

Review Questions

1. What is the primary purpose of creating a data model for a database?

2. List three things accomplished through the process of creating a data model.

3. What are the three phases of data modeling and what order are they performed in?

4. What are business rules and what role do they play in application development?

5. What is an Entity-Relationship Diagram, what is an Enhanced Entity-Relationship Diagram and which phases of the modeling process does each of them resemble.

6. What is the difference between a data entity and an attribute?

7. How do data entities and attributes relate to the tables and fields in the working database?

8. What does a one-to-many relationship indicate?

9. What is another name for the physical data model?

10. What is the difference between a data model and a database model?

Exercises

Look for additional examples of data models from everyday life and take them through the three data models shown here. Here are a few to start with:

1. Take the example of Job Search Plus and turn it around, imagining the process from the viewpoint of either a recruiter or an employment website like Monster.com. What business rules would need to be designed into the database to enable the recruiter to evaluate multiple applicants for multiple jobs? What rules would enable the website to store an indefinite number of opportunities from many different companies and areas? Keep in mind that both the recruiter and the website need to work with

various amounts of historical data as positions close and applicants are processed.

2. Your book collection would probably be easy to model as a database with the book as the main concept but what if you expanded the collection to include DVDs and music?

   o Would you store books and other media together in one collection or treat them as separate entities?

   o What details would need to be stored on each item to uniquely identify it for any report you might want to create?

   o What information would you want for your own purposes?

3. Taking the media collection example a step further, how does the data model change if the collection is in a public library and the items are available for lending?

   o What information do you want to store for borrowers and how would you identify them?

   o How would you account for multiple copies of the same book and determine if each copy is in or out of the library?

   o How would you design the model so that you could link a borrower to the specific copy of the book he or she had borrowed?

   o Would you maintain a borrowing history for each person and if so, how?

Don't worry if these examples seem like brain teasers at this point. Part of learning to model data is facing new challenges and on a couple of my early and difficult projects, it took me a few days to come up with the right model that would account for all the aspects of a system. The important thing is to get your mind in the right mode and start thinking of data in terms of something that can be organized for easier understanding.

Terms to Remember

Attributes - In a data model, attributes describe each entity or category of data. For example, the attributes of a 'Customer' entity might include customer name, address, phone number and other items that would describe a specific customer.

Business Rules - Conditions of the business or organization such as company policies, work flows, financial practices or legal requirements that define the requirements for an application.

Conceptual Model - In the process of modeling data for a relational database, the conceptual model provides a basic picture of high-level concepts or subjects within the data collection and how they relate to each other. For example, an order database would have concepts for both customers and orders with a one-to-many relationship between them as there might be many orders for each customer.

Data modeling - The process of defining the required data within a system and creating a structure in which the data can be stored, easily referenced and retrieved.

Database normalization - The process of organizing data within related tables in a relational database and applying rules which minimize or eliminate duplication and inconsistency within the data stored.

Entities - In a data model, an entity describes a subject or category for which data needs to be stored. These entities can relate to each other based on how they interact and how data is moved within the system. For example, the data model for a school database might include Student, Course and Instructor entities which would enable information on individual students, instructors and courses to be stored within the system.

Entity-Relationship Model - A diagram that depicts the data entities in a system and the relationships between them. Most closely relates to the conceptual data model.

Logical Model - The logical model builds upon the conceptual model, translating the different concepts and subjects within the data collection into data entities with attributes that describe specific aspects for each entity. For example, the customer concept within the model for an order database would become a customer entity with attributes such as name, address, contact person and more.

Relational database - A general purpose database model in which information is categorized within related tables for easy retrieval and reference.

Physical Model (Schema) - This phase of data modeling defines the tables and fields needed to store information within a relational database. At a minimum, the schema includes the definitions of tables, table fields and relationships between tables. It can also include the field types and sizes, indexes, keys, custom data views, functions and other items within the physical database.

Chapter IV

Database Normalization

From Design to Reality

In the last chapter, I showed you how two types of data modeling are used to organize information for storage within a database, starting with the most basic, conceptual model and then adding detail with the logical model. In this and following chapters, I'll show you the final steps in modeling the data and organizing it into the physical tables and other structures contained within a finished database.

Remember that the type of database being discussed here is called a *relational database* which uses tables and fields to organize information by category. These tables are linked to each other within the database management software so that the relationships between the categories of data can be maintained. This type of data organization was introduced in 1970 by a computer scientist named Edgar F. Codd. Dr. Codd developed a set of rules by which data could be organized to avoid duplication and inconsistencies, thereby ensuring the accuracy of the data and simplifying its maintenance. These rules also make adding new types of information easier because there is already a context to build on and a set of guidelines to follow. The process by which these rules are applied is called *database normalization*.

Looking Back

Let's take another look at the entire logical model for the Job Search Plus application. Figure 4.1 shows the data model that breaks the information down into entities, or categories of data, and the attributes that describe the entities.

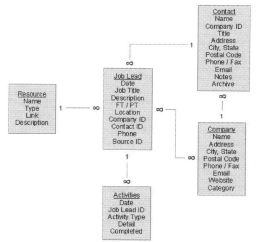

Figure 4.1 - The logical data model is the starting point for designing the tables and relationships that form the database.

The Normalization Process

While there are several rules in database normalization, also referred to as *Normal Forms*, there are only a few that you really need to be concerned with as you learn to develop databases. If you implement these, you will have a very stable and well-organized database. As these rules were developed by a computer scientist and have been restated by other computer scientists and database experts, their official definitions use language that can be a little confusing. It's important for you to be aware of some of the terms used in order to understand the concepts involved regardless of whatever statement of these rules you come across later. With all the different processes that require databases, these rules can be applied in different ways, sometimes selectively.

The Normal Forms are presented as the *First Normal Form*, *Second Normal Form* and so on because they are cumulative; each successive form requires the database to comply with the previous forms. You might also see them abbreviated by database professionals as 1NF, 2NF, etc..

First Normal Form (1NF)

The First Normal Form requires the following:

- All fields within the tables represent single data values that have been reduced to the smallest useful piece of information. This condition is referred to as *atomicity*. Fields cannot contain multiple values. These single values are referred to as *scalar* values.

- The tables cannot have repeating fields or groups of fields. A table should not have multiple fields for the same attribute for the purpose of tracking multiple items.

Atomicity reduces data to the smallest units that still have meaning when presented within a table just as an atom cannot be broken down any further and still represent the same element. This can be a matter of interpretation based on the data and the needs of the application.

In Job Search Plus, the Companies and Contacts tables include addresses with city and state values for each company. I could store the address in a single field, i.e. '123 Lark Drive, Ocala, FL 34470' and this might work very well for the application until I needed to sort the list of companies by city, state or ZIP code. One of the big advantages to an electronic database is the ability to sort data for quick retrieval and analysis. For this reason, the address is broken down into multiple fields. Remember that these fields represent *attributes* of the company or contact shown in the table.

Address	City	State	Zip
123 Lark Drive	Ocala	FL	34470

Figure 4.2 - The First Normal Form requires data to be broken down into the smallest meaningful pieces of information.

Breaking the address down into these separate attributes such as City and ZIP Code allows for a sort or selection to be performed on any of the fields. I can find all of the companies in a specific city or state with a single database query which you'll see in a later chapter.

Breaking down the values into smaller parts also helps to avoid duplication within the database which is one of the main purposes of normalization. It's easier to search on the string '123 Lark Drive' or a ZIP code than it is to search on the entire address which is more likely to have inconsistent formatting that could evade a search. This means that information is less likely to be entered twice by mistake.

The next question might be "What about the Address field?".The Address contains multiple parts that could be separated into different fields, allowing the data to be sorted by street number or name. This would usually be an example of *over-normalization*. Except in some very specialized applications, the work required to reassemble the address each time it needs to be used outweighs the benefits of being able to sort on parts of the address. Also, the street name on its own would no longer directly represent an attribute of the company or contact being represented or a recognizable value whereas an address like "123 Lark Drive" is directly recognizable as an address and references whatever is at that address.

The second condition of the First Normal Form is that the tables cannot have repeating fields or groups of fields. An example of this would be the one-to-many relationship between the Job Leads and Activities data. If this data was being presented on a spreadsheet, a common practice might be to have multiple fields titled 'Activity1', 'Activity2', 'Activity3', etc. to allow for more than one activity. There are a couple problems with this approach. First, it limits the number of activities that can be stored. How many activities do you allow for by adding extra fields and how many fields do you risk having to leave empty because specific leads don't have enough activities to fill them? The second problem is that it becomes very difficult to search the data on the "many" side of the relationship. In order to see all the activities for a job lead, you would have to search each of the activity fields in turn and then assemble the data somehow.

Lead Date	Company	Job Title	Location	Activity1	Activity2	Activity3
04/01/13	Premier Paper	Salesperson	Orlando, FL	Sent resume ...	Follow-up call ...	Scheduled interview ...

Figure 4.3 - The First Normal Form prohibits repeating fields of the type shown here.

The solution to the repeating fields is already indicated in the data model and that is to have two tables; one for the job leads and another for activities. These two tables will be linked so that each record in the Activities table can be associated with a specific job lead and each job lead can be associated with one or more activity records. This one-to-many relationship also exists between the Companies and Contacts data where there can be multiple contacts in each company. In this way, simple requests can be issued to the database for information such as:

- All the activities associated with a specific lead or company
- All activities within a specific date range with a reference to the associated lead
- All contacts within a specific company
- An alphabetized list of contacts with the company name for each contact

Once the requirements of the First Normal Form are met, the physical data model looks something like Figure 4.4.

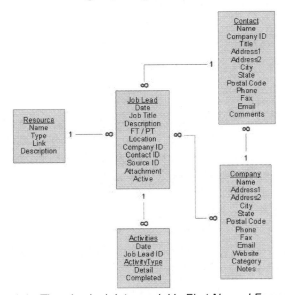

Figure 4.4 - The physical data model in First Normal Form (1NF)

Notice that the Company and Contact tables both have Address1 and Address2 fields which appears to violate the prohibition on repeating fields. These are exceptions I've made to the First Normal Form. In real life, many addresses contain two lines and these two lines refer to different parts of the address. Also, I can be sure there won't be a third line.

A second example is the Location field in the Job Leads table. Although you don't see the data at this point, this field is intended to hold a value that indicates the actual location of the job which might differ from the company or contact addresses. For this application, I decided that a free-form value such as 'Spokane, WA' or 'New York City' was needed as a flexible way to indicate the actual work location as opposed to the address listed for the company and I am willing to accept the limitations on sorting this might cause because the field is simply meant for the user's information on specific leads. While adherence to the Normal Forms is important, the usability of the application and the needs of the user take precedence.

As I said earlier, the Normal Forms are cumulative and must be applied in order. As you're about to see, the completion of the First Normal Form makes it possible to carry out those that follow.

Second Normal Form (2NF)

The Second Normal Form requires that the database *meet the conditions of the First Normal Form* and that:

- All fields that are not part of a table's key must be functionally dependent on the entire key.

Most tables in a relational database have a field or combination of fields that serves to uniquely identify each record in the table. This is called the table's *primary key.* A primary key is a special index field within the table. Index fields assist the database in searching or sorting information on that field and the primary key does this while also uniquely identifying each record. Tables can also have fields that store values from *another* table's primary key in order to reference records within that table. These fields are referred to as *foreign keys*. You can see an example in Figure 4.6 where the Contact entity has a field labeled 'CompanyID'. Each contact record will store an ID value in this field which matches a primary key value in the Company table. The CompanyID field in the Company table is the table's primary key while the matching field in the Contacts table is the foreign key that points back to the Company table.

A table can actually have more than one index field, including the primary key, that indicates values which must be unique for each record such as a driver's license number or a product serial number. There can be only one *primary* key that uniquely identifies a specific record to other tables, however. A key or index definition can also contain more than one field so that one of the field values might be duplicated within a table but no two records can have the same *combination* of values in those fields. This is called a *composite key.*

Sometimes there's a field within a table that provides a naturally occurring unique value. For example, in a small library database, the ISBN assigned to each book would be a unique value that could be used as the primary key because it is unique. However, this might cause a problem if the library has more than one copy of a specific book so that the ISBN is no longer unique within that collection. If the library used the ISBN *and* another field such as a copy number, this would be an example of a composite key. There might be two records with the same ISBN within the database, but they would have different numbers indicating which copy was represented in each record.

ISBN	Title	Author
978-0871403773	Letters to a Young Scientist	Edward O. Wilson
978-1449325947	CSS3: The Missing Manual	David Sawyer McFarland
978-0307743657	The Shining	Stephen King

ISBN	Copy	Title	Author
978-0871403773	001	Letters to a Young Scientist	Edward O. Wilson
978-1449325947	001	CSS3: The Missing Manual	David Sawyer McFarland
978-1449325947	002	CSS3: The Missing Manual	David Sawyer McFarland
978-0307743657	001	The Shining	Stephen King
978-0307743657	002	The Shining	Stephen King

Figure 4.5 - Some potential primary keys occur naturally. Other times, artificial values are needed to uniquely identify a record.

In an employee database, a company-assigned employee number could be used so long as the company procedures ensured that it was unique and that specific numbers were never reused. The Social Security number or driver's license number, being unique values, might seem like good primary keys but I need to stress that confidential information should *never* be used as a table's primary key. This is because the key cannot always be hidden from anyone who needs to view the records. A unique index could still be placed on these fields to ensure they are not duplicated within the table.

More often, an extra field is added to the tables which provides an artificial unique value for each record as it's created. This is called a *surrogate key*. The database management software can generate an automatically incrementing number or unique string of characters as each record is created. This is referred to as a *globally unique identifier (GUID)*.

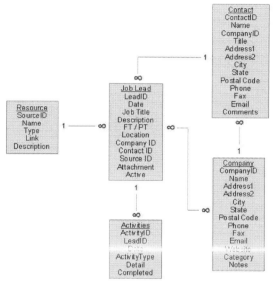

Figure 4.6 – The Second Normal Form (2NF) adds table keys and ensures that all non-key attributes (fields) relate to that key.

Looking at the current tables in the Job Search Plus database, many of them do *not* have naturally unique values that can be used as primary keys. The Job Lead table has no fields that might be unique on their own. The combination of company and job title would often be unique until the user tries to re-apply for the same job at the same company. While composite keys can be used as primary keys, I don't like to do this because this means that both fields within the key must be duplicated in any table that wants to reference them. I also avoid using using values that are subject to change. This means that the Job Leads table gets a surrogate key. The same applies to the Company, Contact, Resource and Activities tables.

With the addition of the primary keys in Figure 4.6, each table gains a new field or two. All of these are surrogate keys meaning their values are actually unique values generated by the database as the records are created. The practical benefits of using primary and foreign keys is that specific information such as the company phone number is stored in one location and referenced as needed instead of being duplicated over and over again. This means less space is taken up in the database and there's less chance of errors being made as information is duplicated.

- Job Leads has it's own primary key, LeadID, and has links to both the Company (CompanyID) and Contact (ContactID) tables to store references to specific companies and contacts. The LeadID field is the primary key while the Company ID, Contact ID and Source ID fields are foreign keys pointing to other tables. For example, a job lead record with a CompanyID of 10 would point to a record in the Companies table with a matching CompanyID value.

- If there is more than one job lead for the same company or with the same contact, there is no need to duplicate the company and contact addresses or other information within the Job Leads table. Instead it's stored in the respective tables and referenced by these foreign key values. If any of the details for a company or contact change, they are changed *once* in the appropriate table and instantly reflected in any reports because of the link between the tables.

- The Activities table has it's own ActivityID primary key and uses the LeadID foreign key to reference a specific job lead record for each activity. This means that the database can return all activity records for a specific lead.

- The Resource table now has a SourceID primary key which is referenced in the Job Leads table to provide information on the source for a job lead.

Given the heavy use of surrogate keys, an easier way to think of the Second Normal Form is that every field outside the table's primary key must directly describe the *subject* of that table and the value of the field must *directly* depend on which item is being represented by the record, even if it's not unique for each record. The company e-mail or address is not *directly* related to the job lead but to the company being referenced and there is no need to store this information over and over again for each job lead at a specific company. In the same way, the job description and location are not *directly* related to the details of each activity for a job lead and there is no reason to repeat these details over and over again for every action taken so they are stored *once* in the Job Lead table and the details of separate activities are stored in the Activities table. The two are then related by the LeadID field.

Third Normal Form (3NF)

The Third Normal Form states that in addition to the requirements of the first two forms being met:

- All fields that are not part of the key must be functionally independent of each other.

Simply, this means that a change to a value in one non-key field must not require a change in another non-key field - no calculated fields and no fields that explain each other. To sum up the meaning of the second and third forms, you could remember it as many database students have over the years:

"Every non-key field must provide a fact about the key, the whole key, and *nothing but the key* (so help me Codd)."

An example of a calculated field might be found in a customer order database where the total price for an order line is stored in a 'Total' field and calculated from the number of items multiplied by the price. Figure 4.7 shows an example of this. The example actually has two separate violations of the Normal Forms; the Total field at the end of the record *and* the ProductName field which depends on the ProductID field. There's no need to store either of these fields because the ProductName field would more properly belong in a separate Products reference table as required by the Second Normal

Form. Whatever program or report is accessing the data can quickly calculate the figure in the Total field as needed.

OrderLineID	OrderID	ProductID	ProductName	Price	Quantity	Total
003	4324	A8791	3' x 3' table	$285.00	2	$570.00

Figure 4.7 - Calculated and related non-key fields are potential violations of the Third Normal Form.

To see why this is a problem, consider what happens if the customer changes the quantity or even the specified item on the order. Multiple fields must then be updated and *any* program that might be written to change this data must be designed with this requirement in mind. The database isn't going to do it automatically. This might seem simple enough but such things can be forgotten in company environments where many hands are in the process and multiple programs are designed over time. What eventually happens is that every new person who ends up working with the data has to be told "Don't use that field, it's not even updated anymore.". Inevitably, someone doesn't get the message so time is wasted on bad information.

Another example of related fields might be the inventory database at your local supermarket which might have a table listing all the products the store carries. This table would have fields for the product name, package type and maybe the UPC or a model number. It would *not* necessarily have fields for the amount of the inventory currently on hand or the last time the item was sold since those values do not relate directly to the product information and are continually changing. These values would be calculated as needed based on the records in other tables of the inventory receipts and sales.

Fortunately, the example model is already in compliance with the Third Normal Form so no changes are needed at this point.

Boyce-Codd Normal Form (BCNF or 3.5NF)

This Normal Form was developed a few years after the original forms by E.F. Codd and another computer scientist, Raymond F. Boyce. Boyce also developed the query language used with relational databases which you'll see later in the book.

This form is rarely needed because it deals with tables that have multiple possible keys that overlap each other. Of the three references I used while writing this chapter, only one mentioned Boyce-Codd. It's considered an extension of the Third Normal Form because, most of the time, the achievement of 3NF will have resolved any potential issues in the tables. Sometimes, however, there are additional fields that can be re-distributed to another table to avoid values having to be duplicated in multiple records.

Course_ID	CourseTitle	Instructor	Schedule	Facility	Days	Start Time	End Time
101	Accounting Principles	Smith	Evening	Collins Bldg	M, W, F	20:00	21:30
102	Beginning Programming	Grady	Daytime	Riverfront Drive	TH	9:00	10:30
103	Advanced Database Design	Hansen	Evening	Collins Bldg	T	18:00	19:30
104	Business Communications	Martinez	Daytime	Riverfront Drive	T, F	14:00	15:30

Figure 4.8 - Class schedule before application of Boyce-Codd Normal Form (BCNF)

That's probably the best way to evaluate a table for BCNF; are there still fields that can be sent to their own tables to avoid duplication or combinations of fields that consistently show the same combinations of values? If so, it's worth looking at whether this change to the database will make it more efficient.

I'll give you a couple examples of normalization that can be done under Boyce-Codd. Figure 4.8 shows a schedule of day and evening classes which take place in two different facilities.

This example meets the first three forms; the fields have single values and there are no repeating groups, allowing for the Days field which isn't worth creating an extra table over (1NF). The CourseID is the key and the rest of the fields relate directly to the course (2NF). Finally, none of the the non-key fields can be said to be strictly dependent on each other (3NF). 'Strictly' is the key word here. Notice that the Collins Building only hosts evening classes and the facility at Riverfront Drive is only used for daytime classes. Looking at the start and end times in terms of a facility schedule, you might also guess that the class times are going to be consistent, at least throughout each semester. This table can be further normalized as shown in Figure 4.9.

The table has now been split into two linked tables with the first holding the classes themselves and the second maintaining the list of available class times in each building. The second table contains time slots at specific locations and these time slots could be changed based on facility needs and conditions. The two tables are linked by the Schedule_ID field. Through this arrangement, many more courses can be scheduled in the course table on different days without duplicating the facility and time information.

Course_ID	CourseTitle	Instructor	Days	Schedule_ID
101	Accounting Principles	Smith	M, W, F	1
102	Beginning Programming	Grady	TH	2
103	Advanced Database Design	Hansen	T	3
104	Business Communications	Martinez	T, F	4

Schedule_ID	Facility	Start Time	End Time	Description
1	Collins Bldg	20:00	21:30	Evening
2	Riverfront Drive	9:00	10:30	Daytime
3	Collins Bldg	18:00	19:30	Evening
4	Riverfront Drive	14:00	15:30	Daytime

Figure 4.9 - Boyce-Codd addresses the possibility of multiple keys in the table.

The second example in Figure 4.10 is an employee table which includes information on former employees and, when applicable, the reasons and dates of their departure from the company.

Employee_ID	First Name	Last Name	Current	Reason for Leaving	Release Date
101	Janice	Petersen	Yes		
102	Robin	Smith	No	Quit	1/25/2012
103	John	Drake	Yes		
104	Robert	Jameson	No	Dismissed	5/17/2012

Figure 4.10 - An example in which certain fields might only be used for a subset of records.

The Third Normal Form states that the change in one non-key field should not require the change of another non-key field and there could be some debate as to whether this table satisfies this rule. If the Current field is changed to 'No', indicating an employee is no longer with the company, it does *not* absolutely require that a reason and date be entered. Still, even if this satisfies the requirements of 3NF and the company, the arrangement leaves a lot of needless blank space in the table as there will usually be more current than former employees. This means that queries and reports will have to be designed to ignore all those blank fields whenever searching for information on former employees.

Another option is to move the last two columns to their own linked table which represents the repeating event of employee separations from the company.

Employee_ID	First Name	Last Name	Current
101	Janice	Petersen	Yes
102	Robin	Smith	No
103	John	Drake	Yes
104	Robert	Jameson	No

Employee_ID	Reason for Leaving	Release Date
102	Quit	1/25/2012
104	Dismissed	5/17/2012

Figure 4.11 - A second table refines the data model by focusing on the subset of former employees.

This arrangement in Figure 4.11 organizes the data so that a dedicated table can be consulted for information on former employees. The table can maintain its own indexes and whatever information is kept specifically on former employees can be quickly searched and sorted as needed. The EmployeeID field can be used both as a primary key for this table and as a foreign key that references the Employees table to access the person's name.

Additional Reasons for Normalization

Outside the Normal Forms shown in this chapter, there are other reasons to split information off into other tables which, in themselves, might point to normalization possibilities that hadn't been spotted already.

- *Security* - Not all data is meant to be seen by everyone using the database. Depending on the database software being used, the safest bet might be to split the data into another table with a primary / foreign key arrangement so that separate permissions can be assigned on the privileged data. Again, this depends on the software being used. Going back to the employee database for an example, information such as Social Security numbers, salaries or even certain contact information might be privileged to the point where it needs to be in a separate table.

- *Table size* - Depending on the application, an excessive number of fields in a table not only makes the table difficult to analyze and support but might indicate that further normalization can be done. If certain fields are rarely updated, such as addresses and phone numbers, they can be moved into another linked table to reduce the size of the original table. This also means that the information can be accessed only when needed and doesn't have to be pulled up every time the main table is accessed. This can help to reduce the demand on the system and speed things up for everyone.

- *Reference* - Sometimes tables exist just to maintain a list of frequently-used values and to ensure that these values are consistently entered. These are often called lookup tables. An example of this would include a table that lists ZIP codes for each city. With this table, a program could fill in the city and state information after the user enters a ZIP code. This table might not even be permanently linked to the other tables but would simply be available for the program to search by ZIP code.

So, In addition to eliminating duplication within the database, proper organization of the information can promote security, manageability and accuracy of your data.

Application Specific Reasons

Let's compare the physical model we have now to the original model for the Job Search Plus application shown in the last chapter. With a couple of exceptions and field names, you can see the two are pretty close.

The most obvious difference is one that I mentioned in the last chapter and that's the apparent duplication of the Companies table in Figure 4.13. This is not a duplication of the table itself but a representation of the two relationships between the Leads and Companies tables.

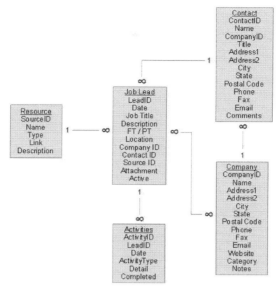

Figure 4.12 - Current data model after application of Normal Forms

A job lead might need more than one company associated with it; the company that's actually looking to hire an employee and a recruiting company acting on the other company's behalf. A job seeker should be able to maintain information on both. With the First Normal Form and its prohibition on repeating fields in mind, I used the same reasoning that I used with the double address fields in the Companies and Contacts tables.

- The Leads table in Figure 4.13 has two fields; a CompanyID and an AgencyID field which represent two attributes of the job lead which are similar but not quite the same. In my years of job hunting experience, I never encountered a lead where I needed to track the information on three companies so I can be reasonably sure these are the only two needed.

- The Leads table has both foreign key fields *and* two relationships to the Companies table with both fields in Leads linking to the CompanyID primary key field.

- Both relationships are one-to-many relationships with each company, especially the recruiting agencies, available for use in many Leads records.

- The Companies table in Figure 4.13 has a True/False or *boolean* field called Agency which indicates if the company is a recruiter. The program that accesses this database can use this field to limit the view to agencies if necessary.

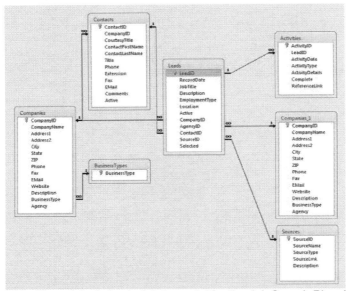

Figure 4.13 - The original physical data model for the Job Search Plus database

The final difference is the Business Types table which lists the different business categories a company might fall into. This might include categories such as health care, aerospace, engineering, finance, etc.. This is an example of a lookup table and can be used by a program to restrict the entry within a field to certain values and to ensure that those values are correctly entered each time. This makes it easier to search on a field because you can be certain the values will be consistent and free of typos. This table has a single field which is also the primary key and links back to the Companies table on a corresponding BusinessType field. Instead of using a number to represent the item within the table, it just uses the entire value such as 'Software' or 'Automotive'.

Updating the new data model with these changes, it looks like the model shown in Figure 4.14. This represents the logical data model as it exists independently of any software with the Normal Forms applied and customizations added to handle specific business rules.

The arrangement of the tables within the model is simply for presentation purposes and doesn't have anything to do with the function. Remember, however, that this doesn't have to be the *final* design. Business needs change over time and a well-designed data model is adaptable to the necessary changes so that it doesn't have to be scrapped and replaced.

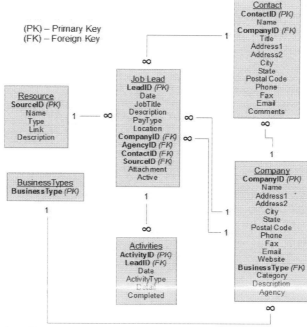

Figure 4.14 - The updated data model after application of the Normal Forms

Learning how to apply the Normal Forms takes practice and happens over the course of multiple projects so if they still seem a little confusing, don't worry. Later in the book, I'll run through a couple more examples to show how they can be applied to different types of data.

Data or Data*base*?

In the last couple of chapters, I've written about the process of creating a *data* model in order to organize categories of information. A data*base* model is something different. While a data model describes how a specific collection of data is organized, a database model describes how a specific database software or technology is *able* to organize and store data. The most popular database model at this point is the relational model that MySQL uses and that you're learning about in this book. It's based on categorizing the data into separate tables, also called *relations*, which are then linked to each other through relationships. The relational model is a good, general purpose approach to organizing data that accommodates a wide variety of uses. There are other types of databases that are used for different purposes. Each database type uses its own set of organizational rules for building the database and this set of rules is referred to as a *database* model.

- The **hierarchical database** model arranges data into multiple levels similar to the directory structure on your hard drive or a company organizational chart. There are parent-child relationships between different types of data just as in the relational model but each child entity can only have one parent. It doesn't allow for tables such as the Leads table in this chapter which looks to both the Companies and the Sources tables for information. The model is still used within XML files as tags within the documents form the same kind of hierarchy.

- The **document-oriented database** is another example where data is grouped into documents instead of records. While the records in a relational database table all have the same fields, a document-oriented database allows for the possibility that not all of the items that need to be stored *can* have the same properties. This is called semi-structured data and documents are stored as entries within the database which is also referred to as a document store.

- The relational model that you've seen in this chapter could be considered a two-dimensional model as it relies on a linked series of tables containing rows and columns. The **multi-dimensional database** model stores data in "cubes" that allow for sophisticated analyses and projections based on totals, averages and other groupings of the data with less effort than a relational database. For example, a sales database could allow for quick analysis of a company's data based on dimensions such as sales region, office location, sales person, year and product with analyses answering questions such as "How many units of this product were sold in each sales region per year for the past five years?". The databases are often accessed through an interface resembling a pivot table where the data is presented based in a flexible table format and based on the question the user is asking. The model is often referred to in connection with Online Analytical Processing (OLAP).

So, essentially, in determining the *database* model, the designer asks "What kind of data is it and which set of rules do we need to use to store it?". Once that's decided, the *data* model is determined as the designer asks "How do we break down the data according to the database model we've chosen?". It's roughly the same difference as asking "What language will I learn?" and "How do I work with the grammar of the language I've chosen?". The relational model I've shown here is the one you're most likely to encounter out in the world but it's good to understand that it's not the only one in case you run into something else one day.

Chapter Summary

In a relational database, data is categorized by subject into related tables. This process, referred to as *data normalization*, helps eliminate duplication and enables the information to be retrieved in an efficient and accurate manner. In this chapter, you saw the process of applying the normalization rules, known as Normal Forms, in order to design the set of tables that will make up the database. You also saw how table keys are used to relate the tables to each other and identify specific information. Normalization can also help create a more secure and manageable database by splitting data into smaller tables that can receive specific permissions. While database normalization provides a systematic way to organize data, it is also done with attention to the needs of the specific data being organized and the organization that owns it.

For Further Study

Review Questions

1. What are the two main objectives of database normalization?

2. Is it possible to apply the Normal Forms to a database independently of each other? Can a database be in Third Normal Form (3NF) without achieving First Normal Form (1NF)? Why or why not?

3. What are the benefits of applying the First Normal Form and ensuring that values within a database are atomic?

4. At what point can the data in a field be considered atomic? Is it possible to carry atomicity too far and how do you know this has happened?

5. You are creating a book database and each book title might have multiple description tags attached to it. The database needs to allow for any number of tag values per

book and the user needs to be able to search on these tags to find books they might like. How do you associate the tags with the books in the database?

6. What is the purpose of a foreign key and how is one created?

7. In an employee database, would you store a person's physical age, their date of birth or both? Why?

8. In the U.S., employers collect data such as race, nationality, veteran status and gender in order to provide reports to government agencies on equal employment efforts. This data is specific to each employee. Would there be any possible benefits to storing such information in a linked table, separate from the general employee information? If so, what?

9. What two purposes are served by a table's primary key?

10. What kind of information should never be used as a table's primary key and why?

Exercises

At this point, you have learned enough to start creating relational database models for any information you might want to record. You still need practice in order to develop a full understanding of the process so it's a good idea to work on some additional examples. For some of these questions, there is not necessarily a right answer but they are things that you need to consider as part of design.

1. You are in charge of planning recreational events for a large group of people. You need a way to record the details of the events themselves, the information for the members of the group, which is continuously open to newcomers, and the attendance for each event. The database will be accessible over a website and the members will be able to indicate if they are attending specific events and leave comments before or after the events. For examples of this, check out websites like Meetup.com and GroupSpaces.com.

- o How would you design the tables to manage the many-to-many relationship between members and events where each member might attend many events and each event will be attended by many people?
- o Members might sign-up for events and then cancel. How would you record this? Would you maintain a history of those decisions?
- o Assuming you have more than one person able to act as an event organizer or administrator, how would you record this information in the database? Would you have a separate table for administrators?
- o How would you set up the tables so that you could get a list of participants for a specific event, either in the future or the past?
- o For security and other reasons, memberships need to be reviewed by an administrator. Members might need to be approved for specific events as well. How would you record these reviews and approvals in the database?
- o Considering this database will be accessible over the web and no website can be absolutely secure, what information will you gather on members as part of their profile? Also consider whether minors will be permitted as members and what information you would want to help establish member recreational interests.

2. You are designing a database to track your exercise sessions and progress toward your fitness goals. At a minimum, you will need to record the details of each session and be able to report on your activity over a specific range of dates. You'll probably want the database to supply information for charts to show your progress and the increasing intensity of your workouts.

- o Assuming you want to record changes in your weight, would you do this in a separate table or would you record it for each workout?

- o How would you design the tables to record separate activities where those like running might be based on time or distance and others such as weight training based on repetitions?
- o Would you record the number of calories burned during each activity in the tables or just record enough information so that the software can calculate it later? This figure can be calculated based on factors such as the activity and your current weight. The complexity of the calculation as factors change over time might cause whatever program was using the data to take longer to generate the reports.

3. You are creating a database to record an inventory of computer and multimedia equipment within a company.

- o How would you structure the tables to hold both a 1.5 Ghz laptop computer with a 15 inch screen and 750 GB hard drive and a 800 x 600 dpi LCD projector?
- o What would you use as the primary key for the equipment table(s)?

4. Using the Job Search Plus example, how would you change the data model if you wanted to maintain a collection of all correspondence and documentation associated with your job search? Rather than simply storing attachments within the Leads table as it does now, you need a way to search through all correspondence by pertinent details such as company, contact and date. You must still be able to link the correspondence to a specific lead but the new data model must allow for the possibility that the job seeker will be sending out inquiries not associated with a specific opportunity.

Terms to Remember

Atomicity - The state in which data is broken down into the smallest parts that are still useful and meaningful.

Composite Key - A table key that is made up of more than one field so that no two records might have the same combination of values.

Database Normalization - The process of applying specific rules to the design of tables in a relational database that seek to eliminate duplicate and inconsistent information.

Foreign Key - A table field that stores an identifying value which points to a specific record in another table. An example would be in a company order database where the customer ID from the customers table is used in the orders table to identify the specific customer on the order.

GUID - Globally Unique Identifier. A value that is guaranteed to be unique in each row of a table. Very often, this is automatically generated by the database itself.

Index - A database structure applied to a specific field in a table to make it easier and faster to search and sort on that field.

Lookup Table - A table that is used mainly for providing a list of frequently used values such as cities or product names in order to ensure that the values are consistently entered and speed up data entry.

Normal Forms - The set of rules applied to database design as part of database normalization. The forms are applied cumulatively with each successive form requiring the previous forms to be in place. Their objective is to eliminate duplication and inconsistency in the data.

Primary Key - A table index that is guaranteed to be unique for each record and can be referenced by other tables to identify a specific record in the original table.

Scalar Values - Single data values stored by themselves within a field.

Surrogate Key - A sequential or random value that can be generated by the database in the absence of a naturally occurring unique value to ensure that each row in a table has a unique identifier.

Chapter V

Servers and Databases

Building the Database

In the last couple of chapters, you learned how to model the data and organize it into a collection of potential tables through the conceptual and logical models. Now it's time to create the *physical* data model or *schema*. This is the part of the process in which the data is actually committed to a specific *database management system (DBMS)*, in this case MySQL. The database, tables and other objects that will actually manage the data are built around the rules, features and even the limitations of that software.

Before we can actually create the tables, however, you'll need to learn a few things about working with the database server which is the top-level object in an enterprise database management system like MySQL.

Accessing the Server

While MySQL can be used to support purely local databases, it's designed to support network-accessible, remote databases and to communicate over a company network or even the Internet. This means that its operations center around the MySQL server software that can manage these communications along with the database operations themselves. Before you can create and work with databases, you need to log in to the database server itself and perhaps even make sure it's running.

As mentioned in a previous chapter, MySQL can be run from the Windows, Linux or OS X command line or as a service that starts and stops with the operating system. You might not be concerned with this if you are accessing a remote MySQL server on your web hosting service or one that's managed by a database administrator elsewhere but if you have setup MySQL on your own machine, you'll need to know where and how it's running before you can work with it.

Definitions

In order to prevent some confusion, let me clarify a few terms that I'll be using in this chapter.

MySQL exists on your machine as a collection of programs. One of these programs is memory-resident and functions as the *database server.* This is a software that is designed to process incoming requests either locally or over a network and to manage the database operations. This software-based server can run on your personal desktop or laptop machine or on a *network server.* The network server is an actual machine, either physical or virtual, that exists *as part of* a larger network and houses various types of software such as database servers that are intended to be accessed through the network. So there is already a distinction there between the *database* server and the *network* server on which it might reside. In day to day operations, however, the term *database server* will often be used to refer to a specific network server that is devoted to running a database management system.

The memory-resident MySQL server needs to be loaded into memory at some point and started in order for you to work with the databases. In a simple installation, this can be done by running an executable file which will load the server into memory and start its processes. MySQL can also be run as a *service* which is a service is a program that's integrated into the operating system and can be started and stopped either when the operating system loads or manually by the user through the OS control panel. Therefore, it's important to remember the distinction between the terms *server* and *service*. A server is the programming and a service represents its integration with the operating system.

Clients are programs or machines of various types that access information on a server and provide an interface through which a user can use those resources. When you connect to the Internet, your browser actually functions as a type of client, sending and receiving information from the web servers whose sites you visit. With MySQL, there are multiple client programs including the command line client which you'll be seeing a lot of in this chapter and various graphical clients. These include MySQL Workbench and phpMyAdmin. All of these programs enable the user to communicate with the server, either pulling down information or changing existing data as needed. If a software developer designs a new reporting program for a specific database, that program functions as a client for the MySQL database server.

The client programs you'll be seeing in this chapter include the following:

- **mysql.exe** - The main command line tool with which you can create and administer databases, user accounts and other objects on the MySQL server. I will often refer to it here as the MySQL command line.

- **mysqladmin.exe** - This command line tool is focused on administrative actions such as checking the server status, adjusting the configuration, and starting and stopping the server.

- **MySQL Workbench** - A sophisticated cross-platform *graphical user interface (GUI)* that can provides a menu-based system for modeling data and working with database objects. It offers a virtually complete solution for database administration and can be used to manage multiple servers and installations.

- **phpMyAdmin** - This is a web application designed in the PHP language that can be used to perform most database and user operations. It's often featured as part of AMP (Apache, MySQL, PHP) and web hosting environments. It is limited by design to a single MySQL server.

- **SQLBuddy** - A very basic web application for performing quick database and user tasks and issuing queries against multiple database servers.

Locating the Files

If you're running your own instance of MySQL, the first step is to know where the files reside and either create some shortcuts or add that location to your system's PATH statement. In **Windows**, this is done through the Advanced System Properties in the Control Panel.

Here's an example of the Windows PATH variable with the MySQL program directory at <u>C:\Program Files\MySQL\MySQL Server 5.6\bin</u> added in:

```
;C:\Users\Andrew\AppData\Local\Code\bin;C:\Program Files\MySQL\MySQL
Server 5.6\bin;
```

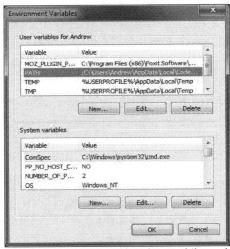

Figure 5.1 - The Windows Path variable can be changed through the advanced system properties.

The program directory will differ based on your installation but look for the bin directory which should hold the executable files such as `mysql.exe` and `mysqladmin.exe` that you'll be using. (The word "bin" is short for "binaries", another word for executable program files.) Multiple directories can be added to the statement and separated by a semi-colon so that those directories are checked whenever a user tries to run a command from the command prompt.

In **Linux Mint** and other versions of Linux, the Path variable can be changed by adding a PATH statement to the `/etc/bash.bashrc` file or either the `.bash_profile` or `.bash_login` files under the user's Home directory. Remember that these are hidden files and you will need to use the CTRL-H shortcut or the **View >> Show Hidden Files** menu option. Look for one of these files that contains a statement like the following

```
PATH="$HOME/bin:$PATH"
```

In this statement, $PATH is the existing path variable and the statement adds the `$HOME/bin statement` to it with $HOME being a variable for the current user's home directory. It essentially says "The PATH *now* equals $HOME/bin *plus* the current PATH variable." You can add a similar statement after it with the directory to your MySQL installation. The *apt* package manager that I demonstrated in the chapter on installing MySQL seems to take care of setting the path to MySQL on its own so it's good to try logging in to MySQL before messing around with the environment variables.

On **Mac OS X**, you can change the path by issuing the following statement in the Terminal environment. To make it permanent, you will need to added it to `~/.bash_profile` using your favorite text editor.

```
export PATH=/usr/local/mysql/bin:$PATH
```

Starting the Server and Logging In

If you're working on your own MySQL installation, you'll need to make sure that the database server has started. The fastest way to determine if MySQL is running on all operating systems is simply to try logging in through the command line with the `mysql.exe` client program using the following syntax:

```
> mysql -h hostname -u username -p
```

example:

```
> mysql -h localhost -u root -p
```

```
password: (enter password here)
```

```
Welcome to the MySQL monitor. Commands end with ; or \g.
Your MySQL connection id is 52
Server version: 5.5.43-0ubuntu0.14.04.1 (Ubuntu)
```

```
mysql>
```

You can actually omit the -h option if you're accessing the localhost as that's the default. You would need to use it if connecting to another named or remote server. For example:

```
> mysql -h mysql.myserver.com -u root -p
```

If MySQL is not running on the machine you would get something like this instead.

```
ERROR 2002 (HY000): Can't connect to local MySQL server through
socket '/var/run/mysqld/mysqld.sock' (2)
```

At this point, you would need to check the status of the database server. There are a couple of ways you can do this, the first being with another MySQL program called `mysqladmin.exe` which is another command line client program that is used to perform various administrative tasks on the server. One of these functions is to *ping* the server or to attempt a basic connection to verify that it's online and responding.

```
> mysqladmin ping -u root -p
Enter password: ******
mysqld is alive
```

If the server is online, you'll get the simple message shown above. If not, then you'll get a similar message as you did when you tried to login through mysql.exe. If you're running MySQL as a service, then the next step is to check to see if the service is running.

In the Linux shell, this can be done with a simple command:

```
$ service mysql status
```

```
mysql start/running, process 1147
```

The simple response shown here provides the service name, its status and the process number. If the service shows as stopped, then you can try to start it with a variation on the same command.

```
$ sudo service mysql start
```

Notice that `sudo` needs to be invoked here; administrative privileges are needed for starting or stopping a service but not for pinging it. Once you've ensured that the service is running, you can try to login again using mysql.exe.

In Windows, if you've installed MySQL as as service, you can verify if the service is running by opening the Windows Control Panel, selecting **Administrative Tools** and opening the **Services** applet. Scroll down through the list of services and look for one associated with the MySQL installation. The name might vary depending on how you installed MySQL on your system but it should start with 'mysql'. Once you find it, you can start, stop or restart the service as needed by right-clicking on the service and selecting the appropriate option from the menu.

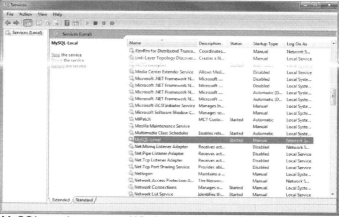

Figure 5.2 - MySQL can be run as a Windows service and either started automatically or manually by the user.

In **Mac OS X**, the simplest way to check if MySQL is running is to open its settings pane from the System Preferences panel.

If you're running MySQL as part of a pre-packaged WAMP system such as EasyPHP or WampServer, then the central administration program for the package should start the server for you or have options from the Windows task bar that will enable you to start it from there. Both packages include the MySQL client and the other programs mentioned here.

- In EasyPHP, the programs are located in the `..\binaries\mysql\bin` subdirectory.

- In WampSever, they're located in `..\bin\mysql\mysql(version)\bin` subdirectory.

Regardless of the installation type and operating system, once you've verified the service is running you can try the mysql command line program again.

The MySQL Command Prompt

Once you successfully login to MySQL, you'll see the welcome message and then just the simple `mysql>` prompt which doesn't provide much guidance for the new user. The first thing to understand about the command line client program and its prompt is that its primary purpose is to accept queries and commands to work with the data on the server. Most client programs that work with the MySQL database server have a query editor in which you can construct these queries for retrieving and manipulating data on the server. The mysql.exe client is the command line equivalent of that. While it's not as user-friendly for the beginner, in experienced hands it can actually be a quick way to manipulate databases and other objects on the server without the overhead of a graphical, menu-driven program. *Structured Query Language (SQL)* is the primary tool that's used to do this although there are some standalone commands that you can issue as needed.

Figure 5.3 shows the MySQL command line in action with a login to the server by a user named "admin". Then there's a query that retrieves the current date and specifies the name for the resulting column and then a `quit` command to exit the MySQL command line. The commands `\q` and `exit` can also be used to leave the program and return to the OS command prompt.

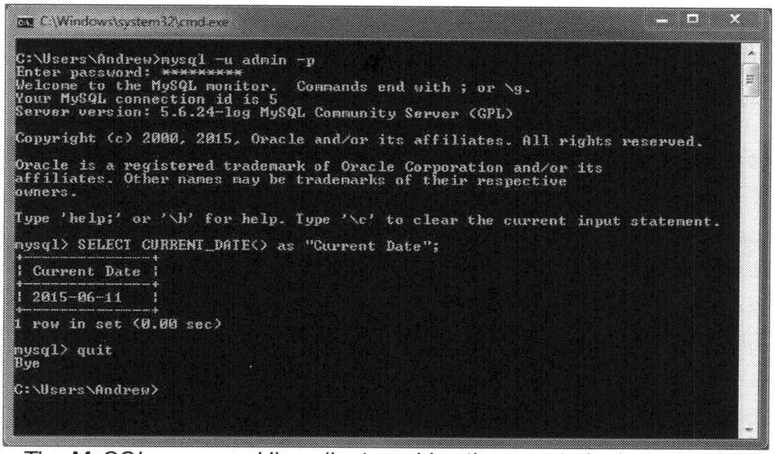

Figure 5.3 - The MySQL command line client enables the user to login to the database server and issue queries and commands to the database server.

In this section, we'll look at a few commands that you can use to get accustomed to working with the MySQL command line. For a full list of functions available in MySQL, see Chapter 12, "Functions and Operators", in the *MySQL Reference Manual*. MySQL has many mathematical, date and text manipulation functions similar to Microsoft Excel and other spreadsheet programs you might have used. You can use these functions as part of database queries or on their own at the command line. I strongly recommend that you take some time to try the following examples and explore the ones available in the MySQL docs to see what else you can do.

The SELECT command in Figure 5.3 is an essential keyword within MySQL and easily the one you'll use most often. It instructs the software to return a specific set of results, either from a database or from manual commands like the ones you're about to enter here. The example query simply returns the current date through the CURRENT_DATE() function. Notice the semi-colon at the end of the command; that signals to MySQL that the command is complete and can be executed. Once the ENTER key is pressed, MySQL carries out the instruction and returns a single row with the requested information. Even at the command line, results are returned in rows and columns. The column header shows whatever label is available - either the function name or a specified column name as shown here which you'll see more about in a minute. The final line shows the count of rows returned and the time it took which can be useful in monitoring both the operation of the server and the efficiency of the query that's been entered.

The use of the word 'set' here is important. As I said before, MySQL is all about reading and manipulating *sets* of data on the server and measures operations in terms of the number of rows affected and how long it took to do it. This is true even when there's only one or even zero rows returned and whether you're using the command line client shown here or graphical tools like phpMyAdmin. The amount of data affected and the efficiency of operations are both very important considerations to anyone working with databases on a regular basis. As you continue learning about SQL queries, you'll see more complex queries that affect greater numbers of columns and tables. These queries can sometimes even reach across databases to carry out operations. The query language is flexible enough to affect tens of thousands of records at a time, almost instantaneously, or to find one specific record among hundreds of thousands and carry out a complex operation on one field. Because of this level of power, it's important not only to learn how to write queries but to learn to write them correctly and *well* in order to safeguard your data and the performance of the server. This is something we'll look at more in a later chapter.

Going back to the example, let's try a slightly friendlier name for the query result.

```
mysql> SELECT CURRENT_DATE() AS 'Today\'s Date';
+----------------+
| Today's Date   |
+----------------+
| 2015-06-06     |
+----------------+
1 row in set (0.00 sec)
```

This example demonstrates a couple of things, the first being the column alias where the 'AS' keyword supplies a specific name for the column header. You can use aliases for both columns and tables within queries and you'll see a lot more of that in upcoming examples. If you're using a single word as an alias, you don't even need to enclose it but you do if it contains any spaces.

The other thing you'll notice is the backslash before the apostrophe in "Today's". This is called an escape character and signals to the command interpreter that the character after it is supposed to be treated in a certain way. In this case, single quotes are being used to delimit the column alias from the rest of the statement and the escape character indicates that the following apostrophe should be treated as a literal character within the string rather than the end of the string. The statement could also be written with double-quotes as in the first example.

```
mysql> SELECT CURRENT_DATE() AS "Today's Date";
+---------------+
| Today's Date  |
+---------------+
| 2015-06-06    |
+---------------+
1 row in set (0.00 sec)
```

In this case, the escape character is not needed since the apostrophe is distinct from the delimiters being used. You could also use the backtick character (`) as a delimiter. This is helpful to know as there are variations in SQL between different database software titles. While MySQL allows any of these delimiters to be used, other software might require a specific one such as the single quote. You also might find yourself reading queries written by database specialists with other backgrounds and query writing habits. Escape characters are used for other purposes which we'll see more of later.

Some queries can get pretty long and can be impractical to write on a single line. One solution is to use multi-line queries.

```
mysql> SELECT CURRENT_DATE(), AS 'Today\'s Date',
    -> CURRENT_TIME AS 'Current Time';
+---------------+--------------+
| Today's Date  | Current Time |
+---------------+--------------+
| 2015-06-06    | 10:45:13     |
+---------------+--------------+
1 row in set (0.00 sec)
```

Again, the semi-colon indicates to MySQL that the statement is finished and can be executed and the client program is going to wait until it sees that semi-colon before doing anything. You could press ENTER a hundred times and it's going to continue giving you another line to work with and show you the -> prompt to indicate that there's a query in the process of being written. Then, if you finish the query or simply enter a semi-colon, MySQL will carry on as normal since it really doesn't care how much whitespace or how many line breaks you put within a query. The command interpreter simply looks at what you've sent to it, disregards any extra space and processes the command. This is true in graphical client tools as well as on the command line.

If you create a new line in the middle of a column alias or another portion of the query delimited by single or double quotes, the new line prompt will indicate that the matching delimiter is needed.

```
mysql> SELECT CURRENT_DATE(), AS 'Today\'s
    '> Date', CURRENT_TIME AS 'Current Time';
+----------------+--------------+
| Today's
Date    | Current Time |
+----------------+--------------+
| 2015-06-06     | 10:45:13     |
+----------------+--------------+
1 row in set (0.00 sec)
```

The above result is not a formatting error, at least not in this book. That is the way mysql.exe will actually print the result to the screen. Therefore, it's best to use your judgement when inserting line breaks. Still, this demonstrates how the program will use different prompts to assist you in writing your queries. The mysql client will also prompt you if you insert a line break after a double-quote (">) or a backtick (`>).

Just as you can split one command between many lines, you can also put more than one command on the same line and run them together. Commands can run in groups to carry out separate but related operations or supply related information that would be difficult to generate from one query.

```
mysql> SELECT NOW() AS "The current date and time is - "; SELECT
CONCAT(USER(), ' is currently logged in.') as "Current User";
+---------------------------------+
| The current date and time is -  |
+---------------------------------+
| 2015-06-06 10:19:28             |
+---------------------------------+
1 row in set (0.00 sec)
```

```
+----------------------------------------+
| Current User                           |
+----------------------------------------+
| root@localhost is currently logged in. |
+----------------------------------------+
1 row in set (0.00 sec)
```

The above example shows one of the text manipulation functions available through MySQL, `CONCAT()`, which you can use to concatenate different values. In the previous chapters, you saw that the first principle of data normalization requires that data be broken down into *atomic* values, or values that cannot be broken down further. This enables stored data to be searched and sorted as needed. Functions like `CONCAT()`, on the other hand, enable you to take that data and recombine it as needed to be presented to reports as shown here.

```
mysql> SELECT CONCAT(LastName, ', ', FirstName) AS "Member Name"
FROM
Members;
+---------------------+
| Member Name         |
+---------------------+
| Richardson, Stephen |
+---------------------+
| Tyler, Joseph       |
+---------------------+
| Greenwood, Donnie   |
+---------------------+
| Hernandez, Maria    |
+---------------------+
4 rows in set (0.15 sec)
```

Because the first and last names are stored in separate fields, they can now be presented in either order required by whatever report or application will be using the data from the query. Put that together with the ability to specify the column heading the way I've done here and you can design some very useful queries.

There's one more thing you should notice in the above queries. MySQL allows you to use either apostrophes, quotation marks or backticks for enclosing text so long as you're consistent when opening and closing any given text string. For the sake of readability, however, it's good to make a decision about which one you're going to use in different situations. In the samples, I've used the single quote to enclose text strings used as arguments within functions and the double quotes to specify column aliases. If you have to read and edit a lot of queries, this can make things much easier. Queries are also case-*insensitive* so you can use CONCAT(), concat() or Concat() as it suits you. When working on the command line, you might decide just to type everything in upper or lower case for the sake of speed. When writing queries in a text editor that you might need to read later, however, it's again a good idea to have a standard to follow. In the above examples, I've put keywords and function names in all caps and capitalized object names and other items as needed. This makes it easier to decipher a query quickly.

Let's take a look at a few more functions that you can use independently of databases.

```
mysql> SELECT CURRENT_DATE() AS "Today's Date",
ADDDATE(CURRENT_DATE(), 30) AS "30 Days", ADDDATE(CURRENT_DATE(),
60) AS "60 Days";
+----------------+------------+------------+
| Today's Date   | 30 Days    | 60 Days    |
+----------------+------------+------------+
| 2015-06-06     | 2015-07-06 | 2015-08-05 |
+----------------+------------+------------+
```

The AddDate() function enables you to add or subtract days from a specified date. To subtract, you can use a negative number of days for the second argument in the function. This query also shows how functions can be used as arguments within other functions with the CURRENT_DATE() function serving as input within the AddDate() functions. MySQL has a selection of date manipulation functions to choose from including the DATEDIFF() function which accepts two dates and returns the number of days between them in terms of the relation of the first date to the second.

```
mysql> SELECT CURRENT_DATE() AS "Today's Date", DATEDIFF('2015-08-
30', CURRENT_DATE()) AS "Days Remaining";
+----------------+----------------+
| Today's Date   | Days Remaining |
+----------------+----------------+
| 2015-06-06     |             85 |
+----------------+----------------+
```

MySQL also has basic calculator functions and mathematical functions that you can use in your queries and follows the PEMDAS order of operations within its calculations (**P**arentheses, **E**xponents, **M**ultiplication, **D**ivision, **A**ddition, **S**ubtraction).

```
mysql> SELECT 25 + 3 / 4 * (3 - 1) + (( 10 + 15 + 20) / 3) as
Result;
+----------+
| Result   |
+----------+
| 41.5000  |
+----------+
```

Breaking this formula down, you can see how MySQL processes it by solving within the parentheses first.

```
25 + 3 / 4 * (3 - 1) + ((10 + 15 + 20) / 3)

25 + 3 / 4 * 2 + (45 / 3)

25 + 3 / 4 * 2 + 15
```

Then the multiplication / division and addition / subtraction operations are carried out in order.

```
25 + 3 / 4 * 2 + 15

25 + 1.5 + 15

26.5 + 15

41.5
```

When typing queries in a command line environment, especially complicated ones like some of these, it's entirely possible that you'll make a mistake and not catch it before hitting ENTER and going onto the next line. There is no way to go back to edit previous lines in mysql.exe but you can cancel the query and start again by using \c. Even though, you can't make changes to lines that have already been submitted, you can access copies of them by using the UP arrow on your keyboard. This way, you can load the faulty line back into the prompt and make the necessary corrections before hitting ENTER. This can also save you time if you're entering multiple similar lines as part of a query.

```
mysql> SELLECT UBSTRING('Mastering the MySQL command line', 14)
    -> \c
mysql> SELECT SUBSTRING('Mastering the MySQL command line', 14) AS
Substring;
```

```
+--------------------+
| Substring          |
+--------------------+
| MySQL command line |
+--------------------+
```

The `SUBSTRING()` function returns a specified portion of a string argument with the second argument representing a place within the original string. The character count is zero-based, meaning that the first character is character 0, the second is character 1 and so on. This is a common practice in many types of programming and, when using a function that accepts a numbered place in any list of objects as one of the arguments, it's important to verify if that numbering starts at 0 or 1.

This is just a sampling of the things you can do on the command line with MySQL and you'll see more examples throughout this book.

Creating Databases

Exploring the Server

Once you have MySQL setup and are comfortable finding your way around the command line, it's time to look around the server and create a database or two. Graphical client utilities will quickly show you a listing of all the objects on the server and allow you to create new ones but it can also be easily done from the command line. First, let's see what databases already exist.

```
mysql> SHOW DATABASES;
+--------------------+
| Database           |
+--------------------+
| information_schema |
| performance_schema |
| phpmyadmin         |
| test               |
+--------------------+
```

Depending on your installation, you might see a list like the one above with a few administrative and test databases already on the server. You will also only see the databases to which your account has been granted access. If you've just installed MySQL, chances are you're logged in as the root user as I am in this example so you can see everything. For the sake of exploring a little more, I now want to see inside one of these databases so I'm going to look at the INFORMATION_SCHEMA reference database which stores information on all the other databases on the server.

```
mysql> USE information_schema;
mysql> SHOW TABLES;
+---------------------+
| Database            |
+---------------------+
| CHARACTER_SETS      |
| COLLATIONS          |
| COLUMNS             |
| COLUMN_PRIVILEGES   |
| ...                 |
```

The USE command instructs the server to run all further commands and queries against a specific database. You could specify the database for each command by putting the database name before each table name and separating them by a period (i.e. INFORMATION_SCHEMA.COLUMNS) but this is much easier and ensures fewer accidental changes to the wrong database and failed queries. Even after switching to a specific database, you can specify a table in another database by appending the database name and this is sometimes done on servers where there are multiple databases containing related information.

Moving further into the database, you can view the columns in a specific table.

```
mysql> SHOW COLUMNS IN CHARACTER_SETS;
+------------------------------------------------------------------------------+
| Field                | Type        | Null | Key | Default | Extra |
+------------------------------------------------------------------------------+
| CHARACTER_SET_NAME   | varchar(32) | No   |     |         |       |
| DEFAULT_COLLATE_NAME | varchar(32) | No   |     |         |       |
| DESCRIPTION          | varchar(60) | No   |     |         |       |
| MAXLEN               | bigint(3)   | No   |     | 0       |       |
+------------------------------------------------------------------------------+
```

Sometimes, the output from a query might be wider than your command window can display, in which case you can display the results vertically by replacing the semi-colon at the end of the statement with \G.

```
mysql> SHOW COLUMNS IN CHARACTER_SETS\G
*************************** 1. row ***************************
  Field: CHARACTER_SET_NAME
```

```
   Type: varchar(32)
   Null: NO
    Key:
Default:
  Extra:
**************** 2. row ***********************
  Field: DEFAULT_COLLATE_NAME
   Type: varchar(22)
   Null: NO
    Key:
Default:
  Extra:

...

4 rows in set (0.01 sec)
```

The keyword FROM could be substituted for IN in this command and it would give the same result. The column display shows not only the names of the columns but their types and sizes, whether they're allowed to hold null values and other characteristics. The SHOW command can actually be used to view lists of many different items on the server and its full options can be found in the *MySQL Reference Manual*. Just from these few examples, however, you are now able to view all the databases on the server, switch to a specific database, get a listing of all tables in the database and then examine the details of a specific table - all from the command line. That knowledge can be invaluable when designing reports or applications that reference the database.

Creating the Database

The syntax for creating a database from the command line is actually pretty simple.

```
mysql> CREATE DATABASE JobSearchPlus;
mysql> SHOW DATABASES;
+--------------------+
| Database           |
+--------------------+
| information_schema |
| performance_schema |
| jobsearchplus      |
| test               |
+--------------------+
mysql> USE jobsearchplus;
```

You can also add a test to ensure that the database doesn't already exist. This is particularly useful when writing scripts that automate the creation of databases and tables which is sometimes done as part of professional software deployment. The test prevents an error which would stop the entire script. You should use relevant names for your databases, long enough to identify the database but not so long to be cumbersome. Names for databases, tables and other objects in MySQL are generally limited to 64 characters with letters (A-Z, a-z), numbers (0-9), the dollar sign ($) and the underscore (_) permitted.

```
mysql> CREATE DATABASE IF NOT EXISTS JobSearchPlus;
Query OK, 1 row affected, 1 warning (0.00 sec)
```

MySQL's response indicates that the query command completed successfully even though the database was already there because the query tested for the condition. There was a warning but this would not stop other queries from being run after this one in a script.

Notice that even though the database name was specified with some letters capitalized, the resulting database was named in all lowercase. When working in Unix or Linux, the database name is case-sensitive, unlike the SQL keywords, so using 'JobSearchPlus' would result in an 'unknown database' error. This is not true in Windows but since MySQL is a cross-platform database where individual databases might be accessed from clients in both operating systems, it's best to treat it as case-sensitive in both.

There are two final options that you might need to consider when creating the database and those are the *character set* and the *collation*. The character set is the simply the set of characters that your database will support which will depend on the language, culture and type of data your database supports. If you're entering data with Russian characters, you might want to use cp866 (DOS Russian) whereas if all your data is in American English, UTF-8 (UTF-8 Unicode), the default in my particular installation, would probably work just fine. Even within a specific language, there might be more than one character set that would work in different situations. You might choose to limit the characters that can be used in the database by choosing ascii (US ASCII) as the character set. You can see the entire list of character sets available in your MySQL installation by using the following command:

```
mysql> SHOW CHARACTER SET;
```

For each character set shown, you'll notice a default collation. The collation of the database determines how different characters are compared to each other for sorting purposes. Although there is a default collation, you can specify a collation of your choice so long as it works with the chosen character set. (Obviously, the hebrew_general_ci collation will not work with the US ASCII character set.) You can see a full list of the collations with the show command.

```
mysql> SHOW COLLATION;
```

You can specify both the character set and collation when creating the database if you need to. They can also be specified for individual tables within a database which we'll see more about in the next chapter.

```
mysql> CREATE DATABASE JobSearchPlus CHARACTER SET = utf8 COLLATE =
ut8_general_ci;
Query OK, 1 row affected (0.02 sec)
```

For many beginners, the defaults should work for any new databases but if you have trouble entering or retrieving certain characters from your database, that's the first thing to consider. For full details on the character sets and collations available through MySQL and how they're used, see Chapter 10, "Globalization", of the *MySQL Reference Manual*.

Leaving the Command Line

MySQL Workbench

At this point you might like to start looking at how to perform some of these functions in other client programs such as MySQL Workbench and phpMyAdmin since a graphical environment makes it easier to visualize the contents of the server. If you have MySQL Workbench installed, you should be able to open it from your Start menu, the equivalent in Linux for the Applications folder in OS X. Workbench features some good data modeling tools and refers to databases as *schemas* in keeping with modeling terminology. After you connect to the server in Workbench, you'll see the screen shown below with the server navigator on one side and the large area for editing queries in the center.

You can run all of the commands and queries that you've seen in this chapter within this space. There's also the advantage that you can freely edit multiple lines before actually running the query so there's less of a chance of making a mistake. You can also enter multiple queries and run one at a time by selecting the appropriate query and choosing the menu option or the toolbar item above the query window. Just as on the command line, you will need to put a semi-colon after most commands to separate them from each other or the query editor will complain about syntax errors. In the figure above, you can see where the CREATE DATABASE and USE commands have been issued and the output messages are shown in the Output box at the bottom of the screen. The USE command resulted in the database (or schema) display on the left hand side being expanded to show any objects within it although none are present at this time.

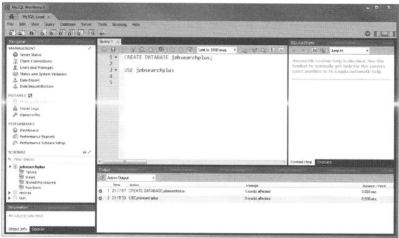

Figure 5.4 - MySQL Workbench provides a more flexible and user-friendly environment than the MySQL command line.

In addition to issuing the commands within the query space, you can right-click within the list of schemas and select the **Create Schema** option or select the toolbar item near the top of the screen to create a new database. The New Schema wizard will appear which simply asks you for the name of the new database and the collation you wish to use which you can change or leave at the default setting. Clicking the **Apply** button will then create the new database.

phpMyAdmin

As in MySQL Workbench, phpMyAdmin's web interface also offers both a query space and on-screen controls to carry out the functions you've seen in this chapter. In Figure 5.5, you can see the tab-based interface which organizes all the server and database management functions into categories.

Under the *Databases* tab, you can easily create a new database by entering the database name, selecting the collation and clicking **Create** button. The new database will then appear in the database list on the left side of the window. The *SQL* tab features a query space like the one in Workbench where you can enter raw SQL commands if you prefer. phpMyAdmin's simplified interface comes in very handy when running MySQL as part of an AMP environment or managing the databases on your web hosting account.

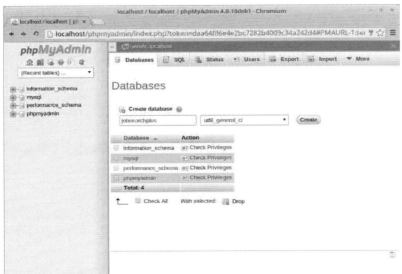

Figure 5.5 - phpMyAdmin includes both on-screen controls and a SQL query space for issuing commands against the server.

SQLBuddy

SQLBuddy offers an even simpler interface than phpMyAdmin although without some of its management capabilities. The *Home* page within its web interface enables the user to create a new interface by entering a database name and selecting the character set. The *Query* page offers an very simple query space that's actually little more than a text box. Even an ultra-simplified interface can be preferable to the command line depending on the user and can speed things up when performing a few quick tasks.

Database Users and Security

When you're studying MySQL with your own local installation, it's perfectly fine to use the root user for everything but if you're creating databases for other people to use, you need to know how to create and manage user accounts in order to keep your server and its data secure.

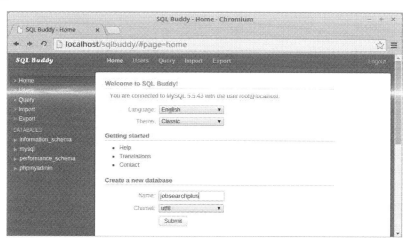

Figure 5.6 - SQLBuddy offers a very simple web-based interface that's useful when performing quick database tasks.

User authentication on MySQL is completely independent of any user names and passwords on the operating system. Even if individual administrators and third-party client programs make use of the user OS logins when creating accounts, *any* user can login to *any* MySQL account so long as they have the username and password. The list of users is stored in the 'user' table of the 'mysql' database which is created during installation.

> **NOTE:** From this point forward, I'll be referring to database objects by the *[database].[table].[column]* syntax (i.e. 'mysql.user.host').

You can see the full list of user accounts by querying the mysql.user table when logged in under the root user.

```
mysql> SELECT user, host from mysql.user;
+-------------------+---------------+
| user              | host          |
+-------------------+---------------+
| root              | 127.0.0.1     |
| root              | ::1           |
| root              | linuxmint-ovb |
| debian-sys-maint  | localhost     |
| phpmyadmin        | localhost     |
| root              | localhost     |
+-------------------+---------------+
```

This is a sample from an installation on a Linux Mint virtual machine. You can see the accounts for the root user, one for phpMyAdmin and another system maintenance account, all of which were setup automatically during installation. Depending on the operating system you're using and your installation type, this list will vary. The user and the host columns are used in combination to identify a specific user with the host indicating where that user is able to login from. The two columns actually form a *composite primary key* for the table and this key is used by other tables from the MySQL database to refer back to a specific user. (Refer back to Chapter IV on data normalization if you need more information on composite and primary keys.) In this example, the root user can login from any one of the hosts listed in the table, although all four of the values in this case actually refer to 'localhost' (127.0.0.1) in different ways. They're useful for connecting to the server from different programs and environments.

On the other hand, the same *username* does not always mean the same *user*. If you are granting access to users on other domains, you could have the following accounts:

```
+-------------+-------------------+
| user        | host              |
+-------------+-------------------+
| joe         | localhost         |
| joe         | otherdomain.com   |
| guest       | %                 |
+-------------+-------------------+
```

The first account would be a user named Joe who logs in on the local system while the second one could be a completely different user named Joe who logs in from the other domain and has a different password. The third account in this list has the '%' for the host value which indicates that the account can login from *any* domain. This could be used as a general guest account for the server or for a user who will be logging in from multiple locations. This host value under which the user logs in is *not* the same as the destination hostname that is used to indicate what server you're logging into when running the mysql client or MySQL Workbench. The hostname in the user table is the one detected by MySQL as the *origin* of the connection attempt.

> **NOTE:** Remote connections can be disabled in MySQL. If you're trying to login to a remote database and the connection keeps failing even though you're sure of the login information you're using, you should verify that remote connections to the server are enabled.

The mysql.user table is the first part of the MySQL authentication process. Whenever a user attempts to connect, MySQL verifies that there is an active user account that is permitted to login from that location. The second part is performed every time a user issues a query or command against the server and MySQL checks the user's permissions to ensure that he or she is authorized to perform that action. We'll be looking at assigning those permissions a little later in the chapter.

Changing the Root Password

After installation, the first thing to verify is whether the root user has been given a password. This is not always done during installation and, even if you're running a local server for study, it's a good idea to make sure it has a password. You will know if there's a password as soon as you login but if you want to verify it, simply issue the following login command, omitting the password option.

```
mysql> mysql -u root;
```

If you get in, then the password needs to be set.

```
mysql> SET PASSWORD FOR 'root'@'localhost' =
PASSWORD('newpassword');
```

This same command can be used to set the passwords for non-root accounts as you create them although the CREATE command will also do that as you'll see shortly. The PASSWORD() function in the above query takes the password you enter and encrypts it so that it can be safely stored in the mysql.user table. You will need to run the SELECT query shown in the last section against mysql.user to see all the accounts and set the password separately for each root account. Choose a strong password that you can remember and keep it in a safe place because it is extremely difficult to recover a lost root password. It's possible to change the other user passwords and privileges through other client programs.

- <u>MySQL Workbench</u> - After logging into the server, choose the 'Users and Privileges' option from the Management section on the left of the screen. This will show all of the user accounts and enable you to change usernames, passwords and assign permissions.

- <u>phpMyAdmin</u> - The Users tab will show all MySQL users and allows for the adding of new users and editing of privileges. Depending on your configuration, you might not be able to log in to phpMyAdmin with a blank password so you might need to use the command line tools or MySQL Workbench in order to set them first.

- <u>SQLBuddy</u> - Select **Users** from the program's main menu to see the user edit screen.

I've known a couple of these programs to throw errors when changing passwords for multiple root accounts while logged in as 'root', so this is something to be aware of and the command line might be the best place to make the changes.

An extra security measure is to actually *rename* the root user since it is the default server user and is therefore well-known to hackers. This can be done simply through the command line as well as through the other client programs.

```
mysql> RENAME USER 'root'@'localhost' to 'primary'@'localhost';
```

Adding New Accounts and Assigning Privileges

As you create new databases, you might want to create user accounts that have access specifically to those databases without having full rights to everything on the server.

```
mysql> CREATE USER 'martin'@'localhost' IDENTIFIED BY 'password';
```

This command does not need the PASSWORD() function shown earlier because it automatically encrypts the password. You can also leave off the IDENTIFIED BY clause in order to create a new account with a blank password although this is not recommended. Once you've created the new user, you'll want to assign some privileges. As an example, you could assign full privileges to the JobSearchPlus database created earlier or permissions to specific tables within it as shown by the two examples below.

```
mysql> GRANT SELECT, INSERT, UPDATE, DELETE ON jobsearchplus.* TO
'martin'@'localhost';

mysql> GRANT ALL ON jobsearchplus.* TO 'martin'@'localhost';

mysql> GRANT SELECT, INSERT, UPDATE, DELETE ON jobsearchplus.leads
TO 'martin'@'localhost';
```

The first statement grants read and write permissions on everything in the database by using the asterisk wildcard and the second statement grants full permissions on the database in the same way. The final statement grants read / write permissions on the 'leads' table only. These GRANT statements will give the user named Martin access to the data in the specified objects and will immediately update the privileges so that the next time he issues a command against the database, he will have the necessary access. MySQL verifies permissions each time a query or command is submitted in order to assess the user's current permissions. It's also possible to manually grant permissions by running `INSERT` and `UPDATE` queries against the tables within the mysql database but the `GRANT` statement is the preferred way since it handles everything automatically and there are fewer possibilities for errors. Manually inserting the permissions also does not immediately update them for the user until the server is restarted or an administrator issues the `FLUSH PRIVILEGES` command.

It's at this point that the other client programs such as MySQL Workbench start to come in really handy as they provide quick access to the various permissions available on databases. It's easier to check and uncheck various permissions for a user than to remember what's available and ensure that you type them right on the command line. Still, you need to know what these permissions enable a user to do before granting them in any program. The Workbench **Users and Privileges** screen divides them into certain categories and here are some brief explanations of the permissions.

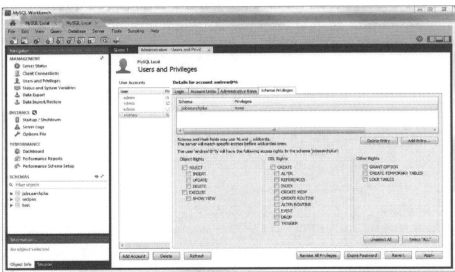

Figure 5.7 - Assigning permissions on SQL Server

- <u>Object Rights</u> - These include the basic read / write permissions on tables; the ability to `SELECT`, `INSERT`, `UPDATE` and `DELETE` rows from a table. The statements for these operations are included in the *Data Manipulation Language (DML)* portion of the SQL language which focuses on the editing of data within the tables. The `EXECUTE` rights enable a user to execute stored procedures on the server and the `SHOW VIEW` permission enables a user to use the SHOW `CREATE VIEW` command which displays the `CREATE` statement for a view.

- DDL Rights - DDL stands for *Data Definition Language* which is the collection of SQL statements that is used to define, create and alter objects in the database including tables, views, indexes and stored procedures. Granting these permissions gives users the ability to make changes to database objects and should be done with care, especially the `DROP` permission which let users delete objects or the database itself.

- Other Rights - The last few rights focus on administrative functions:

- The `GRANT OPTION` permission enables a user to grant permissions on the database to other users and would generally be reserved for an administrator or the the person responsible for a database.

- Temporary tables reside in memory and are only visible to the person or process who creates them. When the connection to the server is closed, they go away. These tables are often used for intermediate sorting and processing of data during complex operations. To create them, a user needs the `CREATE TEMPORARY TABLES` permission.

- The `LOCK TABLES` permission enables a user to place read and write locks on tables in order to prevent other users from accessing the tables at specific times for the sake of performing large updates or other operations.

To assign permissions in Workbench:

1. Click on the **Users and Privileges** option under **Management**.
2. Click on the **Schema Privileges** tab.

3. Click the **Add Entry** button beneath the **Privileges** list box.

4. The **New Schema Privilege Definition** box will appear, select the database (schema) you want to apply the permissions to.

5. Select the privileges you want to grant the user and click **Apply**.

This creates an entry for that database with the requested privileges. This entry can be removed or replaced as needed by the administrator. Multiple entries can be created for each user. In addition to granting privileges on the database and individual tables, it's possible to grant permissions on specific columns within a table but, given the potential amount of work involved in administering users, it's probably best not to get this detailed on the permissions. As mentioned in a previous chapter, columns can also be hidden by putting them in other tables. It's also possible to create a table *view* with just the permitted columns and grant rights on that and there will be more about that in upcoming chapters.

The **Administrative Roles** tab under the **Users** section in Workbench enables you to assign global permissions to various users based on the function they will be performing. These rights apply to the server itself and all databases on it. You can also assign specific permissions to tailor their access as needed.

Figure 5.8 -The Administrative Roles tab in MySQL Workbench assigns both global permissions on all databases and sets of permissions based on function.

The **Users** tabs in both phpMyAdmin and SQLBuddy perform many of the same functions as the **Users and Privileges** section in Workbench. You can create new users and edit the profiles and permissions of current users. The role-based permissions and presentation of database-specific permissions differ somewhat between the three programs with Workbench providing the most detailed set of options. For managing the permissions of any significant number of users, I would probably recommend Workbench but all three are worth exploring.

If you should decide that you don't want one or more users to have specific permissions, there's also the REVOKE command with which you can remove permissions.

```
mysql> REVOKE DELETE ON jobsearchplus.* FROM 'martin'@'localhost';

mysql> REVOKE ALL PRIVILEGES, GRANT OPTION ON *.* FROM
'lacey'@'localhost';
```

You could combinations of GRANT and REVOKE on a specific database in order to tailor a user's permissions. For example, you could grant all permission on a database and then remove the permissions to delete data and objects.

```
mysql> GRANT ALL PRIVILEGES ON jobsearchplus.* TO
'william'@'localhost';
mysql> REVOKE DELETE, DROP ON jobsearchplus.* FROM
'william'@'localhost';
```

Going back to the command line, you can verify the set of privileges assigned to a user at any time with the SHOW GRANTS command.

```
mysql> SHOW GRANTS FOR 'andrew'@'%';

GRANT USAGE ON *.* TO 'andrew'@'%' IDENTIFIED BY PASSWORD ...
GRANT ALL PRIVILEGES ON `jobsearchplus`.* TO 'andrew'@'%'
```

It's important to be careful when deciding what rights to grant the users you create. For security reasons, you should never grant permissions on the 'mysql' administrative database to a user you don't want to have the same privileges as the root user as all of the user account information is stored there.

For a full list of permissions available in MySQL and more detail on each, refer to Chapter 13, section 13.7.1.4 of the *MySQL Reference Manual*.

For Further Study

Review Questions

1. How do you ensure that you can run the mysql.exe command line client program from any directory on your computer?

2. What is the name of the subdirectory in which the MySQL executable programs are stored?

3. What are two ways in which you can increase the security of the MySQL root account and what command line syntax is used to accomplish them?

4. What is the advantage of installing MySQL as a service rather than starting the server from the command line each time?

5. What commands can you use to leave the MySQL command line and return to the operating system?

6. What is the purpose of the SELECT command in SQL?

7. What keyword do you use to specify an alias for a column in a SQL query?

8. What character is used as an escape character in MySQL and what is its purpose?

9. What character is used to end a query or command in MySQL?

10. You are writing a query at the MySQL command line and after pressing ENTER on a line, MySQL presents a command prompt of ->. What does this signify?

11. What result will MySQL return for the following query - SELECT (25 + (6 / 2) * 3) ^ 2 AS "Result" ?

12. You're entering a multi-line query on the MySQL command line. You make a mistake but don't catch it until you're on the next line. How do you cancel the query and start over? How can you access the previous lines so you don't have to retype them?

13. What keyword can you use at the command line to view all databases on the server, all tables within a database and all columns within a table?

14. What command is used to change the server's focus so that all further commands are directed to a specific database?

15. What database and table stores the information for all user accounts in MySQL?

16. What are two reasons that a MySQL server might have multiple accounts with the same username?

17. What is the difference between the hostnames 'localhost' and '127.0.0.1'?

18. You run a query on the mysql.user table and find user accounts with the hostname listed as "%". What does this mean?

19. What are the two steps that MySQL uses to authenticate users and verify their permissions on the server? When does it perform these steps?

20. What function is used to encrypt a plain-text password in order to save it in the user account?

21. How would you create a user with a blank password?

22. Why is the GRANT statement preferable to the INSERT and UPDATE statements for granting permissions to users?

23. What is the difference between Data Manipulation Language and Data Definition Language?

24. What would be the reason for granting permissions to a user and then immediately revoking permissions?

Terms to Remember

AMP environment - A software stack that includes the Apache web server, the MySQL database software and either PHP, Python or Perl as a programming language.

Client - Hardware or software that is designed to interact with a server and often provides an interface through which a user can access the server resources.

Column alias - An alternate name that can be specified for a column of data within a set returned by the database.

Database server - Hardware or software that houses a database management system (DBMS) and manages the local and network communications with that DBMS as well as the design and operation of the databases themselves. The term can be used to refer to a memory-resident portion of the DBMS that performs these functions or to the hardware that has the DBMS installed on it.

Graphical User Interface (GUI) - A program that provides an interface, usually menu-based, through which a user can access specific functions.

Hostname - The name used to identify and communicate with a device on a network.

Localhost (127.0.0.1) - The identifier that a computer or network server uses to objectively refer to itself as a location on a network.

Network server - A network machine, either physical or virtual, that maintains connections and manages communications between its own software and the rest of the network.

Ping - The process of sending a signal to a network resource in order to verify that the resource is responding or to verify the integrity of the network connection. This might also refer to the program or utility used to send the signal.

Schema - Also known as the physical data model. This is the third and final stage of data modeling in which the model is realized as a working database in a specific database software with the tables, indexes and other objects conforming to the rules of that software.

Service - A memory-resident program that is integrated to some degree with the operating system and supports other programs on the computer. A service can be set to start and stop with the operating system or be started manually by the user.

Set - A collection of rows returned or affected by a command or query in MySQL.

Sudo - A Linux program that enables the user to run single commands with administrative permissions.

Structured Query Language (SQL) - A scripting language that enables users to query a database server and issue commands as needed. The language contains commands and keywords to manipulate data on the server, define databases, tables, and other objects and manage permissions and other administrative settings on the server.

Chapter VI

Tables and Indexes

Introduction

As you've seen, there are a number of utilities and MySQL clients that you can use to create and manage your database. You could actually create all of the tables and other database objects through the MySQL command line client shown in the previous chapter. While this would be needlessly difficult and prone to errors, it's still important to understand that any graphical client program that you use such as phpMyAdmin is ultimately providing an interface for you as the user while issuing the same SQL commands to the database server in the background that you could issue on the command line.

For the demonstrations in this chapter, I'll mostly use MySQL Workbench as it is a complete solution for creating and managing database systems within MySQL. In addition to creating the database structures, it has some great tools for data modeling and creating diagrams of your system. Workbench also emphasizes the actual SQL commands that it sends to the server and you can use it to create complete sets of SQL scripts for a database and all of its data. You can then use these scripts to export the database from one server to another. This program was developed by Oracle as an interface for MySQL and is, in many ways, the counterpart to Microsoft's SQL Server Management Studio.

As in previous chapters, it's a good idea to follow along with these examples and try them out on your own MySQL installation. If you have not setup MySQL and created the example database yet, I recommend taking the time to do it and referring back to the previous chapters as necessary.

Storage Engines

One of MySQL's advantages as a database software is that it features multiple database storage engines. The storage engine is the part of the software that manages the database tables and their storage on the local computer or network. In this case, the storage engines also apply different rules and data formats to the database files. Each storage engine is appropriate to a different type of data with a couple of them being multi-purpose. To add even more flexibility, the storage engine is set at table level rather than for the entire database which means that tables which serve different functions within the database can have different storage engines. This means specific tables can be maintained in a way that will be most efficient.

Prior to MySQL v.5.5.5, the default storage engine was MyISAM which allows for storage of up to 256 terabytes (TB) of data, although the size limit for this and other engines is sharply limited even further by the operating system and its file storage. MyISAM is best when used for large database systems known as data warehouses where the emphasis is on fast reads of existing data and less on frequent writes and updates. MyISAM also supports data compression so that the tables take up less space on the server.

MyISAM's weakness for the relational databases that you see in this book is that it does not support the foreign keys which enforce links between tables. Corresponding primary and foreign key values can still be stored in the tables by whatever program or software is writing to the database so that records in one table could refer to records in another and these references can be manually maintained. There is no enforcement on this, however, so an orders table could refer to non-existent row IDs in the customer table or a record could be deleted from a products table and any records in other tables that referenced that product ID would still remain. A storage engine's support of foreign keys and the assurance that it will maintain primary and foreign key references is also known as *referential integrity*. This lack of referential integrity is also true of most of the other storage engines in MySQL.

In MySQL v.5.5.5 and later, the default engine is now InnoDB. While this engine only supports up to 64 TB of data rather than the 256 TB of MyISAM, it does support foreign keys and will enforce referential integrity. Its read and write operations are also ACID-compliant with the ability to rollback transactions on errors and protect the data in the event of a system crash so that data consistency is ensured. (See Chapter II - "Choosing and Installing MySQL" for a more detailed explanation of ACID-compliance.) InnoDB tables also feature a *clustered index* which physically orders the data in a table on the primary key so as to speed up searches on that column. It's still possible to join InnoDB tables with tables of other formats in SQL queries, although the results would be subject to whatever manual referential integrity measures were applied to the non-InnoDB tables.

There are several other engines available in MySQL, although the ones available between installations will vary. You can see the engines available in your installations on the command line or through another utility.

```
mysql> SHOW ENGINES;
+------------+----------+----------------------------------+--------------+-----+------------+
| Engine     | Support  | Comment                          | Transactions | XA  | Savepoints |
+------------+----------+----------------------------------+--------------+-----+------------+
| Federated  | NO       | Federated MySQL Storage Engine   | NO           | NO  | NO         |
| MyISAM     | YES      | MyISAM Storage Engine            | NO           | NO  | NO         |
| BLACKHOLE  | YES      | /dev/null storage engine ...     | NO           | NO  | NO         |
| CSV        | YES      | CSV storage engine               | NO           | NO  | NO         |
| MEMORY     | YES      | Hash based, stored in memory ... | NO           | NO  | NO         |
| InnoDB     | DEFAULT  | Supports transactions ...        | YES          | YES | YES        |
+------------+----------+----------------------------------+--------------+-----+------------+
6 rows in set (0.00 sec)
```

Engines can be added and removed as needed and the Support column indicates whether that particular engine is part of your installation. While InnoDB is the default and will be used in this book's examples, it's good to know a little something about a few of the other engines for comparison.

- **Federated** - This engine is designed to allow for communications with remote MySQL clients. The actual tables reside on the remote server and queries are directed against it while the local server maintains a copy of the table definition and a connection string to the remote server.

- **Blackhole** - Appropriately named, this engine does not retain any data that's sent to it but simply reports on the success of the write and disposes of the data. SELECT statements return sets of zero records. It's often used for testing server performance

- **CSV** - This engine writes the table data to CSV (comma separated values) text files on the server which can be viewed by a text editor independently of MySQL. Because of the plain-text format, the tables can be directly read and even updated by spreadsheet programs such as Microsoft Excel and other database applications.

- **Memory** - The Memory storage engine stores all table data in the server's volatile memory rather than on disk. This can be very useful for temporary and lookup tables that need to be accessed quickly but it also means that the amount of storage is limited to how much of the server's memory can be spared for data tables. The data will go away if the machine shuts down for any reason.

A complete list of the storage engines available through MySQL and their capabilities is available in the *MySQL Reference Manual*.

Models and Schemas

With MySQL Workbench, you can take two different approaches to building a database. The first is to model the database within Workbench as we did in the earlier chapter on Normalization. If you select **File >> New Model** from the main menu, the program will bring up the model editor where you can create the major objects with the model including tables, views and users. Using this approach, you can refine the model and experiment with ideas before you actually create any tables or commit the design to the server. You can also save the model in its own file for reference. Once your model is complete, you can then use the **Database >> Forward Engineer** menu (or the CTRL-G shortcut) to create the physical database (also called the *schema*) and all of its objects. As indicated by the menu option, this is called *forward engineering*.

There are two problems with forward engineering in Workbench. The first is that the modeling interface doesn't always tell you when specific details of the model that you build, such as column default values, cannot actually be written to the database design on the server. When you forward engineer the model, Workbench does allow for the editing of the SQL commands before it issues them to the server to create the objects and it does enable you to edit and retry failed commands. This might be a bit frustrating and daunting for the beginner, however. The second problem is that Workbench is not always able to re-open the file in which it saves the model information. This file is actually a compressed ZIP file with an MWB extension and it contains an XML file with all of the model information. For various reasons, Workbench is sometimes unable to reload these files so I don't recommend relying on the MWB file for storing model information until after the database has already been created. The model file should only be used for reference and documentation on the database and should not be the only documentation.

The other approach is to actually create the database and its tables first and then generate the model and *EER diagram* from the database. This is called *reverse engineering*. The model then serves as documentation for the database on the server. You can also make changes either to the model or the database itself and then synchronize one with the other. This can also be very useful when analyzing a database created by someone else.

As we create the Job Search Plus tables in this chapter, I will be showing you how to create the tables on the server and then reverse engineer the database into a model for documentation. The process for creating tables on the server and within a model is pretty similar so it's not hard to reverse the process if you want when creating your own databases.

MySQL Workbench

Getting Started

Make sure that your installation of the MySQL server is running on your machine and start up MySQL Workbench if you have it installed. If you really want to work through the command line client or another graphical client, I'll be providing the SQL commands that you can use to accomplish these tasks as well.

MySQL Workbench is able to store the information for connections to multiple MySQL servers and, when you start the program, the home page will display tiles for any connections that have already been set up. If the connection information has not been entered for your MySQL server, you can click on the Add icon at the top of the screen or select the **Database >> Manage Connections** menu option. Each of these will take you to different options screens, either of which will enable you to create and save a new server connection.

You will need the hostname, which can be either 'localhost' or '127.0.0.1' for a server on your local machine. The domain name or IP address of a remote machine can be used as well. You will also need the user name and password. Workbench is able to store the password for you or you can choose to enter it each time. For training purposes, it's okay to use the 'root' user account at first although, at some point, it's a good idea to create another user with all rights to the database that you'll be creating and use that one. The port number for MySQL defaults to 3306 so this should be the right one to use unless you have multiple MySQL installations running on the same machine. Even with multiple servers, they can use the same port number so long as only one is running at a time. Finally, choose a name for your connection that you will recognize, especially if you're working with multiple connections.

Once you connect to the server through Workbench, the program immediately displays the connection workspace with the server and schema navigator on the left and the query editor where you can enter raw SQL queries and commands for execution. You can see an example of this workspace in Figure 6.2. The program allows for multiple query windows to be open at once in case you are working with multiple databases or scripts and you can open a new Query tab from the **File** menu or through the CTRL-T shortcut. The Output window at the bottom of the screen will show the messages that result from any commands you send to the server so it's important to pay attention to this window for details on any failed commands. This workspace can be modified through the **View** menu where you can hide either the Navigator or the Output window if you want more space to focus on the queries.

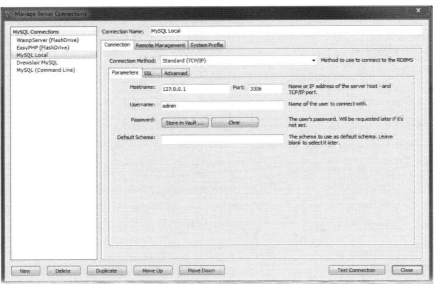

Figure 6.1 - MySQL Workbench enables the storage and management of connections to multiple MySQL servers.

Executing Queries

MySQL Workbench provides a menu interface that can be used to easily create database objects on the server. The program also features the query editor with which you can write and run complex queries and SQL scripts much easier than on the command line. The editor offers auto-completion of SQL keywords and object names for reference and to speed up entry of commands. Despite the availability of the menu commands, it's still important to be proficient in the SQL language in order to truly understand how the database is being managed. SQL knowledge also helps in the occasional situation where the graphical interface isn't handling things as you need it to.

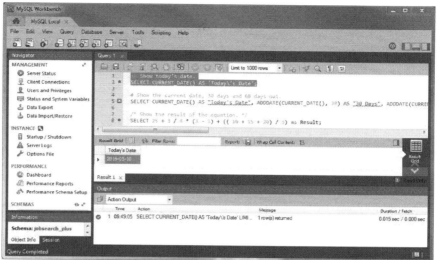

Figure 6.2 - MySQL Workbench provides a workspace that enables management of databases and servers through a menu interface and through direct queries and commands to the server.

In order to get a feel for the query editor, try typing in the following queries from the last chapter along with the comments above them. Be sure to put a semi-colon after each of the queries to indicate to Workbench that they are separate statements.

```
-- Show today's date.
SELECT CURRENT_DATE() AS 'Today\'s Date';

# Show the current date, 30 days and 60 days out.
SELECT CURRENT_DATE() AS "Today's Date", ADDDATE(CURRENT_DATE(), 30)
AS "30 Days", ADDDATE(CURRENT_DATE(), 60) AS "60 Days";

/* Show the result of the equation. */
SELECT 25 + 3 / 4 * (3 - 1) + (( 10 + 15 + 20) / 3) as Result;
```

You can run any or all of these statements using the **Query** menu in Workbench or the toolbar just above the query area. It's important to get familiar with these commands and to know what you're running at all times, especially if you're running action queries that change data. Selecting a statement within the query editor will effectively limit the execution to that statement regardless of the menu or toolbar option used and is the safest way to run queries. One thing that you might immediately notice, as shown in Figure 6.3, is that the Workbench query editor indicates errors on the second statement which uses the double-quotes as delimiters for the column names. This statement will still work but Workbench's error checker doesn't like the syntax.

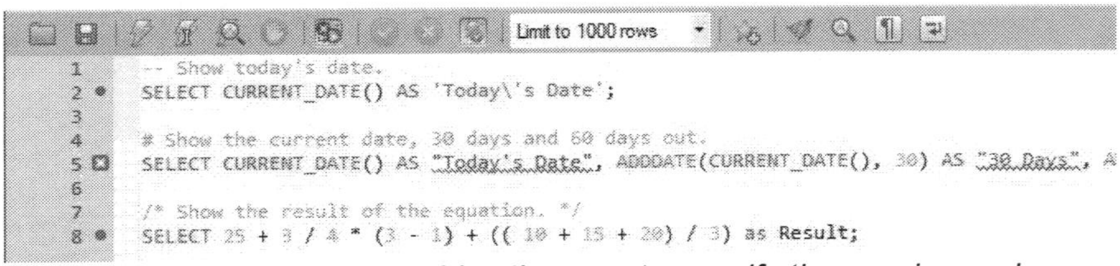

Figure 6.3 - The query toolbar enables the user to specify the queries and commands to be sent to the server while the editor provides basic error-checking of queries.

Also notice the three different ways in which comments are declared within MySQL The double-dash and the pound sign will mark single lines as comments whereas the forward slash and asterisk braces are good for multi-line comments. These lines will be completely ignored by MySQL, even if you have them selected in the editor. Commenting out action queries and commands when you don't want them running is also a good precaution against unwanted changes.

After you run any or all of the commands, you'll see the Result Grid appear under the query area in the Output pane as shown in Figure 6.2. Each query or command that you run will show in a different tab and any output messages will be displayed in the Output window below that. This makes it pretty easy for you to run any commands you need to and quickly see the results.

If you have not already created the Job Search Plus database as shown in the last chapter, now is a good time to do it. After the previous queries you entered, type in the following commands:

```
CREATE DATABASE jobsearch_plus;
```

Then use the mouse to select that statement in the query editor as if you were going to copy it and use any of the query execution options to run it. Alternately, you can also place the cursor somewhere within the command and use the CTRL-ENTER shortcut to execute that specific query. The list of schemas on the left of the screen might not update right away. The Output pane should show that the database has been successfully created but if you want to see for yourself, right-click within the Navigator sidebar under **Schemas** and use the **Refresh All** option to refresh the list of databases on the server.

Creating the Tables

The Table Header

Remember that before you can work with a database in MySQL, you need to set it as the default database so that all statements will be directed to it. In Workbench, you can right-click on the database in the Navigator sidebar under Schemas and use the **Set as Default Schema** menu command or execute the following statement in the query editor.

```
USE jobsearch_plus;
```

I will be using lowercase capitalization for all database objects with underscores to separate words within titles. Remember that object names are case-sensitive under Linux so it's a good idea to name objects with this in mind.

The first table we'll create is the main job leads table which I will simply call 'leads'. If you look at the listing for your new *jobsearch_plus* database under **Schemas** in the Navigation sidebar, you'll see that it has subsections for the tables, views, stored procedures and functions. Right-click on the Tables section and select the **Create Table** menu command to open a new table editor screen.

The table editor in Workbench is fairly straightforward although there are a few options that will need explanation. Figure 6.4 shows the editor with the completed Leads table design displayed and I'll be showing you how to duplicate this design in the next couple of sections. Start by entering the following options at the top for the table definition:

- Table Name: leads
- Collation: Schema Default
- Engine: InnoDB
- Comments: Main job leads table

Again, the storage engine is selected at table level and you can select different engines for tables that serve different purposes. For all the tables in this relatively small database, however, we will be using the InnoDB engine in order to support the foreign keys. It is not necessary to fill in the Comments field although it can help to document the database.

Figure 6.4 - The table designer in MySQL Workbench provides a graphical interface with which to specify settings and options.

After you define the table itself, it's time to create the individual fields; all tables must have at least one field defined in order to be saved to the database. Each field has a number of options and flags you can use to define it and what kind of data it accepts.

- **Column Name** - This is the name that will identify the column. It should be just long enough to clearly explain the column but short enough to be easily referenced. Column names can start with A-Z, 0-9 or the underscore character. MySQL has many reserved words and keywords such as 'date' and 'name' that should not be used on their own for these names in order to avoid confusion. You can find a complete list of reserved words in the *MySQL Reference Manual*.

- **Data Type** - The data type determines the type of data a column can hold, how many characters can be stored in it and the format. I will be explaining more about them in the following section.

- **Primary Key (PK)** - This option sets the primary key for the table. This flag forces the value to be unique for each record and prevents null values from being allowed so the NN and UQ flags are not required to be set.

- **Not Null (NN)** - The Not Null option requires a value to be entered within the field. Attempts to insert records without providing values for required fields will fail.

- **Unique Index (UQ)** - Columns can be set to require unique values in each record. This option actually creates an index on the field and we'll look more at indexes in a later section.

- **Is Binary Column (BIN)** - Used on non-numeric fields. This flag indicates that the column can hold binary data which may contain special characters.

- **Unsigned Data Type (UN)** - For numeric fields, this limits the field to non-negative numbers only which increases the upper limit of the number that can be stored within the field.

- **Zero Fill (ZF)** - For numeric fields, this automatically inserts a zero in the field when no other value is entered.

- **Auto Increment (AF)** - Often used for the primary key, this flag inserts a number in the field starting at 1 and incrementing the value for each record entered.

- **Default** - In addition to using the Zero Fill flag, it's possible to set a default value for the field such as the current date or a text value.

Data Types

The second column within the table editor shows the *data type* for each field. Data types are used by database software in order to enforce rules on the data being entered so that the appropriate operations can be performed on it when necessary. For example, when a field is defined as a date field, the database will ensure that any value entered complies with one of the recognized date formats. In the same way, the fields marked with a data type of VARCHAR(x) can be limited to a certain number of alphanumeric characters and the INT(x) data fields can be limited to integer values (whole numbers) or defined with a given number of decimal places. The primary key uses an INT data type AI (AutoIncrement) flag set to automatically provide a unique value for each field.

MySQL has a wealth of data types to choose from in order to customize your database. You'll see some of them used and the reasoning behind their selection as we continue to design the tables in this application. Here are a few of the standard types that you'll see most often.

- **Integers** - There are a few different types of integers in MySQL from the TINYINT type which can store values up to 255 to the BIGINT type which can store numbers to 18,446,744,073,709,551,615. The difference between the *TINYINT, SMALLINT, MEDIUMINT, INT and BIGINT* fields is in the number of bytes used to store each value within the database and, consequently, on your computer or network. The wider a range of values that a type can store, the more bytes are required to store the number and the more space it takes. When designing a table that will contain a lot of rows, you might use the regular INT type which uses 4 bytes per value and can store values from -2,147,483,648 to 2,147,483,647. This is also referred to as a 32-bit integer (4 bytes x 8 bits per byte = 32 bits). Using the correct type of integer and limiting the range of values entered can also help to ensure the accuracy of the data.

- **Dates** - Dates and times are also covered by multiple data types within MySQL and differ in the number of bytes used to store the values and the degree of precision allowed by the data type. If you need to store the complete date and time down to the second, you might use the DATETIME or TIMESTAMP type whereas if you just need the date, then you would use the regular DATE type.

- **CHAR(x) / VARCHAR(x)** - VARCHAR actually stands for "varying character" and both of these types store alphanumeric data such as names and addresses. The difference is that VARCHAR is used when the length of the data is uncertain but you still know the maximum number of characters. CHAR, on the other hand, is used when there won't be much variation. With both types, the number of characters allowed in the field is specified when defining the field. Therefore, when storing a phone number or license plate number, you could use a CHAR type since these won't vary much. When storing something like the job title in the leads table, VARCHAR is better since there will be a lot of variation. With the VARCHAR types, MySQL and other databases only use as many bytes as necessary to store the value that is entered. The CHAR type allocates the number of bytes specified when the field is defined for *every* value that is stored.

These are just a few of the types available in MySQL and you'll see quite a bit of variation between different database software titles. Sometimes, this can make transferring data between systems a challenge. The software sometimes helps by making its own decisions about what types certain data fits into but it's a good idea to be very familiar with the different data types and their limitations.

Allowing Nulls

The Not Null (NN) column flag in the MySQL table editor specifies whether null values will be prohibited on a table field. A null value indicates that the data simply doesn't exist or is not applicable. It is not the same as a value of '0' or a False value but instead indicates that the data has not been provided or cannot be provided. Whether or not to allow null values in each field is one of the decisions you have to make when designing tables in a database. You have to allow for fields for which the user just doesn't have a value to enter. At the same time, some fields cannot be null because they contribute to the essential definition of a record or must be unique. For the Leads table, there are a few fields that cannot be null as you will see when we define them in the next section.

- The primary key identifies the record. In this table, the field is auto-incremented and therefore filled in automatically.

- The date on which the job lead is entered into the system can be filled in with the current date automatically.

- The job title, which is an essential part of the job lead, must be entered.

- The Active field which indicates if a job lead is still active or has been closed is a BIT field which stores a 1 or 0. It has a default value of 1 (True) and therefore does not need to be null.

Notice that for each field I require, I consider where the data is going to come from. In this case, the only one that can't use an automatically supplied value of some kind is the job title and I can be certain that the user will be able to supply that value.

Conversely, for every field that I allow to be null, I have to consider how this is going to impact the system. The Leads table will allow a job lead to be entered without a company or contact which would sometimes be necessary since some job leads are listed without any identifying information. There are a couple of considerations involved that are specific to the application. The company and contact information is actually made up of three foreign keys; *company_id* which indicates an employer, *agency_id* which indicates a recruiter or other type of third-party agency and *contact_id* which is the current primary contact for the position. Any combination of these fields might be used to indicate who the job seeker should contact about the job lead and I want the user to have the most freedom to enter a specific lead in the way that they need to. I don't want to tell the user how to run their job search or make them work to accommodate the software. The rest of the fields that allow nulls are not essential to the job lead record or can be entered at a later time without causing a problem.

Columns and Indexes

Here are the field specifications for the Leads table which you can fill in if you're creating the tables yourself. Refer to Figure 6.5 for an example of the first few fields. You can select the data type from the dropdown list in the table editor or type them in directly as shown here. Select the PK and AI checkboxes for the primary key field and the NN checkbox for any fields marked as 'Not Null'. Default values can be entered as shown for the three relevant fields.

- *lead_id*, INT(11), Primary Key, Auto-Increment
- *record_date*, DATETIME, Not Null, Default = 'CURRENT_TIMESTAMP'
- *job_title*, VARCHAR(75), Not Null
- *job_description*, VARCHAR(1024)
- *employment_type*, ENUM('Full-time','Part-time','Contractor','Temp','Seasonal','Internal','Freelance','Volunteer')
- *location*, VARCHAR(50)
- *active*, BIT(1), Not Null, Default = 1
- *company_id*, INT(11)
- *agency_id*, INT(11)
- *contact_id*, INT(11)
- *source_id*, INT(11)
- *selected*, BIT(1), Not Null, Default = 0

There are a few design choices worth noticing here. You'll see that the integers in the table are declared as INT(11). The number in the parentheses indicates the display width for the field value, not the actual size of the value. In other words, the value in the table can be displayed using 11 digits. This is the default display width for integers in MySQL.

The recording date for the lead is actually set to a DATETIME field to allow the CURRENT_TIMESTAMP function to be used as a default. This is the exception to the rule that the default value for the field must be a constant value and cannot be a function or expression such as `CURRENT_DATE`.

Column Name	Datatype	PK	NN	UQ	BIN	UN	ZF	AI	Default
lead_id	INT(11)	✓	✓					✓	
record_date	DATETIME		✓						CURRENT_TIMESTAMP
job_title	VARCHAR(75)		✓						
job_description	VARCHAR(1024)								NULL
employment_type	ENUM('Full-time','Par...								NULL

Figure 6.5 - Fields can be quickly created in the table designer by specifying the necessary settings.

The employment type field is set to an ENUM type which specifies a list of allowed values within the field. It also stores an index number instead of the actual text value but displays the text value when reading from the table. This saves storage space. The list of allowed values can be retrieved from the *information_schema.COLUMNS* administrative table within your MySQL installation as shown below.

```
SELECT SUBSTRING(COLUMN_TYPE, 5)
FROM information_schema.COLUMNS
WHERE TABLE_SCHEMA='jobsearch_plus'
    AND TABLE_NAME='leads'
    AND COLUMN_NAME='employment_type';
+-------------------------------------------------------------------+
| Values                                                            |
+-------------------------------------------------------------------+
| ('Full-time','Part-time','Contractor','Temp','Seasonal')          |
+-------------------------------------------------------------------+
1 row in set (0.00 sec)
```

This string can be broken down into separate values by whatever program is accessing the table and presented to the user as a list of values from which to select. The alternative to this is to have a separate lookup table that lists the values which would be linked to the Leads as you'll see later.

The *active* and *selected* fields are BIT fields meaning that the field can store a series of up to 64 bit values, ones and zeros. In this case, the field is storing a single bit value in order to represent a True or False condition. The *active* field indicates if a job lead is still active so its default value is 1 (True) and the *selected* field can be used to select multiple job leads for the software to run reports or other operations on.

You can save the table at this point by clicking on the Apply button at the bottom of the table editor. Workbench will confirm the changes to the table by showing you the SQL statement that will be used to create the table.

```
CREATE TABLE `jobsearch_plus`.`leads` (
  `lead_id` INT(11) NOT NULL AUTO_INCREMENT COMMENT '',
  `record_date` DATE NOT NULL COMMENT '',
  `job_title` VARCHAR(75) NOT NULL COMMENT '',
  `job_description` VARCHAR(1024) NULL DEFAULT NULL COMMENT '',
  `employment_type` ENUM('Full-time','Part-
time','Contractor','Temp','Seasonal',
     'Internal','Freelance','Volunteer') NULL DEFAULT NULL COMMENT
'',
  `location` VARCHAR(50) NULL DEFAULT NULL COMMENT '',
  `active` BIT(1) NOT NULL DEFAULT b'1' COMMENT '',
  `company_id` INT(11) NULL DEFAULT NULL COMMENT '',
  `agency_id` INT(11) NULL DEFAULT NULL COMMENT '',
  `contact_id` INT(11) NULL DEFAULT NULL COMMENT '',
  `source_id` INT(11) NULL DEFAULT NULL COMMENT '',
  `selected` BIT(1) NOT NULL DEFAULT B'0',
  PRIMARY KEY (`lead_id`)  COMMENT '')
  COMMENT = 'Main job leads table ';
```

If you take this statement line by line, it's actually not difficult to interpret the settings of the various columns. If it looks a little complicated, then take a look at the same statement with some of the settings removed. It will still create a table with the same fields but without some of the settings.

```
CREATE TABLE `jobsearch_plus`.`leads`
  (`lead_id` INT(11),
  `record_date` DATE,
  `job_title` VARCHAR(75),
  `job_description` VARCHAR(1024),
  `employment_type` ENUM('Full-time','Part-time',
  'Contractor','Temp','Seasonal','Internal',
  'Freelance','Volunteer'),
  `location` VARCHAR(50),
  `active` BIT(1),
  `company_id` INT(11),
  `agency_id` INT(11),
  `contact_id` INT(11),
  `source_id` INT(11),
  `selected` BIT(1),
  PRIMARY KEY (`lead_id`)
  COMMENT = 'Main job leads table ';
```

This is an example of how easy it is to create an object within MySQL with a single statement. While the graphical tools you've seen so far in this chapter come in handy, it's a good idea to at least be able to read the accompanying SQL statements because you will encounter them if you spend any time working with databases.

After the columns are defined, it's time to place some indexes on the table. Indexes are used to assist in sorting and searching on the fields and this is the guideline to use when deciding which columns to index. Although they do increase the efficiency of table operations, indexes also use resources and too many indexes on the wrong fields can be counterproductive. When deciding what columns to index, there are a couple of guidelines to follow.

- You should index columns that will have a variety of values and will be searched and sorted on often. In the Leads table, the *job_title* and *record_date* fields would be good examples of this.

- Do not index fields that only hold a couple of values such as the *leads.active* field. This requires the database to do extra work maintaining the index on a field that is easily searched anyway.

- Too many indexes can also be a bad thing. Every index represents work that the database has to do whenever data is entered or changed because these indexes must be maintained. It's good to be selective when choosing indexed fields.

One index is already present on the table; under the InnoDB engine, the primary key is a clustered index which determines the order in which the rows are actually stored in the table. There are a few more fields within the job leads table that are eligible for indexes - *record_date*, *job_title* and *employment_type*.

All three of these fields are likely to be sorted or searched on and indexes will assist with that. As for the other fields, the *job_description* field is designed to hold long descriptions that aren't as likely to be searched in this application. The InnoDB and MyISAM engines do support full text searches of these fields if you want to search for specific strings. The *location* field could be searched but it's designed to more of a free-form description of the job location so searches would not be as effective. The two BIT fields, *active* and *selected*, should not be indexed as they can only contain a 1 or a 0. An index is not needed to search or sort on these fields. The remaining fields will be receiving indexes but as foreign keys that will link this table to other tables so we'll look at that later.

Click on the **Indexes** tab at the bottom of the table editor as shown in Figure 6.6 in order to create the indexes for the three fields above. You'll see the table header information at the top and the list of existing indexes which will show the table's primary key. Double-click on the next available line in the index list and enter a name for a new index. For indexes other than foreign keys and the primary key, I like to use the field name followed by an underscore and "idx" to indicate which field or fields will be affected. After you enter a name, press the TAB key to move to the Type option. This option can be set to one of the following values:

- PRIMARY - One or more fields can be selected as the table's primary key although only one index entry can be marked with this option.

- UNIQUE - Requires the values in a field or combination of fields to be unique for each record. Multiple indexes can use this option.

- FULL-TEXT - Available on text fields only and searches the entire text in a field for matching values.

- INDEX - A standard index that assists in searches and sorts on that field.

After you select an index type, you can check the fields to be included in the index under the **Index Columns** listing. All three of the indexes we're creating here are single-column indexes. You could also create multi-column indexes for various reasons such as if you wanted to create a unique index on two columns so that no two rows would have the same *combination* of values. Next to the column name, you can use the "#" option to set the sort priority of each field within the index. In other words, in a multi-column field, you can choose which column will be sorted on first, second, etc..

The **Order** option for the index can be set to ascending or descending ('ASC' or 'DESC'). This option is included for future expansion but is not actually used yet as of MySQL v.5.7 and all indexes are sorted in ascending order so you can leave this as ASC. The **Length** option lets you index the first few characters of text fields in case you have fields where only the first few characters are different between rows. Otherwise, it's safe to leave this option blank.

The set of **Index Options** on the right of the Indexes tab are less frequently used and it's safe to leave these at their defaults. The **Storage Type** option determines how the index will do comparisons between field values. In the InnoDB engine, only BTREE is allowed for this option. The **Key Block** size lets the user set the number of bytes to allocate for pages which are the units of data that MySQL transfers between the storage disk and memory at one time. The **Parser** option lets a user specify a software plug-in to be used when indexing the fields.

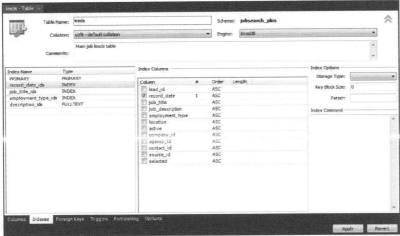

Figure 6.6 - Proper use of indexes makes sorting and searching on specific columns faster.

If you already saved the table after defining the columns, you can click **Apply** again to save the indexes that were added here and Workbench will use the ALTER TABLE statement to add the index definitions. Again, it's pretty straightforward with the ADD INDEX statements sending the index name, the field(s) to be indexed and the sort order to the table.

```
ALTER TABLE `jobsearch_plus`.`leads`
  ADD INDEX `record_date_idx` (`record_date` ASC),
  ADD INDEX `job_title_idx` (`job_title` ASC) ,
```

```
   ADD INDEX `employment_type_idx` (`employment_type` ASC)
   ADD FULLTEXT INDEX `description_idx` (`job_description` ASC)
COMMENT '';
```

If you add the indexes when you first save the table, the syntax is a little different with the KEY clauses added on after the column definitions. This CREATE statement was actually generated by Workbench from a copy of the table that had already been created. You'll notice that certain settings like the blank field comments and the sort order of the indexes are not included.

```
CREATE TABLE `leads` (
  `lead_id` int(11) NOT NULL AUTO_INCREMENT,
  `record_date` datetime NOT NULL DEFAULT CURRENT_TIMESTAMP,
  `job_title` varchar(75) NOT NULL,
  `job_description` varchar(1024) DEFAULT NULL,
  `employment_type` enum('Full-time','Part-time','Contractor',
    'Temp','Seasonal','Internal','Freelance','Volunteer') DEFAULT
NULL,
  `location` varchar(50) DEFAULT NULL,
  `active` bit(1) DEFAULT b'1',
  `company_id` int(11) DEFAULT NULL,
  `agency_id` int(11) DEFAULT NULL,
  `contact_id` int(11) DEFAULT NULL,
  `source_id` int(11) DEFAULT NULL,
  `selected` bit(1) NOT NULL DEFAULT b'0',
  PRIMARY KEY (`lead_id`),
  KEY `record_date_idx` (`record_date`),
  KEY `job_title_idx` (`job_title`),
  KEY `employment_type_idx` (`employment_type`)
  FULLTEXT KEY `description_idx` (`job_description`),
  ) ENGINE=InnoDB DEFAULT CHARSET=utf8 COMMENT='Main job leads table
';
```

Remaining Tables

Looking back at the logical data model that was developed in Chapter IV, there were six data entities within the model, each of which could become one or more tables in the physical schema. Now that we've built the main job leads table, let's look at how the other tables come together.

Activities

```
CREATE TABLE `jobsearch_plus`.`activities` (
  `activity_id` INT(11) NOT NULL AUTO_INCREMENT,
  `lead_id` INT(11) NOT NULL,
  `activity_date` DATETIME NOT NULL DEFAULT CURRENT_TIMESTAMP,
  `activity_type` VARCHAR(30) NOT NULL,
  `activity_details` VARCHAR(1024) NULL,
```

```
`complete` BIT(1) NULL DEFAULT 0,
`reference_link` VARCHAR(255) NULL DEFAULT NULL,
PRIMARY KEY (`activity_id`),
INDEX `activity_date_idx` (`activity_date` ASC),
INDEX `activity_type_idx` (`activity_type` ASC));
```

The Activities table stores individual activities on each job lead such as resume submittals, follow-ups and interviews. You can use the CREATE statement above to duplicate the table, either through the query editor or the table editor. Notice the table includes both an *activity_id* field as the primary key and a *lead_id* field which will act as a foreign key linking the table back to the job leads table. The *complete* field indicates if an activity has been completed and allows for upcoming activities and reminders to be scheduled. The *reference_link* field can hold a hyperlink to supporting documentation as needed.

In addition to the primary key, the table has two indexed fields - the *activity_date* and *activity_type* fields which indicates what kind of action was performed. These are both fields which might be search or sorted on.

Activity Types

```
CREATE TABLE `jobsearch_plus`.`activity_types` (
  `activity_type` VARCHAR(30) NOT NULL,
  PRIMARY KEY (`activity_type`));
```

This is a lookup table that supplies values such as 'Contact', 'Resume submittal' and 'Follow-up' to indicate what was action was performed on the lead. It demonstrates the alternative to the *employment_type* ENUM field in the *leads* table. The *activity_type* primary key in the statement shown above will be referenced by the Activities table as the official list of activity types that can be entered for a job lead. This ensures consistency within the Activities table so that searches are more reliable. The list of activity options is also easier to retrieve and present to the user with the following query.

```
SELECT activity_type FROM activity_types ORDER BY activity_type;
```

This would present an alphabetical listing of all the types entered in the table and could be used by a program to populate a dropdown control. This is a simple lookup that will store the actual text within the

Activities table rather than an ID number. This won't be a problem as this is a relatively low volume application where there will probably be less than a thousand actual job leads. It might become an issue to consider in tables containing many thousands or tens of thousands of records.

Sources

```
CREATE TABLE `jobsearch_plus`.`sources` (
  `source_id` INT(11) NULL AUTO_INCREMENT,
  `source_name` VARCHAR(50) NOT NULL,
  `source_type` VARCHAR(50) NOT NULL,
  `source_link` VARCHAR(255) NULL DEFAULT NULL,
  `source_desc` VARCHAR(1024) NULL DEFAULT NULL,
  PRIMARY KEY (`source_id`) COMMENT '',
  INDEX `source_name_idx` (`source_name` ASC) COMMENT '',
  INDEX `source_type_idx` (`source_type` ASC) COMMENT '');
```

The Sources table will also be referenced by the Leads table and provides information on job lead sources including websites, newspapers and agencies. It's a small table, providing basic reference information on the resources a person is using in their search. In addition to the name and type of resource, there's space for a hyperlink to an online resource and a basic description. The only fields that really need to be indexed are the source name and type.

Companies and Contacts

```
CREATE TABLE `jobsearch_plus`.`companies` (
  `company_id` INT(11) NOT NULL AUTO_INCREMENT,
  `company_name` VARCHAR(75) NOT NULL,
  `address1` VARCHAR(75) NULL DEFAULT NULL,
  `address2` VARCHAR(75) NULL DEFAULT NULL,
  `city` VARCHAR(50) NULL DEFAULT NULL,
  `co_state` CHAR(2) NULL DEFAULT NULL,
  `zip` CHAR(10) NULL DEFAULT NULL,
  `phone` CHAR(14) NULL DEFAULT NULL,
  `fax` CHAR(14) NULL DEFAULT NULL,
  `email` VARCHAR(50) NULL DEFAULT NULL,
  `website` VARCHAR(50) NULL DEFAULT NULL,
  `company_desc` VARCHAR(1024) NULL DEFAULT NULL,
  `business_type` VARCHAR(30) NULL DEFAULT NULL,
  `agency` BIT(1) NOT NULL DEFAULT b'0',
  PRIMARY KEY (`company_id`) COMMENT '',
  INDEX `company_name_idx` (`company_name` ASC),
  INDEX `city_idx` (`city` ASC),
  INDEX `state_idx` (`co_state` ASC),
  INDEX `zip_idx` (`zip` ASC),
  INDEX `business_type_idx` (`business_type` ASC));
```

```
CREATE TABLE `jobsearch_plus`.`contacts` (
  `contact_id` INT(11) NOT NULL AUTO_INCREMENT COMMENT '',
  `company_id` INT(11) NOT NULL COMMENT '',
  `courtesty_title` VARCHAR(25) NOT NULL COMMENT '',
  `contact_first` VARCHAR(35) NULL DEFAULT NULL COMMENT '',
  `contact_last` VARCHAR(35) NOT NULL COMMENT '',
  `title` VARCHAR(50) NULL DEFAULT NULL COMMENT '',
  `phone` CHAR(14) NULL DEFAULT NULL COMMENT '',
  `fax` CHAR(14) NULL DEFAULT NULL COMMENT '',
  `email` VARCHAR(50) NULL DEFAULT NULL COMMENT '',
  `comments` VARCHAR(1024) NULL DEFAULT NULL COMMENT '',
  `active` BIT(1) NOT NULL DEFAULT b'1' COMMENT '',
  PRIMARY KEY (`contact_id`) COMMENT '',
  INDEX `company_idx` (`company_id` ASC) COMMENT '',
  INDEX `last_name_idx` (`contact_last` ASC) COMMENT '',
  INDEX `first_name_idx` (`contact_first` ASC) COMMENT '');
```

Contact management is an important part of running a job search and Job Search Plus helps with this. The Companies and Contacts tables enable the user to enter full information on the people and companies they come into contact with during the search. Although there are a lot of fields in each table, few of them are actually required so that new contacts can be entered quickly and information can be added over time as needed. The *companies.agency* field is required and defaults to 0 (False), indicating that the company is not a placement agency. The *active* field in Contacts indicates whether the person is still available as a contact at the company and defaults to 1 (True).

The two tables will be linked by the *company_id* field so that a company can be selected for each contact and a company *is* required for each contact. Again, only basic fields that might be searched on receive indexes.

Business Types

```
CREATE TABLE `jobsearch_plus`.`business_types` (
  `business_type` VARCHAR(30) NOT NULL COMMENT '',
  PRIMARY KEY (`business_type`) COMMENT '');
```

The final table in the application is a lookup table for various types of businesses such as technology or marketing companies. It functions very much the same as the Activity Types table. This table will be referenced by the Companies table to indicate what business category a company falls under.

Linking the Tables

An important step in building a relational database is to actually relate the tables to each other and ensure that records in one table will correctly refer to the related records in another. In the case of the Job Search Plus database, this means that if one of the Activity table records refers to a specific record within the Leads table, that record should actually exist. This is referred to as *referential integrity* and protects the data against incorrect references caused by update and delete actions within the database. Related tables are often referred to as having a parent-child relationship with the primary key table being the parent and the table holding the foreign key being the child.

- If the user attempts to delete a record in the parent table (the Leads table, for example), referential integrity ensures that if other tables are referring to that record, the deletion is prevented or the user is given the option of deleting the associated records.

- If a naturally occurring primary key value, such as a book ISBN number, is corrected or otherwise updated in the parent table, referential integrity ensures that the value is updated wherever it's referenced in the child tables.

- Finally, referential integrity ensures that the user cannot insert a record in a child table that contains a foreign key value that does not exist within the parent table. For example, in a customer order database, an order line could not be inserted that referenced an order ID value that did not exist in the main Order table.

In each of the cases mentioned above, referential integrity ensures that you don't end up with a lot of *orphaned* records within the child table. See Figure 6.7 for an example of this.

Orders			Order Lines		
OrderID	CustomerID		OrderLineID	OrderID	Product
1001	107		101	1001	Pencil Set
1002	120		102	1001	Staples, 1000ct.
1003	254		103	1004	Binder, 6 inch
1004	(Order Deleted)		104	1004	Copy paper, 500ct.
1005	332				

Figure 6.7 - Referential integrity between tables prevents orphaned record that refer to other records that no longer exist.

The foreign key settings for a table are maintained under the Foreign Keys tab of the table editor and are created on the child table in each relationship. For example, the Leads table has four foreign keys assigned to it which reference the Companies, Contacts and Sources tables in order to get extra information on the job lead. Entering a new key is just a matter of following the steps within the Foreign Keys tab.

1. Enter a name for the foreign key. This can be prefixed with FK and include the field name and "idx", i.e. *FK_company_id_idx*.

2. The **Referenced Table** setting provides the table supplying the primary key value.

3. Once a primary key table is chosen, Workbench will provide a list of fields in the current table to use for the link. Select the foreign key field from the current table and then select the corresponding primary key from the other table under the **Referenced Column** setting.

As an example, the *FK_company_id_idx* foreign key that's highlighted in Figure 6.8 references the Companies table to get company information for the lead. Both the Leads and the Companies tables have a *company_id* field which is used to link the two tables together.

The Foreign Key options settings specify how the database is to respond if the primary key value in a table is changed. This would be most likely in the Activity Types and Business Types tables where the primary key is a text value that is referenced and stored in another table as a foreign key. The database needs to know how to respond if, for example, the business type of 'Research' was changed to 'Research and Development' or if the business type of 'Retail' was removed from the table altogether. There are four options for both of these:

-   Restrict - If there are rows in a child table that reference the key value, the update or deletion to the primary key will not be allowed.

- Cascade - Any rows in child tables will be updated or deleted to reflect the change to the primary key value.

- Set Null - The foreign key column in the child rows will be set to NULL, removing the referenced value.

- No Action - This option originates in standard SQL. In MySQL, it's the same is Restrict. Changes that violate referential integrity will not be allowed.

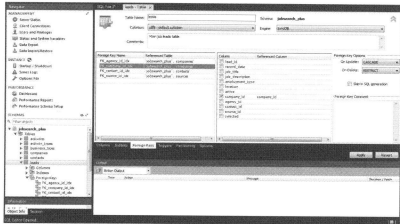

Figure 6.8 - The Foreign Keys tab enables the easy addition for foreign keys to a table in MySQL Workbench.

In all of the relationships in Job Search Plus, I've set the Update option to `CASCADE` and the Delete option to `RESTRICT` meaning that updates to primary key values will be allowed and will cascade to child tables as needed but deletions will not be allowed if there are dependent child rows. This is my preference in order to maintain historical data within a database although other options might be more appropriate for different applications. This is another instance where a little forethought is needed. If you have a reference table in which the rows might change over time, you need to decide if you're going to allow these changes to cascade to other tables that reference that table or if, for example, you want to include an extra field in the reference table that can be used to signal applications that specific rows are no longer to be used, allowing for them to be kept for reference by historical data.

Looking at the SQL, the following statement was generated when the four foreign keys were added to the Leads table. You can see that it adds both an index and a constraint for each foreign key. The ADD CONSTRAINT syntax specifies that the values in the specified fields of the Leads table must match available values within the referenced tables and sets the options for each foreign key. For a diagram of the tables and relationships, refer to Figure 6.9 in the next section.

```
ALTER TABLE `jobsearch_plus`.`leads`
  ADD INDEX `FK_company_id_idx_idx` (`company_id` ASC)  COMMENT '',
  ADD INDEX `FK_agency_id_idx_idx` (`agency_id` ASC)  COMMENT '',
  ADD INDEX `FK_contact_id_idx_idx` (`contact_id` ASC)  COMMENT '',
  ADD INDEX `FK_source_id_idx_idx` (`source_id` ASC)  COMMENT '';
  ALTER TABLE `jobsearch_plus`.`leads`
  ADD CONSTRAINT `FK_company_id_idx`
    FOREIGN KEY (`company_id`)
    REFERENCES `jobsearch_plus`.`companies` (`company_id`)
    ON DELETE RESTRICT
    ON UPDATE CASCADE,
  ADD CONSTRAINT `FK_agency_id_idx`
    FOREIGN KEY (`agency_id`)
    REFERENCES `jobsearch_plus`.`companies` (`company_id`)
    ON DELETE RESTRICT
    ON UPDATE CASCADE,
  ADD CONSTRAINT `FK_contact_id_idx`
    FOREIGN KEY (`contact_id`)
    REFERENCES `jobsearch_plus`.`contacts` (`contact_id`)
    ON DELETE RESTRICT
    ON UPDATE CASCADE,
  ADD CONSTRAINT `FK_source_id_idx`
    FOREIGN KEY (`source_id`)
    REFERENCES `jobsearch_plus`.`sources` (`source_id`)
    ON DELETE RESTRICT
    ON UPDATE CASCADE;
```

If these keys were defined when the Leads table was first created, the CREATE statement would look like the one shown below. If the referenced tables were not present, MySQL would return an error when the Leads CREATE statement referenced the non-existent tables. Database creation scripts can contain the following statement to turn off the verification of foreign keys so that the full CREATE statement can run even if the dependency tables are not present.

```
SET FOREIGN_KEY_CHECKS=0;
```

Setting this variable back to '1' turns the foreign key constraints back on but does not verify anything that was done while the constraints were turned off.

```
CREATE TABLE `leads` (
    `lead_id` int(11) NOT NULL AUTO_INCREMENT,
    `record_date` datetime NOT NULL DEFAULT CURRENT_TIMESTAMP,
    `job_title` varchar(75) NOT NULL,
    `job_description` varchar(1024) DEFAULT NULL,
    `employment_type` enum('Full-time','Part-time',

'Contractor','Temp','Seasonal','Internal','Freelance','Volunteer')
DEFAULT NULL,
    `location` varchar(50) DEFAULT NULL,
    `active` bit(1) DEFAULT b'1',
    `company_id` int(11) DEFAULT NULL,
    `agency_id` int(11) DEFAULT NULL,
    `contact_id` int(11) DEFAULT NULL,
    `source_id` int(11) DEFAULT NULL,
    `selected` bit(1) NOT NULL DEFAULT b'0',
    PRIMARY KEY (`lead_id`),
    KEY `record_date_idx` (`record_date`),
    KEY `job_title_idx` (`job_title`),
    KEY `employment_type_idx` (`employment_type`),
    KEY `FK_company_id_idx_idx` (`company_id`),
    KEY `FK_agency_id_idx_idx` (`agency_id`),
    KEY `FK_contact_id_idx_idx` (`contact_id`),
    KEY `FK_source_id_idx_idx` (`source_id`),
    CONSTRAINT `FK_agency_id_idx`
  FOREIGN KEY (`agency_id`) REFERENCES `companies` (`company_id`)
ON UPDATE CASCADE,
    CONSTRAINT `FK_company_id_idx`
  FOREIGN KEY (`company_id`) REFERENCES `companies` (`company_id`)
ON UPDATE CASCADE,
    CONSTRAINT `FK_contact_id_idx`
  FOREIGN KEY (`contact_id`) REFERENCES `contacts` (`contact_id`)
ON UPDATE CASCADE,
    CONSTRAINT `FK_source_id_idx`
  FOREIGN KEY (`source_id`) REFERENCES `sources` (`source_id`) ON
UPDATE CASCADE
  ) ENGINE=InnoDB DEFAULT CHARSET=utf8 COMMENT='Main job leads table
';
```

The next table to be linked into the database is the Activities table which maintains links to the job leads and activity types tables.

```
ALTER TABLE `jobsearch_plus`.`activities`
ADD INDEX `FK_lead_id_idx_idx` (`lead_id` ASC)  COMMENT '';
ALTER TABLE `jobsearch_plus`.`activities`
ADD CONSTRAINT `FK_lead_id_idx`
  FOREIGN KEY (`lead_id`)
  REFERENCES `jobsearch_plus`.`leads` (`lead_id`)
```

```
  ON DELETE RESTRICT
  ON UPDATE CASCADE,
ADD CONSTRAINT `FK_activity_type_idx`
  FOREIGN KEY (`activity_type`)
  REFERENCES `jobsearch_plus`.`activity_types` (`activity_type`)
  ON DELETE RESTRICT
  ON UPDATE CASCADE;
```

The Activities table already has an index for the *activity_type* field so it only needs to add one more index for the *lead_id* column and then foreign key constraints for both columns.

The Companies table is then linked to the Business Types lookup table for reference.

```
ALTER TABLE `jobsearch_plus`.`companies`
ADD CONSTRAINT `FK_business_type_idx`
  FOREIGN KEY (`business_type`)
  REFERENCES `jobsearch_plus`.`business_types` (`business_type`)
  ON DELETE RESTRICT
  ON UPDATE CASCADE;
```

Finally, the Contacts table is linked to the Companies table in order to get the company information for each contact person. Again, there's already an index on the *contacts.company_id* field so only the constraint is needed.

```
ALTER TABLE `jobsearch_plus`.`contacts`
ADD CONSTRAINT `FK_company_id_idx`
  FOREIGN KEY (`company_id`)
  REFERENCES `jobsearch_plus`.`companies` (`company_id`)
  ON DELETE RESTRICT
  ON UPDATE CASCADE;
```

Here we run into a problem, however. The Leads table already has a foreign key on it with that name so when Workbench goes to run this statement, the following error is returned:

```
ERROR 1022: Can't write; duplicate key in table '#sql-3b4_3'
```

Even though Workbench displays these keys as associated with specific tables, they still exist as database objects so they have to be uniquely named. This is where some planning is required. The simple solution is to change the name of the key.

```
ALTER TABLE `jobsearch_plus`.`contacts`
ADD CONSTRAINT `FK_contact_company_id_idx`
```

```
FOREIGN KEY (`company_id`)
REFERENCES `jobsearch_plus`.`companies` (`company_id`)
ON DELETE RESTRICT
ON UPDATE CASCADE;
```

Documenting the Database

The Model Editor

As mentioned earlier in the chapter, MySQL Workbench provides tools with which you can create a model and diagram of an existing database. This is called *reverse engineering* the database because it analyzes the system and generates the necessary documentation to recreate the database if necessary. In Workbench, this means gathering all the details on the tables, views and other objects and creating a diagram that displays selected objects with the relationships between them.

1. To start the reverse engineering process, select **Database >> Reverse Engineer** from the Workbench menu or use the CTRL-R keyboard shortcut. This will start the program wizard to guide you through the process.

2. You will need to re-connect to the database server using your user name and password.

3. The wizard then prompts you to select one or more databases to be modeled.

4. The relevant objects are then retrieved from the database and you'll be given the option to import all of them or select specific objects. There's also an option on the same screen to diagram the database.

When the wizard finishes, it will place all of the selected objects within the newly-created model as well as on a new EER (Enhanced Entity-Relationship) diagram. Workbench attempts to display the diagram objects and their relationships in a coherent order but it's likely that you'll need to move the objects around a little to get the best result. You can click and drag the objects as needed to prepare the diagram for presentation.

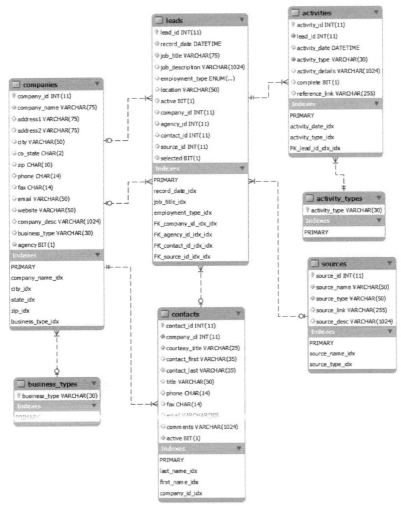

Figure 6.9 - MySQL Workbench provides modeling and diagramming tools which enable you to visualize the database.

The diagram in Figure 6.9 provides quite a lot of information about the structure of the Job Search Plus database. Each entity represented displays the columns along with their data types, sizes and icons indicating if the field is required or is being used as a foreign key.

- The key icon indicate the table's primary key.

- Blue diamonds indicate that the fields are required.

- Pink diamonds indicate foreign keys.

- Red diamonds indicate foreign keys that are also required fields.

The relationship lines themselves also indicate whether the fields involved are required and what type of relationship exists between them. You'll notice that the relationship line between the Companies and Leads tables where a Company ID is *not* required in Leads is different from the relationship between the Leads and Activities tables. The Activities table *is* required to reference a specific Leads record to indicate on which job lead the activity was performed.

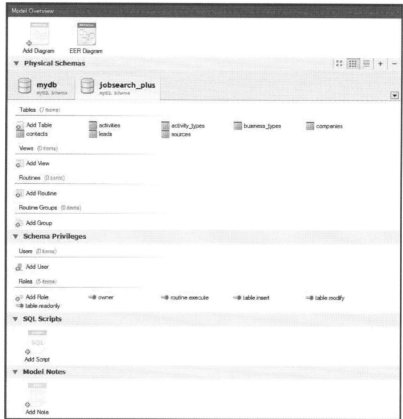

Figure 6.10 – The Model Overview in MySQL Workbench provides a single view of all the objects within the schema.

All of the relationships in this database are one-to-many relationships and, in the cases where the field on the *one* side of the relationship is not required such as between the Contacts and Leads tables, the relationship line indicates this.

If you hover your mouse over one of the relationship lines when viewing the diagram within Workbench, the program will display more details on the specific relationship. Again, this type of notation is specific to Workbench and other documentation systems will have different styles but it's worth noticing how it's done here for future reference

Once you have both a database and a model created, it's possible to make changes in either one and then synchronize those changes in the other. The **Database >> Synchronize** Model option (CTRL-SHIFT-Z) will bring up the synchronization wizard which is very similar to the modeling wizard described earlier. Figure 6.10 - The Model Overview in MySQL Workbench provides a single view of all the objects within the schema.

This wizard favors updating the database from the model but it's very easy to change the direction of the update by using the command buttons on the selection screen shown. The wizard's review screen will show the SQL to be used for the update and you can edit the SQL there or simply click on **Execute** to run the changes.

The database model in MySQL Workbench as shown in Figure 6.10 can include additional notes as well as SQL scripts used in the maintenance or update of the database. Again, there are sometimes problems with saving and reloading model files so it's probably best not to completely rely on the model to store your notes and other information but it can be a convenient place to store items temporarily during the design process.

Scripting and Export

I've previously mentioned the use of SQL scripts in MySQL Workbench and other client programs. These are simply collections of SQL statements that are stored in the same file and are intended to be run in sequence, often to create or alter one or more objects within the database. Scripts are often used in order to deploy changes to the database structure that accompany a software change and they also represent another way to document your new database. Since a SQL script is stored as plain text on the disk and can be opened in any text or query editor, there isn't much danger that the file will become inaccessible.

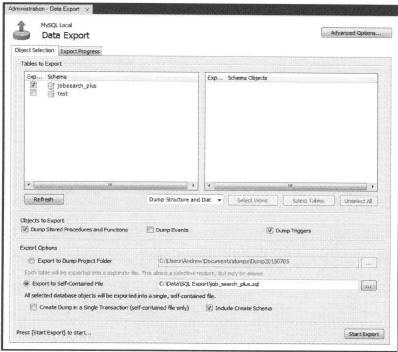

Figure 6.11 - With the Data Export function, you can export the entire database structure and data to a file as a backup or to import the database elsewhere.

Figure 6.11 shows the export options screen which you can access by clicking on the **Data Export** option under the Management section of the Navigator pane or through the **Server >> Data Export** menu commands. The screen enables you to specify exactly how and where you want the script created and what should be included. In the example, I've instructed the program to include stored procedures, functions and triggers even though the database doesn't contain any at this point.

I've also specified that the script should be saved to one self-contained file on disk since I don't want to work with a collection of files. I've chosen to include a `CREATE SCHEMA` statement that will create the database itself if it doesn't exist yet. With these options, I'll have one file that I could copy to another computer to create the entire database from scratch. The screen also provides the option to export the structure, the data or both and I've chosen both even though there is no data in the database yet.

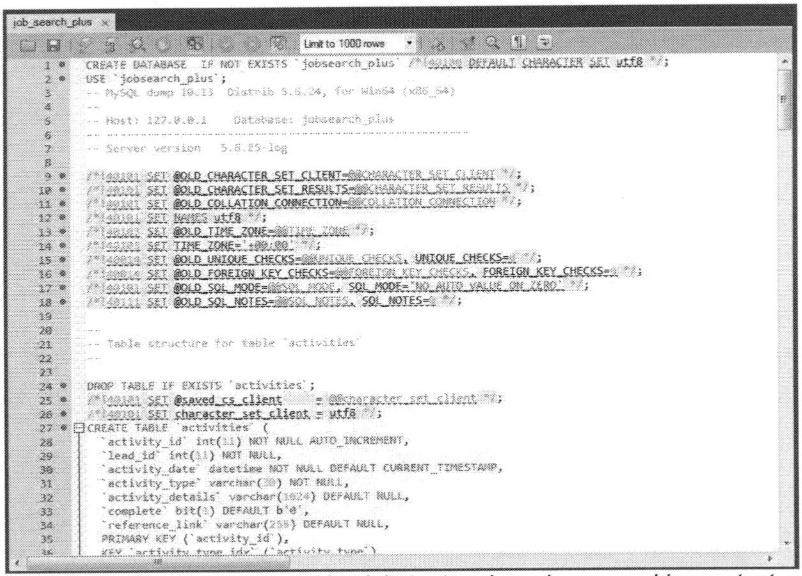

Figure 6.12 - SQL scripts are stored in plain text and can be opened in any text or query editor.

In Figure 6.12, you can see the beginning of the exported script. If you scroll through a script that you create, you'll notice more statements like the first one that include qualifiers like `IF NOT EXISTS`. These statements are added so that the script can be run and re-run as necessary without worrying about a lot of errors that would keep a script, especially a long one, from finishing.

Backing up the Files

If you want to backup the actual database files from your disk, you will need to determine the data directory for your installation of MySQL. You can do this by running the following query:

```
SHOW VARIABLES WHERE Variable_Name like "%dir%";
```

The results will include an entry for the variable name 'datadir' which indicates where the actual data files are stored. This directory will have subdirectories for each database and you can backup the files as needed. Depending on your installation, restoring the files might be as simple as copying the files back into the same directory and restarting the server although you might also need to set permissions on the files depending on your operating system.

Chapter Summary

In this chapter, you learned about referential integrity and the various types of relationships that can be created between database tables in order to ensure consistency between tables. You also learned about the documentation features of MySQL Workbench that enable you to create diagrams and other documentation of your completed database.

After working with the abstract concepts involved in modeling your data, creating the actual tables comes down to laying out the tables and columns in a specific software. While mapping out columns and indexes requires a certain amount of planning and foresight to anticipate the needs of the data that will be entered, seeing the final database design come together makes the effort spent in organizing the data worth it.

In addition to mastering the menus and commands of a specific client software such as MySQL Workbench, it's important to at least be able to understand basic SQL commands and queries. MySQL clients use these commands to create the tables and other objects within a database and that's where the real work is done independently of any interface. The Data Definition Language commands within SQL cover the creation and editing of all objects and are used behind the scenes by client programs.

For Further Study

Review Questions

1. What is the purpose of a data type? Which data types would use use to store the following?

   o A driver's license number

   o A renewal date for a club membership

   o A product price

   o A ZIP code

  o A True / False value indicating if an employee is still with the company

2. What is the difference between a CHAR and VARCHAR field?

3. What is the difference between the MyISAM and InnoDB storage engines?

4. What does a null value indicate in a table?

5. What is the difference between the Memory and Blackhole storage engines?

6. How are `CURRENT_DATE()` and `CURRENT_TIMESTAMP()` used in MySQL and what is the difference between them?

7. Determine whether null values should be allowed for each of the following and, if not, whether there is a default value that can be supplied for each new record.

  o A book's date of purchase in a library database

  o A recipe title in a cooking database

  o An indicator of whether an employee is a military veteran

  o A student's initial enrollment date

  o A product brand name in an inventory database

8. What is the purpose of referential integrity and how does it use a foreign key within a table?

9. What are the advantages of using a lookup table to provide possible values versus an ENUM field and vice-versa?

10. What is the difference between forward and reverse engineering in MySQL Workbench?

11. What is the purpose of the USE command in SQL?

12. In a pair of related tables, is the primary key held by the parent table or the child table?

13. What are two possible responses from the database if a user attempts to delete a record in a parent table for which there are associated records in the child table?

14. What is the purpose of a lookup table in a database and how does it use referential integrity?

15. What is the difference between the INT and TINYINT data types?

16. What is the purpose of adding an index to a table?

17. What is the difference between a clustered and non-clustered index? Which type is represented by the table's primary key?

18. What are the three ways in which you can declare a comment in SQL?

19. Which of the following fields should and should not be indexed within a table?

- o A person's last name

- o A person's gender

- o A product description field

- o A book's copyright year

- o A customer street address

20. Name three examples of a field or combination of fields in any kind of database that would not be used as a primary key but could be the subject of a unique index.

Exercises

1. If you have access to an AMP environment on a Linux system or through a WAMP such as EasyPHP, try creating the Job Search Plus database through another program such as phpMyAdmin. Remember that all client programs ultimately use SQL commands, which are supplied in this chapter, to create the objects. You should also take some time to explore the menus and features available in other client programs and try using both the SQL and the menus to create the necessary objects.

2. In this chapter, we created the database first and then used reverse engineering to create a model and diagram. Now try forward engineering - in MySQL Workbench, use

the **File >> New Model** menu option or CTRL-N shortcut to create a new data model and use the menu options within the new model to create all the necessary options. The table editor within the model editor is very similar to the full table editor that we used in this chapter. After you lay out the tables and relationships, use the **Database >> Forward Engineer** (CTRL-G) to create the actual tables and relationships on the server.

3. After you've created your own copy of the Job Search Plus database, use the Data Export feature to create a SQL script that will export the structure and all data and take some time to examine the statements within the script to get more familiar with the SQL language. As an extra step, try changing the few instances of the database name in the script to something like 'jobsearch_test' and running it in order to create a duplicate of your database.

Terms to Remember

Auto Increment - The ability of the database to insert an automatically incrementing value for a field in each new row of a table. This can be used for primary key values and other fields that require unique values.

Binary Column - A field that can hold binary data with special characters to accommodate the storage of images and other files.

Clustered index - An index that determines the order in which rows are physically stored within the database.

Data Types - Specifications for different kinds of data to be stored within a database. These types can include dates, alphanumeric data, numbers, etc.. The data type assigned to a field determines the values that can be stored and operations that can be performed on the data.

EER Diagram - Enhanced Entity Relationship diagram. A diagram that shows all of the tables and other data entities within a database along with the relationships between them.

Indexes - A reference maintained on one or more table columns by the database in order to assist in finding and sorting information within the table.

Localhost - The hostname used to refer to the local computer or server.

Non-clustered index - An index that does not affect the physical order of the rows but maintains a list of pointers to values within the column.

Null - A field within a table row that does not contain any value. This indicates that the value does not exist or has not been provided.

Orphaned records - In tables that have a parent-child relationship, child table rows that reference a non-existent primary key value in the parent table are said to be orphaned records. This might result from the deletion of the referenced row in the parent table or an error when creating the child table row.

Parent-child tables - A set of tables in which the parent table contains a primary key that is referenced by foreign keys in the child tables.

Query - A request for information from the database.

Referential integrity - The process of ensuring that a foreign key value in a child table does not reference a non-existent primary key value in the parent table.

Table - The basic data object within a database which stores data in rows and columns.

Unique index - An index for which each value in the column or combination of columns must be unique within the table.

Unsigned Data Type - With numeric data types such as integers, the range of allowed values covers both negative and positive values. Specifying that the numbers in a table column are unsigned limits the values to positive numbers and increases the upper limit of the field. For example, a TINYINT normally allows values from -128 to 127. When specified as unsigned, the range is 0 to 255.

Chapter VII

Reading and Writing the Data

Structured Query Language

As you've seen by this point, every operation performed on the database can be represented as a query or a command that is directed to the server. Whether you are retrieving a list of databases or tables, or changing data in the tables themselves, the server accepts specific commands in order to perform these actions. That's where Structured Query Language (SQL) comes in. Many of the commands you've seen so far have been included in subsets of this language that focus on defining objects on the server and controlling access to them. The most well designed and secured set of tables wouldn't be of much use, however, without the ability to transfer data and that's where SQL comes into play.

The basics of SQL's *Data Manipulation Language (DML)* are fairly easy to learn. The language is based around English verbs such as Select, Insert and Delete and a basic sentence structure. The commands specify the fields and tables to be referenced, the relationships between them, filters and sorts to apply and values to write. These operations are stated in a very logical way and many are based on operations that you'll remember from math class. SQL and Transact-SQL (T-SQL), which is used for more complex database operations, are actually specialized computer programming languages known as *fourth-generation languages (4GL)*. If you become proficient in them, you'll be able to say that you have experience with computer programming.

There are some minor differences in SQL syntax depending on the database software you're using and MySQL has its own implementation of the language. I will continue to use the Job Search Plus application as an example database. You'll see how to insert some data into the tables created in the previous chapters and retrieve that data in a way that can be used in reports. The *MySQL Reference Manual* also includes a complete reference to Structured Query Language as it's implemented in MySQL. This chapter will provide you with a solid introduction to those commands that you will work with most often.

Beginning Examples

Before introducing you to the elements of SQL, I want to show you some working examples of SQL. Figure 7.1 shows the completed tables and relationships for Job Search Plus as diagrammed in phpMyAdmin.

A diagram like this is very useful when working with a new database although, in my experience, it's not always available. Sometimes, when reviewing an existing database for the first time, it's up to the individual developer to evaluate the existing relationships by looking at many tables and noting the fields that they have in common which can indicate primary-foreign key relationships.

If you have been creating your own copy of the Job Search Plus database as shown in previous chapters and have an AMP environment running like EasyPHP that includes phpMyAdmin, you can create a diagram like this one by selecting the database within phpMyAdmin and then selecting the **Designer** tab. This diagram provides much of the information available through the MySQL Workbench reverse engineering tools shown in the last chapter and it's a good idea to get experience with various tools and to get accustomed to generating documentation. As I've indicated, it's a valuable and much-needed skill in any organization where database and software design is being performed.

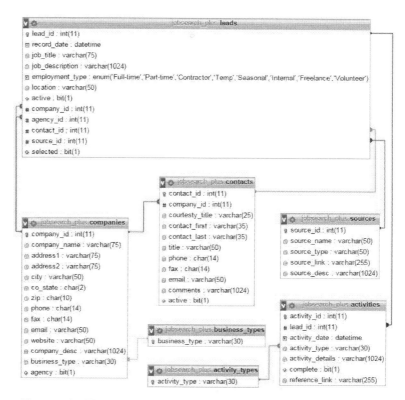

Figure 7.1 - The completed Job Search Plus schema in phpMyAdmin

Adding Data to the System

An important part of designing any database application is running some sample data through it, making the necessary design changes and then testing those changes as well. This testing ensures the system meets the needs of both the data and the users. In a relational database, testing often requires adding reference data and other supporting information. Before you can add a new job lead in Job Search Plus, or at least a complete record of one, you need to add records of companies and sources. Programs are often designed to issue the appropriate commands to the database as the user adds supporting information through whatever interface the program provides. This was the case with the Job Search Plus program that I originally designed. In MySQL client programs, you can do it either by opening a new query window and typing in the commands manually or by using whatever menu commands are available through the programs.

```
USE jobsearch_plus;

INSERT INTO companies
(company_name, city, co_state)
VALUES ('Jameson Corporation', 'Boston', 'MA');

INSERT INTO jobsearch_plus.companies
(company_name, city, co_state, zip)
VALUES ('Alexis Systems', 'Manchester', 'NH', '03103');

INSERT INTO `jobsearch_plus`.`companies`
(company_name, city, co_state, agency)
VALUES ('Northeast Technologies', 'Rochester', 'NY', 1);
```

Above are three examples of simple INSERT commands which add records to the Companies table. The three commands use slightly different methods to refer to the table, which I'll explain shortly, and different values for the three records. Let's analyze some of the features of the queries shown here.

- The USE statement at the top of the window directs MySQL to work with a specific database and to direct all commands to it. This needs to be specified since a server can contain many databases. When the database is being accessed from an external software, the database will typically be specified as part of a connection string in the program code.

- In the examples, I've formatted the INSERT statements for readability with plenty of line breaks. SQL completely disregards line breaks and whitespace and doesn't care what format you use when typing in queries and commands. These commands could be put on one line with no line breaks and would still run. Still, it's best to use some kind of formatting because batches of commands can get long and hard to read otherwise.

- In the Companies table, the *company_name* field is the only required field that doesn't have a default value so I could have just specified values for that field. The State field is actually named *co_state* because 'state' is a reserved word in some database systems and, even though that's not the case in MySQL, it's a good idea to avoid ambiguous names. If you must use reserved words or spaces in table or field names, you will need to place backticks around the names to help MySQL parse the names correctly. For example, the INSERT query would look something like this:

```
INSERT INTO Companies (`Company Name`, City,
`State`)
VALUES ('Galactix International', 'New York', 'NY');
```

- You can see the loose sentence structure of SQL in these two queries where the INSERT syntax is basically *INSERT INTO (<field names>) VALUES (<specify values>)*. Fields and values are separated by commas. This simplified syntax makes SQL relatively easy to learn.

- Alphanumeric and date values such as the company name must be enclosed in single quotes when being specified in a query. These indicators enable the SQL parser to identify them as literal values. This is not required for numeric values such as the *agency* field value.

- The second query demonstrates how a database can be specified without the USE command or how to reference a different database than earlier specified. The database name must be added before the table name with the two separated by periods.

Executing Commands

The query window in MySQL Workbench and the SQL tab in phpMyAdmin can be used to write single queries or create scripts that will create and populate entire databases and make a variety of other complex changes. After you've written and proofed the commands, you can run the entire contents of the query window or select portions depending on what you're trying to do. The old saying "Measure twice, cut once." is especially relevant when it comes to running commands on a database. The wrong command can do a lot of damage to your data very quickly, especially with the UPDATE and DELETE commands you'll see later. It's better to take an extra few seconds and verify that the query is correct rather than make the wrong changes that can only be fixed by restoring a backup.

Workbench will alert you immediately if there's a syntax error in your statement by marking it with an error icon next to the line and underlining the offending portion of the statement in red. It will also do this if you omit a semi-colon at the end of a command and the program sees the next command as a continuation resulting in a syntax error. phpMyAdmin's SQL editor is not as sophisticated and acts more like the MySQL command line client, throwing back error messages from MySQL in response to failed statements and giving you a chance to re-run the statements. MySQL Workbench also has an intellisense feature that will automatically complete names of tables, fields and functions as you type based on what it finds on the server. This can be very helpful in avoiding simple syntax errors from misspelled names.

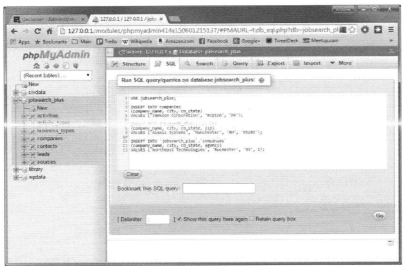

Figure 7.2 - The SQL editor tab in phpMyAdmin enables you to run multiple queries and commands against the server.

Trying This At Home

If you're working with your own copy of the Job Search Plus database, here are some commands to run in any of the client programs to start populating the Companies table.

1. First, try running the previous `INSERT` commands shown in Figure 7.2 on the database to create the two companies, plus a few more so you have a selection of companies to work with.

```
USE jobsearch_plus;

INSERT INTO companies
(company_name, city, co_state)
VALUES ('Jameson Corporation', 'Boston', 'MA');

INSERT INTO jobsearch_plus.companies
(company_name, city, co_state, zip)
VALUES ('Alexis Systems', 'Manchester', 'NH', '03103');

INSERT INTO `jobsearch_plus`.`companies`
(company_name, city, co_state, agency)
VALUES ('Northeast Technologies', 'Rochester', 'NY',
1);

INSERT INTO jobsearch_plus.companies
(company_name, city, co_state)
VALUES ('Nautica Supply', 'Chicago', 'IL');

INSERT INTO jobsearch_plus.companies
(company_name, city, co_state)
VALUES ('Denton Publishing', 'Boise', 'ID');

INSERT INTO jobsearch_plus.companies
(company_name, city, co_state)
VALUES ('Galactix International', 'New York', 'NY');
```

2. Now run the following query to see the records as they exist in the table.

```
SELECT * FROM companies;
```

If you've run the commands that I've shown you so far, the results of the following `SELECT` query when run in phpMyAdmin should look like Figure 7.3. The `SELECT` query uses the asterisk wildcard to instruct MySQL to return *all* fields in the table. The query could also be written as follows:

```
SELECT company_id, company_name, city, co_state
FROM companies;
```

This would return just the name, city and state fields. Notice the *companies.company_id* field and the values that have been automatically assigned to the records. This is result of the field being set as an Identity field with an auto-increment value. The rest of the fields outside this query, except for the *agency* field which has a default value of '0', are null.

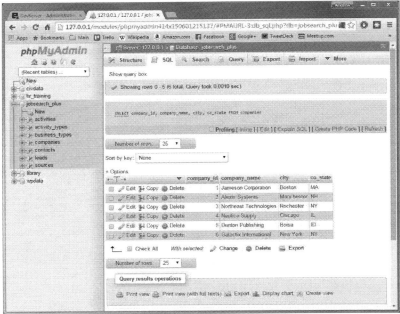

Figure 7.3 - phpMyAdmin also enables you to perform multiple operations based on query results including editing and deletion of rows.

If you refer back to the database diagram in Figure 7.1, you'll see that the *companies.business_type* field is dependent on the *business_types* lookup table which supplies the possible values for the field and uses referential integrity to ensure that these values are consistently entered. Software that's accessing the database can retrieve the possible values from this table and present them as choices to the user. If you're manually entering values through MySQL, you'll need to know which values are present in the *business_types* table.

To see how this works, run the following query:

```
UPDATE companies
SET business_type = 'Information Technology'
WHERE company_name = 'Alexis Systems';
```

This UPDATE query looks for a record where the *company_name* field matches the specified value and then attempts to update the *business_type* field to 'Information Technology'. The WHERE clause is a very important part of many command statements as it protects your data by limiting a command's actions to the correct records. In this query, I could have used the *company_id* field instead and specified the right value like so:

```
WHERE company_id = 2
```

This would be safer and more precise, especially if the table contains more than one entry for 'Alexis Systems'. When retrieving a company record, an external program would store the *company_id* value for reference and use it in queries like this one. This comes a bit more naturally to a computer program whereas a human is used to using names for reference.

In any case, since the *business_types* table does not have an entry for "Information Technology", MySQL will throw back the following error:

```
#1452 - Cannot add or update a child row: a foreign key constraint
fails (`jobsearch_plus`.`companies`, CONSTRAINT
`FK_business_type_idx` FOREIGN KEY (`business_type`) REFERENCES
`business_types` (`business_type`) ON UPDATE CASCADE)
```

This is the result of trying to insert a record that violates referential integrity; the command is aborted. Now run the following command on the database:

```
INSERT INTO business_types (business_type)
VALUES ('Information Technology');
```

This inserts a record into the *business_types* table with the value of 'Information Technology'. Now try running the previous UPDATE command again and it should be successful since the *business_types* table contains a matching record.

For an additional exercise, modify the above INSERT statement to add the following records to the *business_types* table:

- Accounting
- Business Services

- Consulting
- Engineering
- Financial
- Manufacturing

Once you have run the commands to insert each of these values into *business_types*, go back and modify the following UPDATE statement to update the rest of the records in the Companies table to reflect the business type of your choice. For example:

```
UPDATE companies
SET business_type = 'Manufacturing'
WHERE company_name = 'Nautica Supply';
```

For practice, use the *company_id* value in the WHERE clause rather than the *company_name* field, either by specifying the company name or looking up the ID value with a SELECT statement.

In the next section, we'll be looking at SQL syntax in more detail along with some sample queries from the Job Search Plus database. If you're working through these examples, it will be helpful for you to have a little more sample data in the database. Here are some queries that you can use to populate the database and to practice typing in SQL. Start by populating the *activity_types* table with the categories of job lead activities that will be allowed in the database.

```
INSERT INTO activity_types (activity_type) values ('Inquiry');
INSERT INTO activity_types (activity_type) values ('Application');
INSERT INTO activity_types (activity_type) values ('Contact');
INSERT INTO activity_types (activity_type) values ('Interview');
INSERT INTO activity_types (activity_type) values ('Follow-up');
INSERT INTO activity_types (activity_type) values
('Correspondence');
INSERT INTO activity_types (activity_type) values ('Documentation');
INSERT INTO activity_types (activity_type) values ('Closure');
INSERT INTO activity_types (activity_type) values ('Other');
```

The next batch of queries will add five job leads to the Leads table. These commands add values to the *company_id* field which references the Companies table so it's important to first add the company records shown earlier and verify the company ID values.

```
INSERT INTO leads
(job_title, employment_type, company_id, location)
VALUES
('Database Administrator', 'Full-Time', 4, 'Atlanta, GA');

INSERT INTO leads
(job_title, employment_type, company_id, location)
VALUES
('Database Programmer', 'Full-Time', 4, 'Atlanta, GA');

INSERT INTO leads
(job_title, employment_type, company_id, location)
VALUES
('Software Developer', 'Full-Time', 2, 'Atlanta, GA');

INSERT INTO leads
(job_title, employment_type, company_id, location)
VALUES
('Database Administrator', 'Full-Time', 5, 'Montgomery, AL');

INSERT INTO leads
(job_title, employment_type, company_id, location)
VALUES
('Data Warehouse Manager', 'Full-Time', 5, 'Montgomery, AL');
```

Finally, we'll add a few activity records on these job leads. These commands use the *lead_id* values automatically generated from the records added to the Leads table.

```
INSERT INTO activities
(lead_id, activity_date, activity_type)
VALUES
(1, '2015-08-03', 'Application');

INSERT INTO activities
(lead_id, activity_date, activity_type)
VALUES
(1, '2015-08-05', 'Contact');

INSERT INTO activities
(lead_id, activity_date, activity_type)
VALUES
(2, '2015-08-03', 'Application');

INSERT INTO activities
(lead_id, activity_date, activity_type)
VALUES
(2, '2015-08-05', 'Interview');
```

SQL Basics

Now that you've seen a few examples of SQL in action, I want to give you an introduction to the basic commands that you will be working with as you manipulate the data within your tables. As I mentioned at the beginning of this chapter, SQL is actually a very capable language that can be used to completely manage a relational database from the creation of the database itself to inserting data to assigning permissions to specific users.

SQL commands are divided into three categories:

- *Data Definition Language (DDL)* - This includes the commands CREATE, ALTER and DROP which create, change and delete various objects respectively. This can include entire databases as well as individual tables, views and stored procedures.

- *Data Manipulation Language (DML)* - These commands are used to read and write data within the tables and are the focus of this section. The SELECT, INSERT, UPDATE and DELETE commands enable you to work with large sets of records or make very precise changes to a single record.

- *Data Control Language (DCL)* - SQL can also write data as part of transactions which can be selectively committed to the database and rolled back if there's an error. DCL includes the COMMIT and ROLLBACK commands as well as the GRANT and REVOKE commands for assigning and removing permissions on database objects.

Although the commands you'll learn about in this chapter belong to the DML category, it's a good idea to remember the other two categories so that you will understand the full scope of the language.

Selecting Data

The SELECT command is the most basic command in SQL. With the available clauses and keywords, it's also a very flexible command for finding anything in your tables based on the content of any field. Many of these keywords are common to other SQL commands but first we'll look at how they're used in selecting data.

```
SELECT l.lead_id, l.job_title, l.employment_type,
  c.company_name, a.activity_type
FROM leads l
LEFT JOIN companies c
ON c.company_id = l.company_id
LEFT JOIN activities a
ON a.lead_id = l.lead_id
WHERE l.location = 'Atlanta, GA' AND l.active <> 0
ORDER BY l.job_title ASC;
```

You've already seen `SELECT` queries in previous examples but the above is an example that uses some of the most common keywords. Let's look at them one at a time.

SELECT ... FROM

First, the query specifies the tables and fields to be accessed and the order in which the fields are to be displayed in the result set. Notice that the Location field is not listed, even though you'll see it further down in the query. It is not necessary to include every field referenced by the query in the result set. Also notice the letters after the *leads* and *companies* table names (i.e. `leads l` and `companies c`). These are called table aliases. Table names can add a lot of text to a query when they're used over and over again and sometimes a recognizable alias makes the query easier to read. Once an alias is defined, you must use it in the rest of the query when specifying the table as you can see in the example.

JOIN ... ON

SQL uses `JOIN` clauses to access relationships between tables, either those formally defined as you saw in the last chapter or unofficial ones that find any corresponding values between the two tables. In the example shown, it means that the query starts with the Leads table and then performs joins to two other tables, *companies* and *activities*. The `ON` keyword specifies the fields on which the tables are to be joined.

The use of the words `LEFT` and `RIGHT` refer to the order in which the tables are going to be accessed and their precedence in the selection of records. The use of the words 'left' and 'right' is symbolic of the relationship between the two tables and has nothing to do with how the tables are placed on a diagram. In the first join in the example query, the values for the *company_id* field are supplied by the primary key of the Companies table. The Leads table uses those values as a foreign key to link a job lead record to a specific company. In the first join, the *leads* table is listed first and is on the left side of the join. Then *companies* is listed second and is therefore on the right. It might be more clear if you think of reading the following sentences from left to right:

'The *leads.company_id* field is joined to the *companies.company_id* field.'

'The *activities.lead_id* field is joined to the *leads.lead_id* field.'

Therefore, a Left Join would start by selecting the records from the first table on the *left* of the relationship, *leads*, and then select any matching records from the second table on the *right* of the relationship. It's called a Left Join because the record selection priority is on the left side of the relationship. A Right Join would start by selecting records from the second table listed, in this case *companies*, and then selecting the matching job leads based on the *company_id* field. Optionally, you can include the word word OUTER in both relationships, i.e. LEFT OUTER JOIN. A third type of join is an Inner Join which only returns records where a value exists in the joined fields from both tables.

To see a good example of the results, we can look at the Job Search Plus database as it's been populated with data so far in this chapter. Right now, there are six companies in the companies table but only one business category defined in the *business_types* table and only one company with a business type set. The following query uses a Left Join between the Companies and Business Types table which will first pull a list of records in the Companies table and then include any corresponding values in the Business Types table.

```
SELECT c.company_name, c.business_type
FROM companies c
LEFT JOIN business_types bt
ON bt.business_type = c.business_type;
```

company_name	business_type
Jameson Corporation	NULL
Alexis Systems	Information Technology
Northeast Technologies	NULL
Nautica Supply	NULL
Denton Publishing	NULL
Galactix International	NULL

The query selects all records from the Companies table and then does a Left Join to the Business Types table it references to get the business type for each company. There is only one defined so it only finds the one for Alexis Systems. The *business_type* column in the rest of the records returned is null. Compare this with the set returned from the same query with an Inner Join.

```
SELECT c.company_name, c.business_type
FROM companies c
INNER JOIN business_types bt
ON bt.business_type = c.business_type;
```

company_name	business_type
Alexis Systems	Information Technology

The Inner Join only returns the record where both fields in the join are populated, omitting the null values. In this particular case, an Inner Join and a Right Join would produce the same results as the Right Join would start with the business_types table, selecting the one value for 'Information Technology', and would then to go to the companies table and find the one record for Alexis Systems with the business type defined.

Finally, notice that in the ON clause, the table aliases are specified before the field names. Very often, you can get away with not specifying the table name or alias when referring to specific fields in a query but it's best practice to do so and if the field name exists in more than one table, the table name or alias is a necessity.

SELECT queries do not have to join tables on the same fields used in the defined relationships between the tables. For example, if two tables contained fields for a product serial number, a SELECT query could join on these fields even if no formal relationship was defined between the tables within the database. The query would simply return whatever data it found that fit the parameters specified. MySQL will even happily run a query that includes joins between completely incompatible fields such as a VARCHAR and a BIT field, although you won't get very meaningful results. It's important to remember that, just like with the spell checker in your favorite word processing program, MySQL will verify that it can *understand* your query, not that the query is necessarily correct.

WHERE

This clause specifies the criteria that each row must meet in order to be included in the results. In this example, we're looking for active records where the Location field equals a particular string. This clause can specify multiple conditions using the AND/OR keywords and parentheses to group conditions for the right result. Some of the possible WHERE clauses in this sample could be:

```
WHERE job_title = 'Driver'

WHERE active <> 0 AND employment_type = 'Full-Time'

WHERE (active <> 0 AND employment_type = 'Full-Time') OR
employment_type = 'Freelance'
```

In the last example, the query uses the parentheses to show only full-time job leads that are still active *OR any* job leads that are designated as freelance opportunities. A full-time lead that had become inactive would *not* be selected and *all* freelance opportunities would be shown regardless of their active status. This is because the Active field is grouped with the 'Full-Time' specification on the employment_type field by the parentheses.

ORDER BY

The final keyword lists any fields used to sort the query results. In the example query, the records are sorted by the job title. Again, you can sort by multiple fields and the results will be sorted according to the priority in which the fields are listed in the SQL statement. The DESC and ASC keywords instructs the query to sort the record in descending or ascending order by job title.

```
ORDER BY l.job_title DESC
```

```
ORDER BY l.job_title ASC
```

Ascending order is the default so it's really only necessary to specify the order if it should be in descending order. The sort order is specified for each field in the ORDER BY statement.

```
ORDER BY c.company_name, l.job_title DESC
```

The above statement would sort the records first by the company name in *ascending* order and then, for each company, by job title in *descending* order so Alexis Systems would come before Nautica Supply but the Database *Programmer* job for Nautica would come before the Database *Administrator* job.

When run in phpMyAdmin, the *original* query returns the results shown in Figure 7.4.

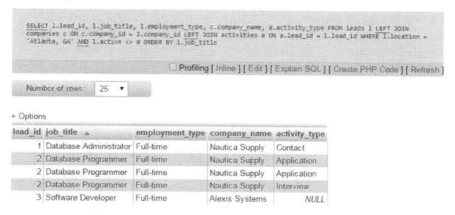

Figure 7.4 - Example query results in phpMyAdmin

As you can see, the query returns five rows because there are *three* active job leads in the database with a *leads.location* value of 'Atlanta, GA' with *five* records in the Activities table referencing those leads. The third job lead doesn't have any corresponding Activities records so the query just returns the record for the job lead itself with a null value for the Activities table field. The Right Join on the Companies table enables the query to reference the appropriate record in the

Companies table for each job lead and retrieve the company name. The Left Join to the Activities table retrieves the activity records for each lead and displays the date and activity type, repeating the information from the Leads table as necessary. Finally, the records are sorted by job title.

If I wanted to omit the record that didn't have any activity information, I could use an Inner Join instead. The following query would only pull records from the Leads table where at least one activity was recorded, omitting the record with the null activity, whereas the Left Join in the above example pulled Leads records regardless of whether there were activities or not.

```
SELECT L.job_title, L.employment_type, C.company_name,
A.activity_type
FROM leads L
RIGHT JOIN companies C
ON C.company_id = L.company_id
INNER JOIN activities A
ON A.lead_id = L.lead_id;
```

In a Left Join, the priority is on the first table listed, in this case the Leads table, so all of its records are pulled. The query then gets whatever records it can from the Activities table and returns null values if none are available. An Inner Join, on the other hand, specifies that only records where the *lead_id* values in *both* tables are equal will be pulled so if there are no Activities records for a specific job lead, the lead cannot be included in the results. Which join is used often depends on what questions are meant to be answered by the results.

Let's take a look at another query to demonstrate two more SQL clauses that you'll sometimes work with. Instead of returning actual leads, this query uses the HAVING clause to perform an analysis on the Leads table and returns a list of locations with a count of active job lead records for each location.

```
SELECT COUNT(L.lead_id) AS `Lead Count`, L.location
FROM leads L
WHERE L.active <> 0
GROUP BY L.location
HAVING COUNT(L.lead_id) > 1;
```

Aside from the GROUP BY and HAVING clauses, this query also uses the COUNT() function which is one of a collection of aggregate functions which can be used to analyze data within the tables. With these functions, you can find averages, totals and minimum / maximum values and much more. In the example, the COUNT() function is used to get a count of job leads and actually returns a column within the results. This column is aliased as 'Lead Count' by the AS statement on the first line.

The GROUP BY clause is used to create groupings within the data based on specific fields and this query is grouping by the Location field in the Leads table. By default, when the GROUP BY clause is not specified, SELECT queries automatically group on *all* fields listed in the SELECT statement. If the GROUP BY clause is specified, then every column included in the SELECT list must either be included in the GROUP BY clause or must be part of an aggregate function so that its value is calculated based on the other field groupings. Otherwise, the query will return an error. This is true in the above query where the Location field is in the GROUP BY clause and the Lead Count is generated by a COUNT() function. The result is to return a count of the job leads for each location value as shown in Figure 7.5.

If I were to add the *leads.employment_type* field to the SELECT statement, I would need to add it to the GROUP BY clause as shown below or the query would fail. This would also affect the results of the query, however, since it would now be grouping on both fields. It would do this by grouping on one field after another, depending on which one was listed first. For example, if Location was listed first, the query would first count the records by Location and then, within each Location group, it would further group by *employment_type*. The final results could contain two rows for the location 'Montgomery, AL'; one with a count of all full-time jobs in that location and another row with a count of the part-time jobs.

```
SELECT COUNT(L.lead_id) AS `Lead Count`, L.location,
L.employment_type
FROM leads L
WHERE L.active <> 0
GROUP BY L.location, L.employment_type
HAVING COUNT(L.lead_id) > 1;
```

On the final line, `HAVING` is used to limit the records returned based on properties of groups defined by the `GROUP BY` clause and cannot be used unless `GROUP BY` is present. The difference between `WHERE` and `HAVING` is that `WHERE` looks at values in individual records *before* the query performs any grouping.

The `WHERE` clause in the example looks at the Active field in each record and only allows records with the correct value to be included. `HAVING` is applied *after* the grouping is done on the Location field and, in this case, it further limits the query to locations that have more than one job lead.

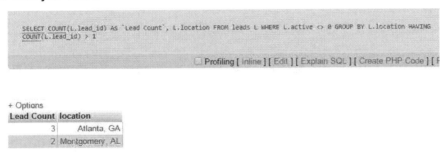

Figure 7.5 - Results of location analysis query in phpMyAdmin

Subqueries

As I mentioned in the last section, when grouping is used to get record counts, averages and other analyses of the data, it can limit the fields returned in a simple query because all included columns must be part of the `GROUP BY` statement or the aggregate functions. Sometimes, however, you might want to include fields for extra information without grouping on them. For example, let's say I want to group by the location as shown in Figure 7.5 but I want all the fields shown in Figure 7.4 - *job_title*, *employment_type*, *company_name* and *description* as well as the location itself. I don't want to group on all of these fields as that would break the Lead Count down in too many ways.

One solution is a subquery using the `IN` keyword as part of the `WHERE` clause.

```
SELECT job_title, employment_type, C.company_name,
  L.job_description, location
FROM leads L
RIGHT JOIN companies C
ON C.company_id = L.company_id
WHERE location
IN
  (SELECT l.location
   FROM leads L
   WHERE L.active <> 0
   GROUP BY L.location
   HAVING COUNT(L.lead_id) > 1);
```

In this example, the `WHERE` statement includes a subquery which generates a list of the locations which have more than one active job lead. The `WHERE` statement of the main query then specifies that only job leads where the Location field matches a value in this list will be returned. Note that the subquery only returns one field, otherwise the query would fail because it wouldn't be clear which value the location was supposed to match. The IN statement could just as easily reference a specific list of values as shown in the examples below.

```
WHERE Location IN ('Atlanta, GA', 'Montgomery, AL')
```

```
WHERE CompanyID IN (1, 3, 5)
```

The `IN` statement is a very handy keyword for specifying a list of values rather than using the `AND` keyword over and over for each value. The output from the above query is shown in Figure 7.6.

+ Options

job_title	employment_type	company_name	job_description	location
Database Administrator	Full-time	Nautica Supply	NULL	Atlanta, GA
Database Programmer	Full-time	Nautica Supply	NULL	Atlanta, GA
Software Developer	Full-time	Alexis Systems	NULL	Atlanta, GA
Database Administrator	Full-time	Denton Publishing	NULL	Montgomery, AL
Data Warehouse Manager	Full-time	Denton Publishing	NULL	Montgomery, AL

Figure 7.6 - Query results using IN statement with subquery

Communicating in SQL

As with any computer or human language, understanding the vocabulary is only the beginning of mastering the language. Effective communication requires you to use proper grammar and to develop a sense for how to construct clear statements that the person or machine you're communicating with will understand. When talking to people, you often have some leeway because a person is able to analyze the words you're using, put them in context and use their own good judgement to decide what you're saying and how to respond. A computer will just take what you say and run with it, for better or worse.

As with other computer languages, there is often more than one way to construct a query or command to the server that will return the same result. The difference between various successful methods lies in their efficiency and the resources they use. You probably won't notice this difference when working with small databases but when you move to a professional environment where tables store many thousands of records, it's a different story. Your understanding of how SQL works can make the difference between efficient queries that operate quickly using minimal resources and commands that lock up your system or even block access for other users. Those are the queries that can prompt calls from your company's database administrator.

One strategy to remember when constructing efficient commands is to ask for no more data than you actually need. When you're trying to get a sense of the data within a table, it's better to use queries like these to grab a few records than to pull the entire table.

```
SELECT * FROM LEADS LIMIT 100;
```

This can also be combined with wise use of the WHERE clause to limit the number of records retrieved. There's no reason to pull an entire table containing three years worth of data when you only need the records created in the last three months.

```
SELECT *
FROM leads
WHERE record_date > DATE_ADD(CURRENT_DATE(), INTERVAL -90 DAY)
LIMIT 10;
```

The DATE_ADD() function is one of many internal functions within MySQL that you can use to carry out calculations without writing additional code. Here, it adds -90 to the date in order to subtract 90 days. You can generally count on database and spreadsheet software to have a function to do this. In the case of MySQL, it also has a DATE_SUB() function which will subtract from a date. The COUNT()

function which you've already seen is another one I use frequently when examining unfamiliar tables to determine their size.

```
SELECT COUNT(*) FROM activities;
```

```
SELECT DISTINCT COUNT(city) FROM companies;
```

The use of the `DISTINCT` keyword limits the query to distinct values so even though there might be 100 records in the table, if there are only five distinct cities represented, the query will return that number. This could be used without the `COUNT()` function to return a list of distinct values.

```
SELECT DISTINCT job_title FROM leads;
```

Another aspect of SQL is that when you issue a command to the server, you are not just requesting data. You are, to some degree, actually instructing the server on *how* to obtain it. Take a look at the following query which uses a subquery to look for records in the Leads table that do not have any corresponding records in the Activities table.

```
SELECT L.lead_id, L.record_date, L.job_title
FROM leads L
WHERE L.lead_id
NOT IN
  (SELECT DISTINCT lead_id
  FROM activities);
```

The query essentially says: "Create a list of distinct LeadID values from Activities and then show me all the records in Leads where the Leads.LeadID is *not* found in that list.".

Now look at another query which returns the same result but uses another method to get there.

```
SELECT L.lead_id, record_date, job_title
FROM leads L
LEFT JOIN activities A
ON A.lead_id = L.lead_id
WHERE A.lead_id IS NULL;
```

This query uses a Left Join which returns all the records in the Leads table and any corresponding records it finds in Activities. Since all Leads records are being returned, that means that if there are no Activities records, then the LeadID value will not exist in the Activities table. A Leads table record is still returned but the recordset returned shows a null for the *activities.lead_id* value. The query limits the returned records to those leads and is basically saying: "Do a join on the Leads and Activities table. Show me the Leads records where no Activities values are returned." This takes full advantage of the ability of SQL to work with table joins and doesn't use a separate query.

Which is better? That depends on a number of factors including how your specific database software works with subqueries, the size of the tables and which fields have indexes placed on them. On very large tables, WHERE clauses could be added to limit the records being read in order to speed up the query. The issue of joins vs. subqueries is one where a lot of database professionals have their own preferences and opinions but there really is no consistent answer, partly because of all the factors that come into play. This is true with any type of programming where there are multiple ways to do various things. The best solution is the one that gets the job done without causing other problems and works over the long term. After that, it comes down to individual preference and style and a familiarity with how your particular database software handles various operations.

UNION Statements

A union query combines two or more SELECT queries with the same fields into a single recordset. The first SELECT statement defines the columns to be returned and the following queries must have the same number of columns with the same data types in the same positions. The keyword UNION is placed between each query to indicate that the results are to be combined. By default, duplicate rows are removed so there is no need to use the DISTINCT keyword anywhere, although it could be added after the UNION keyword for clarification. The phrase UNION ALL will retain duplicate rows.

A union query is useful when the specifications for the data to be retrieved include a large number of variables or when you need to obtain results using different variables from different joined tables. Sometimes, if a particularly complex query is not giving you the results you need, it might help to break it down into a series of smaller queries and then join them through a UNION statement. The example below retrieves one result set with all job leads where Alexis Systems is listed as the company, the city for the lead is Boston or the source is the Northeast Referral Network.

```
SELECT l.record_date, l.job_title, l.employment_type,
  l.location, c.company_name
FROM leads l
LEFT JOIN companies c
ON c.company_id = l.company_id
WHERE c.company_name = 'Alexis Systems' OR c.city = 'Boston'

UNION

SELECT l.record_date, l.job_title, l.employment_type,
  l.location, c.company_name
FROM leads l
LEFT JOIN companies c
ON c.company_id = l.company_id
LEFT JOIN sources s
ON s.source_id = l.source_id
WHERE s.source_name = 'Northeast Referral Network';
```

This could actually be done in the second query just by combining all three conditions into one WHERE statement but the union query splits the actions and, with more complicated queries, makes the logic a little easier to follow and test. There are also times when the number of conditions that need to be applied simply cannot be combined into one statement and this is when UNION queries come in very handy.

Storing SQL Queries as Views

One of the features of MySQL and other database software is the ability to store often-used queries on the server as SQL *Views*. Views can use joins to combine data from multiple tables and can be referenced and queried just like the tables they draw from. They can be used to serve up data for specific reports or provide limited access to tables for specific users.

The basic syntax to create a view is pretty simple and this example uses one of the earlier queries to present active leads from areas that have more than one job lead.

```
CREATE VIEW jobsearch_plus.multi_lead AS

SELECT job_title, employment_type, C.company_name,
  L.job_description, location
FROM leads L
```

```
RIGHT JOIN companies C
ON C.company_id = L.company_id
WHERE location
IN
  (SELECT l.location
   FROM leads L
   WHERE L.active <> 0
   GROUP BY L.location
   HAVING COUNT(L.lead_id) > 1);
```

The `CREATE VIEW` line above is really the only thing needed to store your favorite `SELECT` query on the server. You can also overwrite an existing view by changing the line slightly.

```
CREATE OR REPLACE VIEW jobsearch_plus.multi_lead AS
```

Once the view has been created, you can query it and link to it just like a regular table.

```
select * from jobsearch_plus.multi_lead limit 2;

SELECT c.*
FROM jobsearch_plus.companies c
INNER JOIN jobsearch_plus.multi_lead ml
ON ml.company_name = c.company_name
WHERE ml.job_title = 'Software Developer';
```

The second example above selects all the fields from the Companies table based on an Inner Join to the *multi_lead* view and specifies to only return the company information for the jobs with 'Software Developer' as the title. Since there's only one job lead like that in the sample data you've seen so far, it returns the company record for Alexis Systems. Note that there is no formal relationship defined in the database between the table and the view. The join on the alphanumeric *company_name* field works anyway because it finds equal values in the specified fields of both tables.

The `CREATE VIEW` syntax will not work with `INSERT` or other commands that change data on the server, only `SELECT` statements. Views can also be shown on database diagrams, although they might just be shown as an object with no attributes.

Inserting Data

Earlier, you saw many examples of the INSERT command which is the primary way of adding information to the database. Using this command, you can insert one record at a time with a simple command.

```
INSERT INTO Sources
(source_name, Source_Type,
  Source_Link, `Description`)
VALUES
('Monster.com', 'Website',
  'http://wwww.monster.com', 'Online Job Board');
```

The above query represents most of the syntax for the INSERT command. It doesn't have any use for the joins and most of the other clauses you saw in the SELECT command.

The statement starts by naming the table and then the fields to be populated. This doesn't mean that you have to name every column in the table; if a field is not required or has a default value, it would be considered optional. The VALUES clause is then followed by values to be inserted into the specified columns which must be listed in the same order as the field names.

The INSERT command can be combined with a SELECT command to insert multiple records at once. You might use this if you wanted to copy data from one table to another such as when importing or archiving data.

```
INSERT INTO Sources (source_name, source_type,
  source_link, source_desc)
SELECT source_name, source_type,
  source_link, source_desc
FROM SourceImport;
```

It's still a very simple syntax where the SELECT fields match the fields in the INSERT statement and supply a set of records for insertion. Note that the auto-incremented primary key for this table is not specified. You could even specify aggregate or other functions in the SELECT statement as shown in the previous section which would write the results of those functions to the table. You could also copy an existing record into another record, changing specific fields if necessary.

```
INSERT INTO leads (record_date, job_title,
  job_description, source_id)
SELECT DATE_ADD(CURRENT_TIMESTAMP(), INTERVAL 1 DAY), job_title,
  job_description, source_id
FROM Supplemental_Leads;
```

The query above copies all records from a table called *Supplemental_Leads* to the main Leads table, inserting the previous day's date into the *record_date* field for each record. The CURRENT_TIMESTAMP() function returns the date and time down to the millisecond although these commands work so fast that you could probably do a few dozen records in only three or four milliseconds. This is something to keep in mind if you have a unique index on a date field for whatever reason. The next command duplicates a specific record, searching by *lead_id* and again inserts the current date.

```
INSERT INTO leads (record_date, job_title,
  employment_type, location, company_id)
SELECT CURRENT_TIMESTAMP(), job_title,
  employment_type, location, company_id
FROM leads
WHERE lead_id = 1;
```

You could also use the IN keyword as part of the where clause to specify multiple records to duplicate as shown below.

```
INSERT INTO leads
(record_date, job_title, employment_type, location, company_id)
SELECT CURRENT_DATE(), job_title,
  employment_type, location, company_id
FROM leads
WHERE lead_id IN (1, 2, 3, 4);
```

MySQL Workbench actually includes a couple features to make it easier to write up SQL commands such as the INSERT commands needed to populate tables. Intellisense will suggest keywords, table names and column names as you type. You can use the down arrow key on your keyboard to select the appropriate keyword or name and then use the ENTER key to add it to the statement.

Another feature is the command template. If you right-click on a table name under the Schema listing and then select **Send to SQL Editor >> INSERT Statement** from the context menu, a command like the following one will be placed in the current query window.

Figure 7.7 - Intellisense in MySQL Workbench helps to complete commands by supplying object names and keywords.

```
INSERT INTO `jobsearch_plus`.`sources`
(`source_id`,
`source_name`,
`source_type`,
`source_link`,
`source_desc`)
VALUES
(<{source_id: }>,
<{source_name: }>,
<{source_type: }>,
<{source_link: }>,
<{source_desc: }>);
```

This can save you quite a bit of typing and it helps if you're a little fuzzy on the syntax of the statements. The statement templates don't take into account that certain fields are auto-generated or not required but they're still easily edited into usable statements.

```
INSERT INTO `jobsearch_plus`.`sources`
(`source_name`,
`source_type`,
`source_desc`)
VALUES
('Northeast Referral Network',
'Professional Network',
'Network for employment referrals in northeastern U.S.');
```

Using Variables

One of the challenges in populating the tables in a database with many foreign keys is getting the right primary key values to reference the correct parent records. Later in this chapter, you'll see an example of how you can use the LAST_INSERT_ID() function immediately after inserting a new record to get the auto increment value assigned to it. You can also use SELECT queries to retrieve the appropriate ID number based on other fields that you know the value of.

```
SELECT company_id FROM companies WHERE company_name LIKE 'Mentoris%'
limit 1;
```

The `LIKE` keyword above will do a comparison on the table and retrieve records where the specified column is *like* the value supplied. In this example, the % wildcard at the end of 'Mentoris' specifies that the statement should look for any value *beginning* with 'Mentoris' and the query is then limited to one row. It could also be used as '%mentoris%' to specify any record with that text anywhere in the value. The underscore wildcard "_" can be used to substitute for a specific character in the string, i.e. 'Databas_ Programmer'.

An exact comparison could also be done with the equals sign.

```
SELECT company_id FROM companies WHERE company_name = 'Mentoris
Training Systems';
```

SQL can also store information in user-defined variables in order to use the information later. Variables are defined simply by using the `SET` statement to assign a value to a variable name that starts with "@". Unlike in other languages, variables in SQL are declared and assigned values all in one statement. They are session-specific, however, which means that if you break the connection with the server, any variables that you've defined go away.

The result of the above query can be assigned to a variable and then used in another statement where it provides the foreign key value needed to insert a record.

```
SET @company_id =
(SELECT company_id FROM companies
WHERE company_name = 'Mentoris Training Systems');

INSERT INTO leads
(job_title, employment_type, company_id)
VALUES
('Executive Assistant', 'Full-Time', @company_id);
```

In the above example, the `SET` statement stores the company ID for Mentoris Training Systems in the @company_id variable which is then used to insert a new row in the *leads* table. A SQL statement can use multiple variables in order to provide the necessary values. For the database designer, this means that a script like the one above can be created with `SET` statements that accept known values and retrieve the necessary IDs. Scripts like this can save the designer work by automating complex operations. Further along in the process, programmers can use variables and other advanced features of the SQL and T-SQL languages to create stored procedures which accept multiple values, do any necessary lookups and then insert data or carry out complex operations. These procedures can then be called by outside programs as needed to process commands from the end users.

Updating Data

The UPDATE command used to change existing data has a few of the options found in the SELECT command that you can use to target specific data for updating. These include WHERE clauses and joins that can be used to gather reference information to select the correct rows to be changed. You've already seen some basic UPDATE commands such as the following which would change the Active bit for any job lead that did not represent a full-time opportunity.

```
UPDATE leads
SET active = 0
WHERE employment_type <> 'Full-Time';
```

A more sophisticated version uses a join to the Companies table to make changes based on the state in which the company is located. In this case, the Active bit for all job leads where the company's address is not in Massachusetts or Connecticut is set to 0.

```
UPDATE leads
SET active = 0
FROM leads L
RIGHT JOIN companies C
ON C.company_id = L.company_id
WHERE c.co_state NOT IN ('MA', 'CT');
```

Note that in the first example, the table to be updated was only specified on the first line but when doing a join to another table, you need to use the FROM clause as shown in the second command. Also note the use of NOT IN which is the inverse of the IN command.

Another option for inserting or updating records is to obtain the value for a foreign key through the use of a subquery.

```
UPDATE leads
SET company_id = (SELECT company_id FROM companies WHERE
company_name = 'Jameson Corporation' limit 1)
WHERE lead_id = last_insert_id();
```

The above query sets the *leads.company_id* value for the last record inserted by doing a select on the *companies* table and looking for a specific name. This would need to be used with care. First, the `LAST_INSERT_ID()` function is not table-specific; it will return the last auto-incremented ID generated for *any* table so this statement would need to be run immediately after the insert to the leads table. Second, the `SELECT` subquery specifies `LIMIT 1` in case there is more than one record matching that criteria. Additional criteria could be added to the `WHERE` clause in order to ensure the selection of the correct record but the `LIMIT` keyword is still a great idea.

Deleting Data

The final SQL command we'll look at here is the `DELETE` command which is used to remove rows from a table. `DELETE` has the same clauses available to it as `UPDATE` including the ability to join to other tables and specify parameters with the `WHERE` clause so that you can be precise when deleting rows.

It's important to remember that checking and re-checking your commands before running them is absolutely essential, especially when you're deleting data. Once you run the `DELETE` command, your data is gone short of restoring backups. A missing `WHERE` clause in a `DELETE` query can lead to that ominous user question; "Why is this query taking so long?". Even with SQL's ability to affect thousands of records in a short period of time, an unqualified `UPDATE` or `DELETE` operation on an entire table with tens of thousands of records can still take just long enough for the user to realize that he or she has just made a *very* serious mistake.

An excellent way to check your `DELETE` commands before running them is to *always* write them as `SELECT` commands first as shown below.

```
SELECT *
FROM activities
WHERE lead_id = 8;
```

At this point, it would be wise to run the query to ensure the right data is selected *before* changing a single keyword as shown here.

```
DELETE
FROM activities
WHERE lead_id = 8;
```

Notice the '*' wildcard is not required on the DELETE command. If you follow this rule whenever you're writing DELETE commands, it will help you to avoid unhappy surprises.

Here are two more examples of what you can do with DELETE. Suppose you have a number of job leads in the database from a website that you later found was fraudulent and you wanted them removed along with the record of the website itself in the Sources table. Referential integrity prevents you from deleting the Sources table record so long as there are corresponding records in Leads so the proper method would be to remove the job leads first and then remove the Sources record. A join can be used in the first delete statement to target the job leads that reference the offending website.

```
SELECT * DELETE
FROM leads L
LEFT JOIN sources S
ON S.source_id = L.source_id
WHERE S.source_name = 'JobCritter.com';
```

```
SELECT * DELETE
FROM sources
WHERE source_name = 'JobCritter.com';
```

Commenting SQL Code

Another way to ensure that DELETE commands and other queries are not run by accident is to mark the entire commands as comments within the query script when not in use. If you are working with multiple queries within a program like MySQL Workbench and have any commands in them that might cause problems if run by accident, it's best to comment them out until you want to run them.

SQL supports single and multi-line comments. A pair of dashes or a pound sign mark the rest of a single line as a comment and this can be done for the purposes of actually leaving explanatory comments or marking out sections of code that are not to be run. MySQL will disregard anything that is marked as a comment.

```
-- This is a comment

# This is a comment

SELECT *
FROM activities
WHERE lead_id = 8;

SELECT TOP 10 *
FROM companies;
-- WHERE co_state = 'MN'
-- The above WHERE clause is ignored
-- because of the comment dashes.
```

Single line comments can be stacked on the same line as shown in the second example above. If the first pair of dashes is removed, activating the WHERE clause, the second pair of dashes will maintain the comment at the end of the line.

Multi-line comments can be used for the same reason but enable the user to mark out multiple lines without having to place dashes at the beginning of each line. The "/*" characters will start a comment and SQL will ignore everything after it until it sees the comment end characters "*/". It does not matter if the characters fall on the same line as other text.

```
/*
This is a multiline comment.
Both lines are ignored by SQL
*/

/* This entire command will be ignored by SQL
   DELETE
   FROM contacts
   WHERE active = 0
*/
```

Chapter Summary

Structured Query Language, also known as SQL, is the main scripting language used to work with relational databases. The three sections of the SQL language can be used to do everything from creating entire databases, tables and other objects to making very precise changes to the data within tables. The commands can be issued from multiple sources including outside programs, query editors such as those found in MySQL Workbench and phpMyAdmin, automated scripts and command line tools. The language uses English keywords in order to specify actions, table and column names and exact specifications for the changes to be made. Data Manipulation Language (DML), the portion of the language dedicated to editing table data, is used to carry out SELECT, INSERT, UPDATE and DELETE operations within tables and is fairly easy to learn in a short time. Because of the power contained within this language, especially in the commands that change or delete data, it is important for a database user to be both experienced and careful in its use.

For Further Study

Review Questions

1. Name two places from which SQL queries and commands can be directed to the database.

2. What is the difference between Data Manipulation Language and Data Control Language?

3. What is the purpose of the USE keyword in SQL?

4. If a table column name conflicts with a SQL keyword, how would you mark it as a column name?

5. What character is placed on either side of a value to mark it as a literal value in SQL?

6. How is the WHERE clause used in a SQL command?

7. How are relationships between tables represented within SQL?

8. How are table aliases used in SQL?

9. What is the difference between a Left Outer Join and an Inner Join?

10. How are parentheses used in WHERE clauses?

11. What is the difference between the WHERE and HAVING clauses in SQL?

12. What is a subquery and how can it be used in a WHERE clause?

13. Name two ways in which the SELECT command would be used to insert records into a table.

14. How would you verify that a DELETE command was specifying the correct data to be deleted before executing it?

15. What are the two ways to create comments within SQL code and how can comments be used to prevent accidental deletions of data?

Exercises

1. Using the database diagram in Figure 7.1, write SQL queries that will generate the following reports:
   o A list of all active contacts including the contact name, company name, contact title, phone number and e-mail.
   o A list of job lead sources and number of leads obtained from each over the past 90 days.
   o A list of activities earlier than five days in the future that have not been completed.
   o A list of companies with no associated contacts.

2. Following up on the exercises shown earlier in this chapter, continue writing commands to populate the tables in your

copy of the Job Search Plus database with information. Write `INSERT` commands to enter basic required information for tables and UPDATE commands to update selected fields with information that might be obtained over the course of the search. For tables with parent / child relationships such as the Leads and Activities tables, you can use the `LAST_INSERT_ID()` function to return the primary key value of the last record inserted in the parent table. For example:

```
INSERT INTO leads (record_date, job_title)
VALUES (CURRENT_DATE(), 'Technical Support');

INSERT INTO Activities (LeadID, ActivityDate, ActivityType)
VALUES (LAST_INSERT_ID(), CURRENT_DATE(), 'Initial Contact');
```

Remember that `LAST_INSERT_ID()` will pull the last auto incremented value for *any* table so the above statements must be run consecutively in order to ensure the right value.

Terms to Remember

- **Execution Plan** - The list of steps that the database software will follow to execute a command or query. The plan will include the amount of system resources needed to execute the command and the relative cost of each step. Used to determine the efficiency of a query.

- **Inner Join** - A table join in which only records where the values on both sides are equal are returned as part of the query result.

- **Intellisense** - A feature of various coding environments in which the editor detects the commands being used as they are typed in by the user and automatically completes them or provides lists of appropriate options. This speeds up code entry and reduces errors.

- **Right Join** - A table join in which specified records from the second table listed in the join (on the 'right' side of the relationship) are retrieved along with any matching records from the first table.

- **Queries** - SQL `SELECT` commands used to read data from database tables.

- **Left Join** - A table join in which specified records from the first table listed in the join are retrieved along with any matching records from the second table.

- **Structured Query Language (SQL)** - A scripting language used to make changes to relational databases including the management of objects and permissions and the editing of table data.

- **Syntax** - The commands and structure of a language.

Chapter VIII

Design Overview: Human Resources and Training Database

Introduction

The principles of database design that you've seen demonstrated in this book require practice in order to truly understand. In order to clarify them, I want to provide a couple more examples in this chapter and the next to show you how these ideas can be applied in different situations.

SpheraTech Manufacturing is an electronics manufacturer with approximately 200 employees. The company wants to put together a custom database application to track employee information and training classes. The system must be able to store complete employee information including contact and position information, hire and termination dates and other information required to manage the workforce. It should also show an employee's history of completed training classes. Some classes might need to be repeated periodically for re-certification or legal reasons so the Training department needs to be able to run reports that show how and when the classes have been held and document which employees have completed them.

Design meetings are conducted with representatives from Human Resources, the Training department and the I.T. design team. This team includes a database administrator, reporting specialist and a couple of application programmers. During the meetings, the Human Resources Manager and other business representatives mentioned several other human resources, training, payroll and maybe even facility security functions that they believe would be nice to have in the system. The I.T. Manager later recommended that the design team keep future expansion of the system in mind when creating the database.

Modeling the Data

Conceptual

Remember that the conceptual phase of the modeling process involves mapping out the concepts represented by the database, also known as *entities*, and the relationships between them. When doing this, it helps to start by going through the requirements and making a list of the items found. The immediate concepts the design team found in the requirements above were the employee data, positions within the company and the training classes.

The concept of an employee within the database is pretty straightforward, although there might be a number of related tables involved as information is added. The positions or jobs within the company and the training classes get a little more complex. A position within the company can mean two different things;

1. The job itself which includes a job description and can be held by multiple people either simultaneously or over many years

2. A person's employment within a position over a specific period of time

The job itself, as defined by the company, represents an entity that can be included in the model. It is an item that can be described with a set of attributes such as a title, set of responsibilities, a department identifier and other information related to pay and job type. A person's *employment* within a position, on the other hand, could be treated as a portion of the employee's overall record at the company. It still needs to be recorded within the database but this can be done within a record or two rather than one or more tables. Other than a start and end date and a couple other details, the employee's presence within a given position does not have many attributes that are specific to it. Even the employee's salary is only partially determined by position and is treated as an attribute of the employee entity. The number of attributes required to describe a concept and whether they can be placed elsewhere in the database is a test you can use to determine if that concept represents an entity within the model.

The concept of a training class is also one that would be defined within the database based on what needed to be recorded. A training class can represent either the course itself which has a title, a course outline and a set of objectives or it can represent the scheduled class in which the course is taught over a period of days or weeks. In one of the requirements meetings, the design team asked about the amount of detail to be kept on training classes and related courses. The Training department decided that both overall course information and scheduled classes should be tracked for documentation purposes since some of the classes satisfy regulatory requirements.

The Training Manager wanted to have a report demonstrating that the classes had been held as often as required and how many people attended. She also wanted to use the database to manage the class schedules and workloads for her instructors. This led into a discussion about documenting information on class instructors and their qualifications. Instructors are sometimes brought in from outside the company so the database will have to accommodate both internal and external instructors as well as external training company information. Training vendors might supply as little as a course syllabus and set of training materials or they might administer the entire training, supplying their own instructors and off-site classes.

In the conceptual model shown in Figure 8.1, you can see the entities and the relationships that resulted from these discussions. Again, this is not a collection of tables at this point and doesn't include information such as the department listing that will be referenced by the employee and position entities. It does give a good picture of the main concepts in the database and serves as a way for the designers to visualize the system so they can move forward with the design.

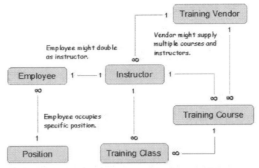

Figure 8.1 - The initial model for the human resources and training database includes both employee and training information.

Adding Details

In practice, the conceptual and logical modeling process aren't strictly separate. Even as SpheraTech's design team was working out the concepts to be included in the database, the business team was talking about information that needed to be included for each of the areas and the database designers were following up with questions of their own. With the conceptual diagram in place as shown in Figure 8.1, this is another example of how the planning might proceed as the team starts mapping out the database.

Figure 8.2 shows the initial list of items to be tracked in the database. It's a lot of information to start with and the design team anticipated a large and sophisticated system. The team's reporting specialist requested sample reports and other data from H.R. and the Training department to get a clearer picture of what the data looked like. The other team members agreed that this was an important step not only for designing the database but also for testing it before the users get to see it. While some adjustments might eventually be needed based on user input, having the database as close to finished and ready for use by the time the users see it seemed like the best policy.

The next step is to start organizing this data according to the data normalization rules that you saw in previous chapters. Since this is looking like a somewhat complex data model, let's start with how the team mapped out the the Human Resources section of the database.

Figure 8.2 - The logical model can start with a simple listing of the information required for each subject.

First Normal Form (1NF)

All fields within the tables represent single data values that have been reduced to the smallest useful piece of information. Fields cannot contain multiple values and tables cannot have repeating fields or groups of fields. A table should not have multiple fields for the same attribute for the purpose of tracking multiple items.

This essentially means breaking down a number of the employee attributes such as the address, phone numbers and emergency contact information into individual fields to be created in the tables. As I mentioned in the chapter on Normalization, it's sometimes reasonable to have more than one field that appears to hold the same type of information such as Address1 and Address2, Phone1 and Phone2 even though the First Normal Form prohibits repeating fields.

Figure 8.3 shows the changes to the employee section of the data model. Aside from the breakdown of the attributes into fields that will hold single values, a second prospective table, *Employee Notes*, replaces the Notes attribute. The H.R. representatives confirmed when asked that there would need to be an employee history maintained for each employee over the period of his or her employment so the designers decided a second table would accommodate the data. Also as a result of discussions with the business, an *Action Type* field was added to the Notes data to indicate specific actions such as status changes, meetings with H.R., benefits administration, etc.. The table will indicate which H.R. representative recorded a specific note and when.

Employees		Employee Notes
SSN	Em. Contact Name	Employee ID
Badge Number	Em. Contact Phone	Date
Date of Birth	Photo	Action Type
First Name	Department ID	Notes
Last Name	Shift	Recorded By
M.I.	Position ID	
Address1	Hire Date	
Address2	Start Date	
City	Current (Y/N)	
State	Term. Date	
Postal Code	~~Notes~~	
Phone1	~~Completed Training~~	
Phone2		
E-mail		

Figure 8.3 - Breakdown of employee data into First Normal Form (1NF)

The 'Completed Training' attribute, while still necessary, is removed from this part of the data model as it will be addressed later by other tables. The 'Job Title' attribute is changed to 'Position ID' in anticipation that the positions and their details will be held in a separate table. There's no need to store the job title in the Employees table when it will be shown in a table dedicated to positions within the company.

Second Normal Form (2NF)

The database must be in First Normal Form and all fields that are not part of a table's key must be functionally dependent on the entire key.

It's time to introduce some table keys into the model.

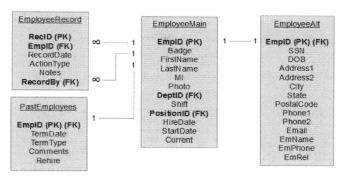

Figure 8.4 - Application of the Second Normal Form

Applying the Second Normal Form was another opportunity for the team to ask questions about the data that needed to be kept. You can see a few extra fields in Figure 8.4 that resulted from these discussions. The employee data is broken down into two tables - *EmployeeMain* for the employment information and *EmployeeAlt* for contact and confidential information that might need to be restricted. The reporting specialist wanted the name 'Employee_Private' but a database designer suggested something a little less conspicuous. Depending on the database software being used, splitting the data like this might not be strictly necessary from a security standpoint but it doesn't hurt and it does reduce the size of the tables. One software developer asked why the employee badge number wasn't used as the primary key and the database administrator reminded him that permanent badges aren't issued at the company until after employee orientation is complete while the employee record would hopefully be created at the time of hire.

The *EmployeeRecord* table holds the employee notes and history and also maintains two relationships to *EmployeeMain*. Instead of storing the name of the H.R. person making the change, the team decided to just store their employee ID and relate back to the main table for their name. There was a minor debate about whether to give the *EmployeeRecord* table it's own auto-incrementing surrogate key or just use the employee ID and the date / time value recorded as a composite key. A coin toss late in the day on Friday resulted in the *RecID* field being added as an auto-incrementing primary key.

The *PastEmployees* table was broken out to avoid a lot of blank termination dates in the *EmployeeMain* table and it was linked to *EmployeeMain* on the EmpID field. Human Resources again confirmed that it would be a good idea to record a couple of details on former employees such as the reason they left the company and whether they were eligible for rehire so these fields were added. The one-to-one relationship assumes there won't be too many people coming back to the company and then leaving again. Even if some do, the *EmployeeRecord* table would be able to maintain an adequate history with the *PastEmployees* table keeping a record of the last separation from the company. This also confirmed the decision not to use the employee badge as the table key since a person's second trip through the company would result in a different badge number.

Also notice the change in a number of the field names. Some companies have naming conventions as part of their technical standards, some don't. Short and understandable names are preferable considering that these names are going to be used in code to retrieve and save the data and that code needs to be maintained. It helps if the names are self-explanatory but aren't so long that they're tedious to work with.

Completing the human resources portion of the data model, Figure 8.5 adds the *Positions* and *Departments* tables to the model.

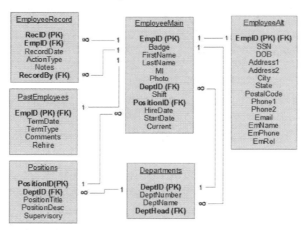

Figure 8.5 - Addition of Positions and Departments tables

The *Positions* table maintains some basic details on all the job descriptions. The *DeptID* field is included in this table as well as in the *EmployeeMain* table. This allows for the the possibility that a position might be specific to a department or might be written more generally to fit multiple departments. The field's presence within the *Positions* table and it's status as a foreign key does not require it to be used. It can hold a null value and simply won't reference any record in *Departments.*

The *Departments* table maintains reciprocal relationships with the *EmployeeMain* table, providing details on the departments and using the *EmpID* field to retrieve the information on the employee serving as the department head.

The Training portion of the database was the next part of the design to be worked out. The team was able to clarify with the Training department that it was not necessary to keep a lot of detail for external trainers as they are certified by the training vendors who assign them. It is necessary, however, to document which courses *internal* trainers are qualified to teach, when they were certified and if the certifications, which might need to be renewed, are current.

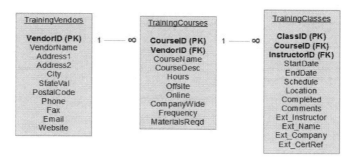

Figure 8.6 - Initial design of the model's training section

Figure 8.6 shows the model for the first three training tables. In keeping with the original conceptual model, the tables allow for many courses to be supplied by each vendor and many classes to be taught based on each course. With these relationships, the company can track the number and details of classes taught based on a specific training course or training materials supplied by a specific vendor.

The *TrainingClasses* table allows for both internal and external instructors or even a combination of both with an InstructorID foreign key field which will be linked back to the *EmployeeMain* table to ensure that only company employees are referenced by the field. It also has fields which enable details on an external instructor to be documented. The *Ext_Instructor* field will be a Yes / No choice to indicate if an external instructor was brought in to teach the class while the remaining fields provide the instructor name, company and any information the business wants to retain on the instructor's certification to teach the class.

Again, the presence of a foreign key field in a table does not mean that the field *always* has to be used. In this example, if a class is taught solely by an external instructor, the *InstructorID* field can simply be left null and it won't reference an employee. While one of the aims of the normalization principles is to eliminate fields with an excessive number of null entries, it doesn't mean they have to be eliminated completely.

This brings us to the next change. The discussions with the Training department and a casual glance at the class schedules they supplied show that the majority of training classes within the company are taught by employees rather than external instructors. This is by design as the company feels it ultimately gets a better value by having course instructors who are familiar with the company environment and culture and can work closely with H.R.. This means that three of those four fields in the *TrainingClasses* table will often be null. So, in the interests of a cleaner design, the team decides to move them off into another related table and turn the *Ext_Instructor* field into a foreign key.

The *ExtInstructors* table makes this portion of the design fully compliant with the Second Normal Form since, other than the *Ext_Instructor* field that indicates the presence of an external instructor, that instructor information doesn't actually relate to the subject of the class itself. The *VendorID* foreign key was also added to the table so that any queries written on these tables don't have to go back three tables just to get the vendor details for an external instructor. It also allows for the possibility that the instructor might not be from the same company associated with the training course.

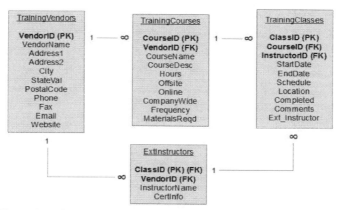

Figure 8.7 - Details on external instructors split into separate table

Many-to-Many Relationships

Not all tables or groups of tables in a database have to be related to each other. It's possible to have a large database where one or more tables sit apart for reference to show another process. In this database, however, the Training and H.R. portions do tie into each other since both reference employee information. To do that, the database designers needed to resolve a couple of many-to-many relationships within the data model. These are relationships where the two entities can occur more than once on each side of the relationships and the relational language does not allow for them to be directly represented within a database. Here are the two that showed up in the model:

- *Employees and Training Classes* - Again, a training class is the actual session or group of sessions during which a training course is taught. An employee will take many training classes over his or her time at the company and there are many employees per training class.

- *Instructors and Training Courses* - An employee who is qualified as an instructor might be qualified to teach many training courses. A course might have many qualified instructors within the company.

Many-to-many relationships are often resolved with an intervening table that will break the relationship down into two separate one-to-many relationships that can be represented within the database. Often this table will include other information that relates to the relationship between the tables.

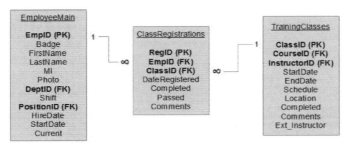

Figure 8.8 - A table detailing employee registrations for classes resolves the many-to-many relationship between employees and training classes.

Figure 8.8 shows how the *ClassRegistrations* table ties the *EmployeeMain* and *TrainingClasses* tables together and resolves one of the problem relationships. The primary keys from each table are used as foreign keys and the table also includes the date the employee registered for the class, whether he or she completed it and other relevant information. With this table, the database can supply a complete record of the employee's attendance of training classes. While it's not shown here, the *InstructorID* field in *TrainingClasses* can link back to the EmpID field in *EmployeeMain* to get the instructor's employee information.

In Figure 8.9, the *TrainingCertifications* table supplies a way to track internal instructor certifications while resolving the many-to-many relationship between employee instructors and training courses.

Third Normal Form (3NF) and Boyce-Codd (BCNF)

"The database must be in Second Normal Form and all fields that are not part of the key must be functionally independent of each other."

At this point, the tables also conform to 3NF and BCNF which looks for multiple possible primary keys within a table. This is due in part to the fact that the tables are heavy on text and date values rather than numeric values which might be used in calculations. The Second Normal Form also encourages the Third Normal Form since the focus is kept on the primary key to start with. After that, keeping the number of fields within reason and being aware of when information can be more efficiently stored where it will only need to be written once helps the table structure to fall naturally into 3NF. Issues related to the Boyce-Codd form are unlikely.

Figure 8.9 - A table detailing instructor course certifications resolves the many-to-many relationship between employees and training courses.

Design Notes

One thing you might have noticed in this example is how important it is to keep the communication open between the designers and the end users. In this case, end users are represented by the team from H.R. and Training. Ultimately, the database has to serve the needs of the users and not just the requirements of the Normal Forms. If the designers are reluctant or unable to talk with the users for whatever reason, it's likely that business requirements will be missed or improperly implemented. This can lead to a lot of expensive man hours spent redoing the design, unhappy users and even a failed project.

The size of the design team on this project is not out of line. Two database specialists and two application programmers to design a user interface for data entry and reporting functions would probably be able to get this application up and running in a reasonable amount of time. A fifth person could even be added to manage communication with the users and document the project. The database administrator is probably going to be working on a number of other projects as well and will act in more of an advisory role, granting one of the software designers the necessary permissions to build the actual database once the design is worked out.

Expansions

A couple weeks into the project, the Training Manager dropped by and mentioned that she had also been looking for a way to track required training on both a department and position level. She asked if, by any chance, this new database could do that as well. A couple of the design team members, enthusiastic about the project so far, immediately agreed. The team then discussed a couple of different ways to add this information.

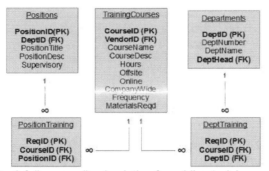

Figure 8.10 - A fully normalized solution for adding training requirements

Figure 8.10 shows the first solution that the team suggested which treats the relationship of the *Courses* table to the *Positions* and *Departments* tables as a couple of many-to-many relationships; many courses might be required for each position or department and many positions or departments might require a certain course. Two new tables are proposed to resolve these many-to-many relationships, one for the position-specific training and one for the department-specific training.

The first question was how the required training would be retrieved for any given employee and the answer was that two SQL statements would be needed. One statement would use the employee's department to access the list of required training courses for that department and the second statement would use the employee's position in the same way, accessing the list of position specific training. The two SQL statements could be combined using SQL's UNION keyword to return a single set of data. The UNION keyword also filters out duplications by default. The entire query could be saved to a stored procedure which could be called with the necessary parameters.

```
DELIMITER $$
CREATE PROCEDURE `getRequirements`(Dept VARCHAR(45), Position
VARCHAR(45))
BEGIN

    SELECT TC.CourseID, TC.CourseName, TC.CourseDesc
    FROM TrainingCourses TC
    INNER JOIN PositionTraining PT
    ON PT.CourseID = TC.CourseID
        INNER JOIN Positions P
        ON P.PositionID = PT.PositionID
    WHERE PT.PositionTitle = Position
    UNION
    SELECT TC.CourseID, TC.CourseName, TC.CourseDesc
    FROM TrainingCourses TC
    INNER JOIN DeptTraining DT
    ON DT.CourseID = TC.CourseID
        INNER JOIN Departments D
        ON D.DeptID = DT.DeptID
    WHERE DT.DeptName = Dept;

END $$
```

The syntax for creating a stored procedure is pretty straightforward as you can see in the example above. The DELIMITER statement defines a delimiter other than the semi-colon that can be used to signal the end of the stored procedure.

This procedure can then be called from within the MySQL as follows:

```
CALL getRequirements('Finance', 'Facility Accountant');
```

The union query above links back to both the *Positions* and *Departments* tables to allow for the names to be used in the stored procedure call. The procedure definition on the first line specifies the required arguments and their data types. The queries could be simplified by using the department and position IDs instead, which will be readily available to whatever program is designed around the database. The stored procedure could then accept the department and position IDs and pass them to the modified queries.

```
CREATE PROCEDURE `getRequirements`(Dept INT, Position INT);
```

While this represented a fully normalized and workable solution, there were some reservations in the group because of the dual tables and the possibility of duplications between them. The *DeptTraining* table could include safety training for the Maintenance department while the *PositionTraining* table might include the same course for the Maintenance Supervisor position which was already designated as being part of the Maintenance department. One of the application programmers suggested that the software could run a duplication check before inserting a requirement and the reporting specialist reiterated that the union query would filter the duplication anyway. The solution's reception within the design team was still lukewarm.

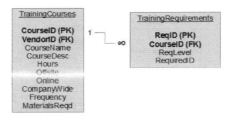

Figure 8.11 - Single-table solution to adding training requirements

Figure 8.11 shows the second solution proposed and that was to have one table called 'TrainingRequirements' that would be related to the *TrainingCourses* table on the CourseID field. The requirements table has a text field called *ReqLevel* that will be limited to 'Department' or 'Position' and a RequiredID field that will hold the appropriate department ID or position ID value. The SQL required to get all requirements for a specific employee still used a union query but the team felt better in general about working with a single table.

```
DELIMITER $$
CREATE PROCEDURE `getRequirements`(Dept VARCHAR(45), Position
VARCHAR(45))
BEGIN
        SELECT TC.CourseID, TC.CourseName, TC.CourseDesc
```

```
        FROM TrainingCourses TC
        INNER JOIN TrainingRequirements TR
        ON TR.CourseID = TC.CourseID
            INNER JOIN Positions P
            ON P.PositionID = TR.ReqID
        WHERE P.PositionTitle = Position
        AND TR.ReqLevel = 'Position'
        UNION
        SELECT TC.CourseID, TC.CourseName, TC.CourseDesc
        FROM TrainingCourses TC
        INNER JOIN TrainingRequirements TR
        ON TR.CourseID = TC.CourseID
        INNER JOIN Departments D
        ON D.DeptID = TR.ReqID
        WHERE D.DeptName = Dept
            AND TR.ReqLevel = 'Department';
END $$

CALL getRequirements('Finance', 'Facility Accountant')
```

The team leader finally decided to try the second solution and see how it worked through the testing phase of the program. If there were problems or the requirements changed later, he reasoned, the two types of training could easily be broken out into separate tables. See the SQL examples at the end of this chapter for a demonstration of how the data will be retrieved from the new table.

Creating the Tables

After all the negotiations and planning, the logical data model developed by the team was worked out into 13 physical tables to start with as shown in the following diagrams and SQL statements. Let's look at the Human Resources tables first.

Most of the fields in these tables are pretty self-explanatory. The information for individual employees is broken up into two tables - *employee_main* and *employee_alt*. The *employee_alt* table also has the *emp_id* field as a primary key but the field is not set to auto increment so the table can store whatever value is generated by the *employee_main* table. The field does have a unique index on it, however, so there's actually a one-to-one relationship between the two tables. The diagram in MySQL Workbench shows a one-to-many relationship by default but this can be changed within the diagram as shown in Figure 8.12.

The *employee_main* table uses a BLOB data type to hold the employee's photo. This is a field that can store binary data of the type that you would find in a graphic, sound or executable file. Employee photos might be stored in JPEG files and whatever program is designed around this database can use this field to store the content of those files. The photos can then be retrieved and displayed as necessary.

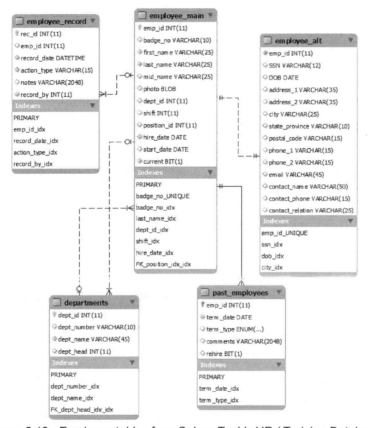

Figure 8.12 - Employee tables from SpheraTech's HR / Training Database

The *employee_alt* table includes the social security number, date of birth and contact information. This separates this sensitive data from the main table and enables the administrators to restrict the rights to the data by setting different permissions. As an added bit of security, the software being used to maintain the database could be set to encrypt the Social Security Number and other very sensitive data, decrypting it as needed so that anyone viewing the database itself will not be able to directly query the table for this information. This is often used for user passwords stored within the database.

The *DOB* (Date of Birth) field in the *employee_alt* table does not need to record what time an employee was born, only the date, whereas the *employee_record.record_date* field uses the DATETIME field to enable multiple records entered on the same day to be properly sorted. The DATE type stores the date only and uses 3 bytes per field where the DATETIME also stores the time down to the second and uses 8 bytes per field. This won't make a lot of difference, even in larger databases, but it's best to use the proper field for your needs.

The database also uses the BIT field a few times to store True / False values. A BIT field stores binary values made up of ones and zeros, i.e. '0101' or '0010'. In this example the field would either store a 1 (True) or 0 (False). The size of a BIT field can be set up to 64 which would hold 64 bits (8 bytes or characters in binary format). If no size is specified, as shown in Figure 8.12, the default is 1. MySQL only uses as many bytes as necessary to store the amount of data as specified by the field definition so if the field only allows 1 bit, MySQL rounds up and uses 1 byte to store each value. The TINYINT data type which stores whole numbers from -128 to 127 (or unsigned values from 0 to 255) could also be used and also uses only one byte.

The *past_employees.term_type* field uses an ENUM field to allow four values to indicate why the employee left the company; 'Quit', 'Dismissed', 'Layoff' and 'Deceased'. This type is also specific to MySQL and might not be available in other database software where a lookup table with referential integrity would be needed to enforce the allowed values.

The indexes placed on the tables, indicated by the KEY statements in the command below, are reserved for fields that are likely to be searched or sorted on. With a few of the indexes in these and the rest of the tables, you'll notice that they are preceded by "FK_" indicating that MySQL added them while adding a foreign key constraint to the tables. When you place a foreign key on a table, MySQL determines if the foreign key field already has an index on it and creates one if there isn't one already. If there's already one present, it uses that one.

The *departments* table has a single foreign key referencing the *employee_main* table and only because it's pulling the *emp_id* of the department supervisor or manager for reference. The departments table also allows for a company-defined department number in addition to the name.

```
CREATE TABLE `employee_main` (
  `emp_id` int(11) NOT NULL AUTO_INCREMENT,
  `badge_no` varchar(10) DEFAULT NULL,
  `first_name` varchar(25) NOT NULL,
  `last_name` varchar(25) NOT NULL,
  `mid_name` varchar(25) DEFAULT NULL,
  `photo` blob,
  `dept_id` int(11) DEFAULT NULL,
  `shift` int(11) DEFAULT NULL,
  `position_id` int(11) DEFAULT NULL,
  `hire_date` date NOT NULL,
  `start_date` date DEFAULT NULL,
  `current` bit(1) NOT NULL DEFAULT b'1',
  PRIMARY KEY (`emp_id`),
  UNIQUE KEY `badge_no_UNIQUE` (`badge_no`),
  KEY `badge_no_idx` (`badge_no`),
  KEY `last_name_idx` (`last_name`),
  KEY `dept_id_idx` (`dept_id`),
  KEY `shift_idx` (`shift`),
  KEY `hire_date_idx` (`hire_date`),
  KEY `FK_position_idx_idx` (`position_id`),
  CONSTRAINT `FK_department_idx` FOREIGN KEY (`dept_id`)
    REFERENCES `departments` (`dept_id`) ON UPDATE CASCADE,
  CONSTRAINT `FK_position_idx` FOREIGN KEY (`position_id`)
    REFERENCES `positions` (`position_id`) ON UPDATE CASCADE
) ENGINE=InnoDB DEFAULT CHARSET=utf8;
```

Finally, the foreign key constraints themselves link to the other tables in the database. The *employee_main* definition above was generated *after* all the tables and relationships were defined so it's showing relationships with other tables you haven't seen yet. On the support site for this book, you'll be able to see the actual script to create the database and tables where the script uses statements to disable the verifications of the foreign keys so that CREATE statements like this one can be run. The verifications are re-enabled after the script completes.

The portion of the diagram for training classes shows how many-to-many relationships are represented within the database.Figure 8.13 - Class and registration tables from SpheraTech's HR / Training Database

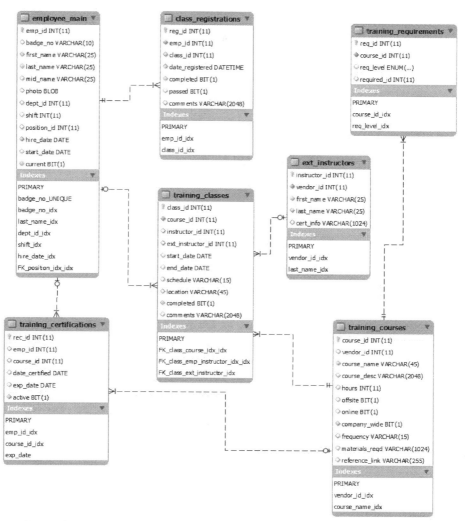

Figure 8.13 - Class and registration tables from SpheraTech's HR / Training Database

Both the *class_registrations* and *training_certifications* tables act as intervening tables to split many-to-many relationships into one-to-many relationships that can be represented.

- There will be many employees in each class and each employee will take many classes so *class_registrations* records the registration in each class for each employee as well as whether they completed and passed the course.

- Each employee will take many courses and there will be many employees taking each course so the *training_certifications* table records an employee's list of certifications and whether each one is current.

The *training_requirements* table enables the company to define required courses for either positions or entire departments as specified by the *req_level* field. The *required_id* field stores the ID of either the department or position specified.

The *training _classes* table maintains foreign keys for both an employee instructor and an external instructor, either or both of which might be used for a class. The *ext_instructors* table holds the necessary information on external instructors and links back to the *vendors* table which is not shown.

The final two tables are mostly lookup tables. The *positions* table shows a list of defined positions within the company and is referenced by the *employee_main* table. The *training_vendors* table holds contact and other reference information on the vendors who supply training curriculum and other course materials to the company.

```
CREATE TABLE `positions` (
  `position_id` int(11) NOT NULL AUTO_INCREMENT,
  `dept_id` int(11) DEFAULT NULL,
  `position_title` varchar(45) NOT NULL,
  `position_desc` varchar(2048) DEFAULT NULL,
  `pay_grade` int(11) DEFAULT NULL,
  `hourly` bit(1) DEFAULT b'1',
  `supervsiory` bit(1) DEFAULT b'0',
  PRIMARY KEY (`position_id`),
  KEY `dept_id_idx` (`dept_id`),
  KEY `pos_title_idx` (`position_title`),
  CONSTRAINT `FK_dept_id_idx` FOREIGN KEY (`dept_id`)
    REFERENCES `departments` (`dept_id`) ON UPDATE CASCADE
) ENGINE=InnoDB DEFAULT CHARSET=utf8;

CREATE TABLE `training_vendors` (
  `vendor_id` int(11) NOT NULL AUTO_INCREMENT,
  `vendor_name` varchar(45) NOT NULL,
  `address_1` varchar(35) DEFAULT NULL,
  `address_2` varchar(35) DEFAULT NULL,
  `city` varchar(25) DEFAULT NULL,
  `state_province` varchar(10) DEFAULT NULL,
  `postal_code` varchar(15) DEFAULT NULL,
  `phone` varchar(15) DEFAULT NULL,
  `fax` varchar(15) DEFAULT NULL,
```

```
`email` varchar(45) DEFAULT NULL,
`website` varchar(255) DEFAULT NULL,
PRIMARY KEY (`vendor_id`),
KEY `vendor_name_idx` (`vendor_name`),
KEY `city_idx` (`city`),
KEY `state_idx` (`state_province`)
) ENGINE=InnoDB DEFAULT CHARSET=utf8;
```

The full design of the database includes a lot of VARCHAR fields which are used for names, addresses and other text fields where there might be a lot of variation in the number of characters needed. The VARCHAR type is designed to only take up as much storage space as necessary to store the data that's actually entered into the field. So, when assigning a field size, you're actually telling the database how many characters to *allow* in the field rather than how many characters to use. It's still a good idea to use reasonable limits since a field that allows 255 characters when no more than 35 will ever be needed fails to enforce helpful limits on the data which could prevent certain errors.

The VARCHAR field will hold 64 KB of data. For a few of the description and comment fields, the team allowed 2048 characters (2 KB) which should be enough to hold a couple pages of text. The size of the field can always be increased later if the users need more space.

Figure 8.14 shows the data model as generated by MySQL Workbench. The full model is a little too large for presentation here so this diagram shows the tables and relations between them. You can view the full model online on this book's official support site listed in the introduction.

Writing the SQL

Populating the Tables

Testing is an important step in any kind of application design. With a database, that involves entering some test data to ensure the tables are going to support the actual business data they were designed for. It's not unusual to discover that a VARCHAR field needs to be lengthened or that an allowed value needs to be added to an ENUM field. The more testing is done before the database goes live with the users, the smoother things will go when it does.

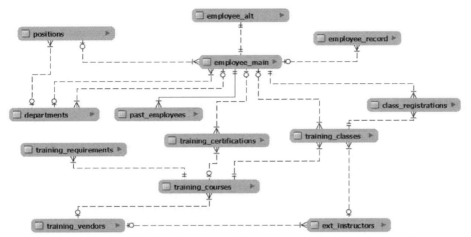

Figure 8.14 - Table-level data model as shown in MySQL Workbench

Because of the layers of foreign keys and references in this database, there's a certain order in which tables need to be populated, at least if it's to be fully tested. The *training_vendors, departments* and *positions* tables are the three that function mainly as reference tables and have the fewest dependencies so those needed a few records in order to provide lookup data for the others. In Figures 8.12 and 8.13, the darkened red and blue diamonds next to certain fields indicate that the fields are required. A quick scan of the full database diagram reveals that the following tables have required fields that are also foreign keys and therefore, the tables can only be populated *after* the parent tables.

- **employee_alt** and **training_certifications** use the *employee_main.emp_id* field..

- **class_registrations** requires the *employee_main.emp_id* and the *training_classes.class_id* values.

- **training_requirements** and **training_classes** require the *training_courses.course_id* value.

- **ext_instructors** requires the *vendors.vendor_id* value.

These six tables are therefore dependent on the parent tables being populated. The design team assigned the initial population of the tables to the reporting specialist with some help from one of the application developers and the understanding that the data would be subject to continuous change during testing. The process of populating the tables with sample data proceeded in the approximate order shown below. You can use the diagram in Figure 8.14 to follow the progression of the data.

1. Add sample data in *positions*, *departments* and *training_vendors*.

2. Add records to *ext_instructors* and *training_courses* using values from the *training_vendors* table.

3. Sample records can then be added to *training_classes* from the course data.

4. The *training_requirements* table can be populated with data referencing the *positions*, *departments* and *training_courses* tables.

5. Add employees by populating *employee_main* and then *employee_alt* for each employee.

6. Add sample data to *employee_record* using the employees from *employee_main*.

7. Record certifications for employees in the *training_certifications* table.

8. Mark at least a couple employees as having left the company in *employee_main* and create sample records in *past_employees*.

9. Schedule the remaining current employees for some training classes by adding data to *class_registrations*.

If this sounds like a complex and time-consuming process, it is. While there are tools that will generate random data for testing database tables, there's really no substitute for entering data resembling what the tables are going to hold in real life and making changes based on realistic scenarios and that simply takes a bit of time. The advantage is that you get another perspective on how the data is going to flow through the application and how the application needs to process it. For example, the team noticed from the final steps above that programming was needed to limit training class registrations to current employees. They also noticed that the program needed some kind of process to cancel class registrations for an employee who leaves the company for whatever reason before the class is completed.

Reporting Queries

With some test data in the tables, the team started writing the queries for the requested reports. The first view designed was for an employee contact list requested by the Human Resources department.

```
CREATE VIEW current_employee_contact_list AS

SELECT
  concat(em.last_name, ', ', em.first_name, ' ', em.mid_name) AS
'Employee Name',
  em.badge_no AS Badge,
  concat (d.dept_number, ' - ', d.dept_name) AS 'Department',
  em.shift, p.position_title,
  ea.address_1, ea.city,
  ea.state_province, ea.postal_code,
  ea.phone_1, ea.phone_2, ea.email, em.emp_id
FROM employee_main em
LEFT JOIN employee_alt ea
  ON ea.emp_id = em.emp_id
LEFT JOIN departments d
  ON d.dept_id = em.dept_id
LEFT JOIN positions p
  ON p.position_id = em.position_id
WHERE em.`current`<> 0;
```

The *current_employee_contact_list* view provides a list of current employees, some basic position details and contact information. The view gathers fields from four different tables into one recordset and has a few features that you need to be familiar with.

The CONCAT() function is a SQL function which concatenates multiple string values into one. It's used twice here to create fields from combinations of other fields. This enables the report writers to pull values together from different tables and fields and present them as needed on reports.

```
concat(em.last_name, ', ', em.first_name, ' ', em.mid_name) AS
'Employee Name', ...
+-------------------------+
| Employee Name           |
+-------------------------+
| Jones, Stephen A.       |
+-------------------------+
```

Column aliases, i.e. 'Employee Name' and 'Department' are used to provide labels for the fields in the resulting recordset. This is a good practice to use. Note that the single quotes are used around the 'Employee Name' alias. This is required because of the space while the 'Department' alias works fine without them. The current field in the WHERE statement is enclosed in backticks. Note that these are not the same as single quotes and are found to the left of the '1' number key on many Windows keyboards. While the view was being typed in, the color coding in MySQL Workbench indicated that 'Current' was a reserved SQL word so the backquotes are used to indicate a field name.

As detailed in the last section, the *current* field is a BIT field that is defined to hold a 1 or 0. The WHERE clause specifies all records where the field *does not* equal 0 in order to limit the recordset to current employees. It might seem that a positive test for a value of 1 would make more sense but testing for *not zero* is actually a good habit to get into when testing for True / False values. This is because some systems might use triple-state values of 1, -1 and 0 or the designer might have used a TINYINT field and values other than 1 might have been written for True. Therefore, when looking for True values, it's safer to use the "<> 0" syntax that says 'Show me anything that isn't marked as False.'

Once the view is in place, it can be called as needed to retrieve the information. Views can also be assigned separate security permissions to grant a group of users the information they need from a database while restricting the main table.

The next report was a list of previous employees who could be considered for re-hire.

```
SELECT concat(em.last_name, ', ', em.first_name) as 'Employee Name',
   em.badge_no AS 'Badge', concat (d.dept_number, ' - ', d.dept_name)
as 'Department',
   em.shift, p.position_title AS 'Position Title', ea.address_1,
ea.city, ea.state_province,
   ea.postal_code, ea.phone_1, ea.phone_2, ea.email
FROM employee_main em
LEFT JOIN employee_alt ea
   ON ea.emp_id = em.emp_id
LEFT JOIN departments d
   ON d.dept_id = em.dept_id
LEFT JOIN positions p
   ON p.position_id = em.position_id
WHERE em.`current`<> 0;
```

Again, the CONCAT() function is used to return the employee name in a single field. This time, the query references the *past_employees* table, a WHERE clause uses the *employee_main.current* field to limit the recordset to past employees and the *past_employees.rehire* to find employees the company is able to bring back. An ORDER BY clause sorts the results by the termination date with the last employees to leave first.

Employee Name	DeptName	PositionTitle	TermDate	TermType
Donaldson, Jerry M	Manufacturing	Inspector	2013-02-09	Quit

Figure 8.15 - Example results of the past employees query

In addition to learning how to construct queries in SQL, it's also important that you are able to read and decipher queries like the ones shown above. One of my past challenges was developing the patience to read other people's code. Even if you don't end up working with a team of developers, there is always the chance you will find yourself searching the Internet for instructions on how to write the query that you need to design your latest report. You will need to be accustomed to reading SQL and maybe other languages in order to recognize and use the answers you need. Also, understand that every developer has their own writing and formatting style and many developers do not break the code down into the neat one-clause-per-line format as I have.

```
SELECT CONCAT(em.last_name, ', ', em.first_name) AS 'Employee Name',
   d.dept_name, p.position_title, er.record_date, er.action_type,
er.notes
FROM employee_main em
INNER JOIN employee_record er
   ON er.emp_id = em.emp_id
```

```
LEFT JOIN departments d
  ON d.dept_id = em.dept_id
LEFT JOIN positions p
  ON p.position_id = em.position_id
WHERE er.record_date > SUBDATE(NOW(), INTERVAL 91 DAY)
ORDER BY em.last_name, record_date DESC;
```

The above query uses the *employee_record* table to show all the activity recorded by Human Resources for employees over the past 90 days. It uses the `SUBDATE()` function in the `WHERE` clause to limit the query to records where RecordDate is greater than the current date minus 91 days. The query then sorts first by the employee's last name and then by the date recorded in *descending* order. So the list goes from A to Z on the employee names and then for each employee, the most recent activities are shown first. The sort order is specified for each field listed in the `ORDER BY` clause with ascending (ASC) as the default.

This query could actually be simplified a little by adding the *EmpID* field to the *CurrentEmployeeContactList* view shown earlier and using that view to replace a couple table joins.

```
SELECT cl.`Employee Name`, cl.Department, cl.position_title AS
'Position Title',
  er.record_date, er.action_type, er.notes
FROM employee_main em
INNER JOIN employee_record er
  ON er.emp_id = em.emp_ID
LEFT JOIN current_employee_contact_list cl
  ON cl.emp_id = em.emp_id
WHERE er.record_date > SUBDATE(NOW(), INTERVAL 91 DAY)
ORDER BY em.last_name, record_date DESC;
```

The *current_employee_contact_list* view referenced above already supplies the employee name in the single field as desired along with the department names and position titles. The benefits of this are mixed since the view that's being called still has to do its own processing and this might actually increase the actual burden on the server. It's possible, however, to write views that supply commonly requested values expressly for this purpose. In addition to simplifying later queries, it provides a consistent source of information to different reports.

The next query returns a list of employees currently certified as internal instructors and the courses they are certified to teach.

```
SELECT cl.`Employee Name`, cl.Department, tc.course_name
FROM current_employee_contact_list cl
LEFT JOIN training_certifications cert
  ON cert.emp_id = cl.emp_id
LEFT JOIN training_courses tc
  ON tc.course_id = cert.course_id
WHERE cert.active <> 0
AND cert.exp_date > NOW();
```

The query starts out with the *current_employee_contact_list* view which effectively limits the recordset to current employees without having to specify it further. It then links to the certifications and courses tables although only the *training_courses* table provides another field for the recordset. The certification table is used in the WHERE clause to limit the employees to those who have certifications which have not expired and are not marked as inactive for any other reason. This demonstrates the need to be thorough in WHERE clauses and take into account all conditions that might affect the data that you're reading or changing.

The database design was really put to the test when it was time to write a query to determine the training requirements that had not yet been satisfied for a specific employee. This meant retrieving requirements for both the relevant department and position and subtracting those that were already met.

```
SELECT course_name AS `Course Name` FROM
  (SELECT tc.course_id, tc.course_name, em.emp_id
    FROM training_requirements trDept
    INNER JOIN employee_main em
    ON em.dept_id = trDept.required_id
    INNER JOIN training_courses tc
    ON tc.course_id = trDept.course_id
    WHERE trDept.req_level = 'Department'
    AND em.emp_id = 2

    UNION

    SELECT tc.course_id, tc.course_name, em.emp_id
    FROM training_requirements trPos
    INNER JOIN employee_main em
    ON em.position_id = trPos.required_id
    INNER JOIN training_courses tc
    ON tc.course_id = trPos.course_id
    WHERE trPos.req_level = 'Position'
    AND em.emp_id = 2)

  AS ReqUnion
```

```
WHERE ReqUnion.emp_id = 2
AND ReqUnion.course_id NOT IN
  (SELECT course_id FROM training_classes tc
   INNER JOIN class_registrations cr
   ON cr.class_id = tc.class_id
   WHERE cr.emp_id = 2
   AND cr.completed <> 0
   AND cr.passed <> 0);
```

A query this large almost needs to start with its own algorithm or series of steps that it needs to follow to achieve a result. In this case, the algorithm could be stated as follows:

1. Create a union query with two `SELECT` statements; the first to retrieve the department-level training requirements for a specific employee and the second to retrieve the position-level requirements. Select the *CourseID* and CourseName fields for each requirement and include the employee ID.

2. From the completed union query, select a distinct list of *course_name* values.

3. In the WHERE clause, narrow the recordset by a specific employee ID.

4. Also in the WHERE clause, use a subquery to specify a list of courses already completed by the employee. Use the NOT IN condition to exclude these courses from the final list returned.

As you can see above, a union query is useful when the specifications for the data to be retrieved included a large number of variables. Each of the statements in the above union query join to the same tables but one joins on the *employee_main.dept_id* and the other joins on the position_id field in order to pull the right data. Pay particular attention to the portions of the query in **bold** to see the differences.

The union query is then enclosed in parentheses and treated as a subquery. Its results are given the alias of *ReqUnion* so that they can be referenced in the rest of the query. The main query in the example simply returns the course names and refers to other fields returned by the union query in the `WHERE` statement as stated in the algorithm steps. The `IN` / `NOT IN` condition statements are particularly useful and powerful when it comes to quickly searching a query result for a specific value.

Because the query is referencing the entire employee table, it could accept another value like the badge number and use that to specify the correct employee but using the table's primary key is the surest way to get the right person's information. The application using the database can be programmed to retrieve this value as needed in order to reference the correct record.

This example query would only represent the "proof of concept" that the data could be retrieved from the tables while they were being tested. The *emp_id* field is stated multiple times in the query and subqueries and, in everyday use, this would lead to errors if all but one of the references were changed. A query like this would belong in a stored procedure which could accept the employee ID as a parameter and reference that parameter throughout the procedure as shown below.

```
DELIMITER $$
CREATE PROCEDURE `IncompleteTraining` (EmployeeID INT)
BEGIN
SELECT course_name AS `Course Name` FROM
  (SELECT tc.course_id, tc.course_name, em.emp_id
    FROM training_requirements trDept
    INNER JOIN employee_main em
    ON em.dept_id = trDept.required_id
    INNER JOIN training_courses tc
    ON tc.course_id = trDept.course_id
    WHERE trDept.req_level = 'Department'
    AND em.emp_id = EmployeeID

  ...

END $$
```

Once this procedure is present in the database, it can be called either through a program like MySQL Workbench or from an external program to retrieve the recordset.

```
call IncompleteTraining(2);
```

Conclusion

In a database of this size and complexity, the design process will probably continue for a while. The business and the system designers will need to work out the user interface that will be feeding data to the database, the full range of data that needs to be stored and the reports that are needed for various functions. As stated early on, the business quickly came up with a list of things that would be nice to have and some of the things on that list might yet end up in this application while others will eventually go into different databases that could still be linked to this one. Still, with the care taken to anticipate business needs and the communication that was maintained between everyone involved, this database serves as a good foundation on which to continue building.

For Further Study

Exercises

1. Review the section on table indexes in Chapter VI and then refer to the portion of the data model shown in Figure 8.12. This model shows a few of the indexes placed on the tables but not all of them.
    - Which fields would you index for faster searches and sorting?
    - Would you create any unique indexes other than the primary keys?
    - Are there any combinations of fields that can be used as composite indexes?
2. The Human Resources Manager wants to start using the database to store the details of annual personnel reviews. What tables would you create to handle this and how would you integrate them into the data model from Figure 8.14? The printed review reports must include the following, either from existing information or the tables you add:

- o Employee Name
- o Department
- o Supervisor / Department Head
- o Job Title
- o Date of review
- o Review categories such as 'Policy Compliance', 'Attendance', 'Teamwork' along with numeric ratings.
- o Supervisor and employee comments
- o Indicators of employee, supervisor and HR sign-off.

3. Write SQL queries to get the following information:
   - o The count of employees per department
   - o A list of employees, their department names, and job titles sorted by department name and employee last name
   - o A list of current employees who do not have any notes in the *employee_record* table.

Chapter IX

Design Overview: Recipe Database

Introduction

I've previously mentioned the importance of testing an application before turning it over to the users. Some of the most rigorous testing an application will receive is when the database designer is creating it for his or her own work. In this example, the owners of a small start-up business decide to combine some design experience with extensive experience in their own field to create their dream application.

Allen and Cindy both have a passion for cooking and have started catering small functions for friends and family. They each have a sizeable collection of recipes either in books or online and decided that they could be far more efficient in their catering work if all the recipes were available in a searchable database. While there are programs they could buy, Cindy has some experience designing databases for other companies and wants a program that will be specific to their own needs. She's also done a little work with MySQL and likes it as a free and open source solution.

Cindy and Allen sat down with some of their favorite recipes to decide on the requirements for the system.

- The program must be able to store detailed recipes with nutritional and other information for retrieval and printing. Printed and e-mailed reports will be needed to review recipes with the other organizers of the functions they'll be catering.

- Recipes need to be categorized for quick retrieval and searchable by major ingredients. Some clients might have special dietary needs and limitations so recipes will need to be marked for conformance to specific diet plans and tagged with warnings about potential allergies.

- The database should be able to store potential substitutions for any ingredients that might be unavailable or inappropriate for a specific function. Substitution ratios or other notes need to be stored as well.

- The database should be able to store comments and ongoing notes on various recipes.

- Multiple versions of the same recipe might be stored within the database and there should be some way to link related recipes.

- The database must be able to supply a list of ingredients in the form of a shopping list.

Modeling the Data

Recipe Information
Recipe Title
Author
Description
Prep Time
Cook Time
Servings
Difficulty (1-5)
Substitution
Directions
Source
Category
Photo
Modified From
Related recipes

Ingredients
    Amount
    Measure
    Ingredient

Nutritional Information (per serving)
Serving Size
Calories
Saturated Fat
Total Fat
Cholesterol
Sodium
Carbs
Fiber
Protein
Sugars

Allergies and Warnings

Tags

Comments

Figure 9.1 - Listing the data requirements is a good starting point for most relational databases.

The list of information to be stored in Figure 9.1 already indicates a few relationships in the data model so, while Allen reviews the recipe collections for anything they might have missed, Cindy starts mapping out the data model.

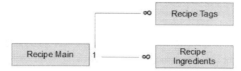

Figure 9.2 – The conceptual model can start with the core information and grow outward.

There are three entities involved in the recipe itself with a one-to-many relationship between the main recipe containing the title, prep times and other top-level information and the list of ingredients. Since the resulting database will need to search on ingredients, each ingredient line should be stored as a separate record instead of in a single list with all the other ingredients. The 'Recipe Tags' entity is meant to support tags of one or two words each that Allen and Cindy can search on for various types of recipes. While each recipe will have one main category, there will be an indefinite number of tags such as 'low carb', 'holiday' or 'chocolate'. Therefore this object is added with a one-to-many relationship.

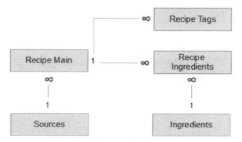

Figure 9.3 – The need for supporting information is more clear when related to the core concepts in the model.

Cindy adds two more entities to the model to cover the supplemental information for recipe sources and the information on ingredients themselves that doesn't relate to their use in a recipe such as the ingredient description.

Although it's not directly shown, you might notice in Figure 9.3 that there's actually a many-to-many relationship within the model between the 'Recipe Main' and 'Ingredients' entities; there will be many ingredients on each recipe and many recipes might use each ingredient. This relationship, which cannot be directly represented in a relational database, is resolved by the 'Recipe Ingredients' entity which splits the relationship into two one-to-many relationships.

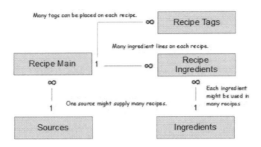

Figure 9.4 – Even in a familiar process, clear documentation is important and this extends to the conceptual model.

As shown in Figure 9.4, a few notes add the finishing touches to the current conceptual model of the database. Even though this database represents an independent project outside a formal development environment, it's a good idea to have good documentation for reference. It also happens that Allen and Cindy have already been talking about the possible future of this database as a marketable software product or the back end for a website and Cindy's keeping all the notes she can.

In Figure 9.5, Cindy has distributed the required attributes from the original list throughout the model which results in the addition of more prospective tables.

- The nutritional information relates directly to the recipe but not all recipes will have it or they might have only some of it so this data is split off into its own table with a one-to-one relationship to the main recipe table.

- There was some discussion about how many photos would be needed per recipe. Cindy and Allen decided to just include one good photo per recipe to save some time. This meant the photos would be stored with the main recipe instead of in their own table. If more photos are kept later, the fields can easily be split off to another table and the data can be moved with a single query.

- Multiple recipes might use the same source such as a cookbook or website but have different authors so there is a field for both in the main recipe table.

- One important feature of the new database is the ability to mark recipes with food warnings such as allergies. It made sense to place these warnings on individual ingredients so that the resulting program can use a recipe's ingredients to search the Food Warnings table for any possible aversions such as peanut or shellfish allergies. Also, by linking the warnings to the ingredients, individual ingredients can be tagged with new warnings as new concerns are identified with specific foods. This is easier than searching potentially hundreds of recipes for multiple ingredients.

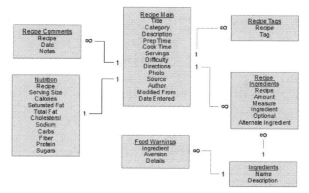

Figure 9.5 – Once the concepts are mapped out, organizing the data to be stored is sometimes just a matter of putting everything in its place.

Figure 9.6 adds three new supporting tables to the model:

- *Categories*, a lookup table for specifying the categories to be referenced by recipes

- *Units* for the measurement units referenced

- *Sources* for a list of sites and other resources for new recipes.

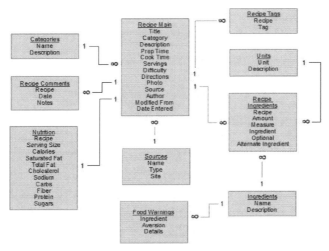

Figure 9.6 – As in the conceptual phase, the logical diagram can grow from the central concepts outward.

Now that the data model covers all the necessary information, the next step is to ensure that the prospective tables conform to rules of database normalization. Cindy updates the model with the table and field names she wants. She then breaks a few fields down into smaller fields and adds the necessary table keys that will be used to relate the tables to each other.

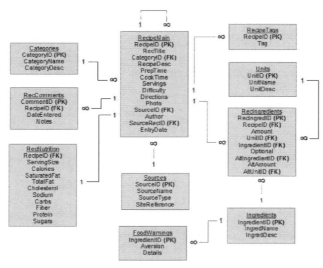

Figure 9.7 – The addition of primary and foreign keys and formal field names makes the model look more like a database.

At this point, as sometimes happens, the data model has fallen naturally into the Third Normal Form. To see how this has worked, let's review the forms as they apply to this model.

First Normal Form (1NF) - *"All fields within the tables represent single data values that have been reduced to the smallest useful pieces of information. Fields cannot contain multiple values and tables cannot have repeating fields or groups of fields. A table should not have multiple fields for the same attribute for the purpose of tracking multiple items."*

In Figure 9.7, all of the information has been broken down into its basic parts. The last field that really needed to be broken out was the alternate ingredient in the *RecIngredients* table which is now split between three fields holding the amount, unit and Ingredient ID for the alternate ingredient.

Second Normal Form (2NF) - *"The database must be in First Normal Form and all fields that are not part of a table's key must be functionally dependent on the entire key."*

This database has a lot of auto-incrementing surrogate keys that are automatically managed by the database. Therefore, it's good to think of the table's *subject* when deciding what information is actually dependent on that table. The Second Normal Form was pretty much ensured during the process of distributing the attributes to be stored between the objects in the original data model. Using her previous normalization experience, Cindy was able to build on the conceptual model by assigning the various attributes such as the recipe source and the calorie count to the right prospective tables.

Third Normal Form (3NF) - *"The database must be in Second Normal Form and all fields that are not part of the key must be functionally independent of each other."*

There are a couple of places in the model that could have lent themselves to calculated fields such as the saturated fat and total fat counts in the *RecNutrition* table or the preparation and cooking times in the main recipe table but the data model didn't go there. These are also static values that are not likely to change once entered for a specific recipe.

Design Notes

At this point, the thing bothering Cindy most about the data model was the *RecIngredients* table with its three fields for the alternate ingredient. After thinking about how the recipes are going to be entered, she realized that it's inefficient and a little limiting. The majority of recipe ingredient records might not have alternate ingredients to list so these fields will be blank for a lot of the records. Also, it only allows for one possible alternative where some items might have more than one possible substitute. This could be seen as a conflict with the Boyce-Codd Normal Form which looks for multiple potential primary keys in the same table.

A possible solution would be to split off these fields into a separate table related to the *RecIngredients* table. This would allow multiple alternative ingredients to be stored and then only when needed. This still limits the system, however. For example, if buttermilk is listed on a recipe as a possible substitute for yogurt, that substitution might work on many other recipes containing yogurt. It won't be seen, however, since it's tied to that specific recipe so it has to be entered for each recipe where it's allowed.

The other solution that Cindy finally decided to try was to create a *Substitutions* table and relate it directly to the Ingredients table. That way, whenever an ingredient shows up on a recipe, the system can do a query to find any possible substitutions that can be applied.

The other minor design question came up when Cindy looked at the model and realized that there was no entry date on individual recipes. This meant there was no way to search on the date when a recipe was entered. The idea of adding a manual date field seemed like one more field to fill out and didn't really seem relevant to the idea of a recipe but it was still needed. The solution was to add a field to the *RecipeMain* table that would default to the current date. This field would not even need to appear on forms and reports but would automatically fill when recipes were entered and could be searched on.

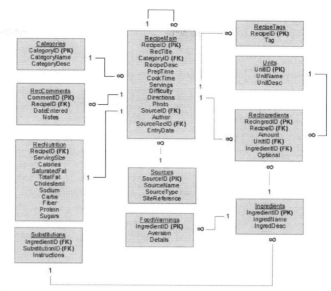

Figure 9.8 – Design changes are easier in the modeling stage than after the database has been constructed.

Working Diagram

Figure 9.9 shows the relationships diagram for the recipe database in MySQL Workbench. The working model now appears to have all the fields it needs in order to support the requirements mentioned earlier.

- The model will accommodate entire recipes and supporting information that can be put into reports for printing and e-mailing.

- With the right SQL queries, the proposed model will allow for recipe searches by category, tags and ingredients. Tags such as 'Party', 'Kid favorite' or 'Low Sodium' can be used to mark the recipes themselves for specific uses. Individual ingredients can be marked for potential food sensitivities.

- The *substitutions* table is able to store any alternate ingredients that can be used.

- The *rec_comments* table can store unlimited comments and notes on any recipe.

- The *recipe_main.source_rec_id* field will be a numeric field that can store the ID of a source recipe. This will enable searches for all recipes derived from a single recipe or a search to find the origin of a specific recipe.

- A simple query can pull the list of ingredients for one or more recipes and present it as a shopping list.

There are a few features in this database that you haven't seen in previous examples. For one, the *recipe_main* table actually has a self-join where the *source_rec_id* field is linked back to the table's primary key so that recipes can be identified as variations of other recipes. In the table's CREATE statement, this looks like any other foreign key with the exception that a cascade deletion is specified.

```
CONSTRAINT `FK_recipes_source_rec` FOREIGN KEY (`source_rec_id`)
  REFERENCES `recipe_main` (`recipe_id`) ON DELETE CASCADE ON UPDATE
CASCADE,
```

The *rec_ingredients* table, which lists the ingredients for each recipe and has a parent-child relationship with *recipe_main*, uses the DECIMAL data type which allows for non-integer numbers such as are needed when specifying measures like half and quarter tablespoons or two-thirds of a cup. This data type also enables the resulting application to adjust the proportions for a recipe based on how many servings are needed. The portion of the data type in parentheses specifies the number of digits allowed in the field. The first value is known as the *precision* and indicates the number of digits overall and the second value, the *scale*, indicates the number of digits that will follow the decimal point. Therefore the definition DECIMAL(6,2) allows a value up to 9999.99 whereas, if values with up to three decimal points were needed, a definition of DECIMAL(7,3) would be required. In MySQL, the NUMERIC data type functions the same as DECIMAL. The *units* table supplies the unit names for *rec_ingredients* such as "each", "cup", "pint", "pound", etc..

There are a few fields that serve as examples where some restriction on the allowed values might be needed but none is actually provided by the database. Figure 9.9 - The MySQL Workbench relationships diagram for the recipe database

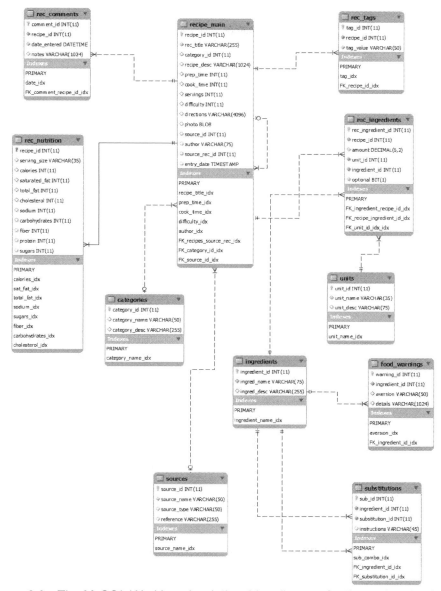

Figure 9.9 - The MySQL Workbench relationships diagram for the recipe database

The level of difficulty in a recipe shown in the *recipe_main.difficulty* field is represented by an integer which could be on a scale of 1 to 5 or 1 to 10 depending on the person designing the app. An ENUM field could be used instead to allow for these values but the Enum type only stores text values which might cause problems when sorting. A lookup table would be overkill for a series of numeric values unless it included a field with descriptions of the difficulty level such as the years of experience needed. Another option is to simply have whatever program is populating this field limit the values that can be entered with a drop down field or a slider control.

The *food_warnings.aversion* and the *rec_tags.tag_value* fields, on the other hand, need to be flexible in accepting new values such as when a new dietary restriction such as "gluten-free" or "organic" becomes popular. At the same time, some validation is needed on the field so the database doesn't end up with variations and mis-spellings that make searching difficult. Again, this is where the program can do some of the work by presenting the user with values that have previously been entered or using controls that provide auto-completion based on these values. Whether to perform validation at the database level or at the program level is the kind of design choice that's common in application design.

Finally, notice the double relationship between the *ingredients* and *substitutions* tables with both the original and substitution ingredient in a record looking back to the ingredients table. This will require both ingredients to be available but also ensure the integrity of the data. A unique index, *sub_combo_idx*, ensures that the same substitution will not be entered twice.

Writing the SQL

Populating the Tables

The *recipe_main* table has only *one* required field and that's the title. While it might not seem very useful to have a recipe record with only a title, this allows for the data to be filled in as it's available and for flexibility in the input queries.

```
INSERT INTO recipe_main (rec_title) VALUES ('Chicken Marsala');

INSERT INTO recipe_main (rec_title, prep_time, cook_time,
directions)
```

```
VALUES ('Absolute Brownies', 25, 35, 'Preheat oven to 350 degrees
F ...');
```

The *recipe_main* table only has two foreign dependencies, *categories* and *sources* which are both small lookup tables that can be populated quickly in order to provide the references for a couple of quick recipes.

To fully test the database, it would be best to populate the dependency tables for both the *recipe_main* and *rec_ingredients* tables. Refer to Figure 9.9 to see how the steps below would impact the individual tables.

1. Add records to the *categories*, *sources*, *units* and *ingredients* tables.
2. Add data to the *food_warnings* and substitutions tables for existing ingredients.
3. Enter the first few recipes in *recipe_main* and then add corresponding records in *rec_nutrition*.
4. Add records to *rec_comments* and *rec_tags*, referencing the existing recipes.
5. Finally, add ingredients for the existing recipes in the *rec_ingredients* table, referencing the *ingredients* and *units* tables previously populated.

In the application that runs off of this database, the *categories* and *units* tables might be pre-populated when the program is first installed with the ability to edit them as needed through the program itself. The user would likely have the option of entering data in the *ingredients*, *sources*, *food_warnings* and *substitutions* tables either separately or when entering new items as part of a recipe.

Basic Queries

For the examples, let's start with a couple of queries to create a basic printout of a recipe.

```
SELECT RM.recipe_id, RM.rec_title, RM.recipe_desc, RM.prep_time,
   RM.cook_time, RM.servings, RM.directions, RM.photo, RN.*
FROM recipe_main RM
```

```
LEFT JOIN rec_nutrition RN
  ON RN.recipe_id = RM.recipe_id
WHERE RM.rec_title = 'Chicken Marsala';
```

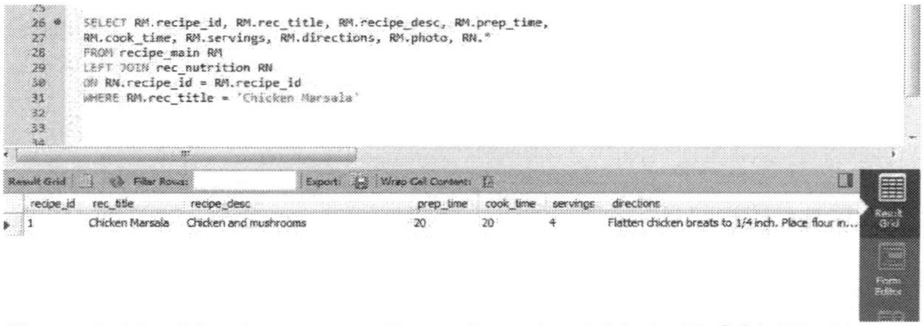

Figure 9.10 - A basic query on the main recipe table in MySQL Workbench

Using this query, it's easy to retrieve basic information for a recipe by title. The list of fields selected includes key fields from *recipe_main* and all fields from *rec_nutrition* as shown by the wildcard character. The WHERE statement determines which recipes will be pulled and could use a few different options in order to find the right one.

```
WHERE RM.rec_title LIKE '%chicken%'
```

```
WHERE RM.prep_time < 30
```

```
WHERE RN.calories < 300
```

Now we can retrieve the ingredients by referencing the ingredients tables and the units lookup. The following query uses a different method to join the three tables involved than you've seen previously; it uses the WHERE clause instead of JOIN statements. This is an older method for declaring Inner Joins in which only records where the primary / foreign key value shows up in both of the joined tables will be selected.

```
SELECT RI.amount, U.unit_name, I.ingred_name, RI.optional
FROM recipe_main RM, rec_ingredients RI, ingredients I, units U
WHERE RI.recipe_id = RM.recipe_id
AND RI.ingredient_id = I.ingredient_id
AND RI.unit_id = U.unit_id
AND RM.rec_title = 'Chicken Marsala';
```

While this syntax still works, it does not represent the current standard and is not recommended because it can cause confusion within the queries. I use it in this example because you might see it when you're reading queries written by other developers who prefer it or older queries that were written when it was more often used. The query is better written as follows so that the `WHERE` statements are reserved for filtering the data, making it easier to see what the query will return.

```
SELECT RI.amount, U.unit_name, I.ingred_name, RI.optional
FROM rec_ingredients RI
LEFT JOIN ingredients I
  ON RI.ingredient_id = I.ingredient_id
LEFT JOIN units U
  ON RI.unit_id = U.unit_id
WHERE RI.recipe_id = 1;
```

By reading through the query, you can now get a clear view of how the tables are being joined and how the records are being filtered so that only the ingredients for the recipe in Figure 9.11 are returned. These results are shown in OpenOffice Base, a free desktop database software from Oracle that can link to MySQL data and other database formats.

	amount	unit_name	ingred_name	optional
▷	4.00	Each	Chicken breast halves, boneless	
	2.00	Tablespoon(s)	Flour	
	2.00	Tablespoon(s)	Olive oil	
	2.00	Cup(s)	Sliced mushrooms	
	2.00	Tablespoon(s)	Butter	
	0.75	Cup(s)	Marsala wine	
	0.25	Teaspoon(s)	Rosemary, dried and crushed	
	2.00	Tablespoon(s)	Parsley, minced	
	2.00	Tablespoon(s)	Parmesan cheese, grated	✓

Record 1 of 9

```
SELECT RI.amount, U.unit_name, I.ingred_name, RI.optional
FROM rec_ingredients RI
LEFT JOIN ingredients I
ON RI.ingredient_id = I.ingredient_id
LEFT JOIN units U
ON RI.unit_id = U.unit_id
WHERE RI.recipe_id = 1;
```

Figure 9.11 - The results of the ingredient query as accessed with OpenOffice Base.

The query output in Figure 9.11 shows the ingredients and marks any optional ones but what about the available substitutions that posed a design challenge earlier? For this, another join is necessary. In the data model, the *ingredients* table was joined to both the *rec_ingredients* and *substitution* tables so that both could retrieve ingredient information as needed. Because of this, the *ingredients* table needs to show up twice so that the query can join both of the tables to it.

```
SELECT RI.amount, U.unit_name, I.ingred_name, RI.optional,
I1.ingred_name AS 'Substitution', S.instructions
```

```
FROM rec_ingredients RI
LEFT JOIN ingredients I
  ON RI.ingredient_id = I.ingredient_id
LEFT JOIN substitutions S
  ON S.ingredient_id = RI.ingredient_id
LEFT JOIN ingredients I1
  ON S.substitution_id = I1.ingredient_id
LEFT JOIN units U
  ON RI.unit_id = U.unit_id
WHERE RI.recipe_id = 1;
```

In this new query, the *ingredients* table is joined to both the *rec_ingredients* and *substitutions* tables to supply the necessary information. Figure 9.12 shows a simple diagram for these relationships.

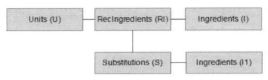

Figure 9.12 - Tables can be used more than once in a query under different joins and aliases.

By having the *ingredients* table in the query twice, under separate aliases, the query can retrieve the ingredient names for both the regular ingredients and the one substitution ingredient based on separate joins. When the query is run, the resulting recordset clearly shows the ingredient list with the available substitution.

amount	unit_name	ingred_name	optional	Substitution	instructions
0.75	Cup(s)	Marsala wine	0	Chicken broth	One for one substitution
4.00	Each	Chicken breast halves, boneless	0	NULL	NULL
2.00	Tablespoon(s)	Flour	0	NULL	NULL
2.00	Tablespoon(s)	Olive oil	0	NULL	NULL
2.00	Cup(s)	Sliced mushrooms	0	NULL	NULL
2.00	Tablespoon(s)	Butter	0	NULL	NULL
0.25	Teaspoon(s)	Rosemary, dried and crushed	0	NULL	NULL
2.00	Tablespoon(s)	Parsley, minced	0	NULL	NULL
2.00	Tablespoon(s)	Parmesan cheese, grated	1	NULL	NULL

Figure 9.13 - The modified ingredients list with substitutions

Because the ingredient substitutions are listed in their own table and linked to the Ingredients table, *any* recipe that calls for Marsala wine will now show an option to substitute chicken broth. Whether or not it works in a specific recipe is, of course, up to the cook. Best of all, the substitution only has to be stated *once* instead of on every recipe and that's one of the main benefits of database normalization - elimination of redundant data, also known as *"write it once"*.

So, with some relatively simple queries, there is now enough information from the tables to create a recipe that can be printed out or written to a file for e-mailing.

Figure 9.14 - Retrieved information can be used to produce reports for presentation and reference. (Simulated)

Custom Searches

Aside from generating print-outs, being able to search for recipes is an important feature in this system. The data model makes it simple enough to search on either categories or specific tags.

```
SELECT rec_title, recipe_desc, prep_time, cook_time
FROM recipe_main RM
LEFT OUTER JOIN categories C
  ON C.category_id = RM.category_id
WHERE C.category_name = 'Desserts';
```

In this query, the join is being done to the *categories* table which supplies the CategoryID key value. Therefore, the join is saying "Start with the *recipe_main* table and perform an outer join to the *categories* table, joining on the *category_id* field in both tables.". Then the WHERE clause works across this join to filter the results on records where the *category_name* field in categories equals 'Desserts'.

To search on tags, the following query starts with the *recipe_main* table and joining on the *recipe_id* field in both *recipe_main* and *recipe_tags*. Since *recipe_main* supplies the key value and is on the left side of the relationship, it uses a Left Outer Join.

```
SELECT rec_title, recipe_desc, prep_time, cook_time
FROM recipe_main RM
LEFT OUTER JOIN rec_tags RT
ON RT.recipe_id = RM.recipe_id
WHERE RT.tag_value = 'Pasta';
```

In these particular queries, the direction actually doesn't really matter and they each work with either Left or Right Joins but in more complicated queries, especially when working with large sets of data, it might make a great deal of difference so it's a good idea to remember how they work.

Finally, there's the table for storing warnings about allergies and other food sensitivities.

```
SELECT I.ingred_name, FW.aversion, FW.details
FROM food_warnings FW
INNER JOIN ingredients I
  ON I.ingredient_id = FW.ingredient_id
WHERE I.ingredient_id IN
(SELECT ingredient_id FROM rec_ingredients
   WHERE rec_title = 'Crab Rangoon');
```

The above query uses a subquery and an Inner Join to retrieve all of the food sensitivities listed for the ingredients on a specific recipe. The Inner Join links the *food_warnings* and *ingredients* tables and we only need to see *ingredient_id* values that are listed in both tables so an Inner Join is just fine. The subquery supplies a list of ingredient IDs on a specific recipe and the main query uses that list to search for food warnings on the correct IDs.

For Further Study

Exercises

1. On the sample recipe, notice that the amounts include values such as '3/4' and '1/4'. While these are valid amounts, fractions cannot be stored as numeric values in the database without converting them to decimal values (3/4 = 0.75, etc..). Doing so, however, would change the the way they appear on the recipe. '0.25 teaspoon(s)', while accurate and not difficult to convert, is not a user-friendly way to present the ingredient line when measuring equipment typically uses fractions.

   o This problem could be resolved with the use of a programming function that would convert fractions to decimals. Assuming the database software does not have such a function and one cannot be written in that software, how would you change the table structure and relationships to provide a solution. Remember the Third Normal Form and it's prohibition on calculated fields and non-key fields dependant on each other.

   o If you have a solution to the first problem, take it a step further and modify the data model to ensure that whatever program uses this database has enough information to scale recipes so that a recipe designed to serve four people can be automatically updated to serve eight, 12 or 100 people.

   o Evaluate this data model to determine if it will accommodate metric as well as U.S. standard measurements.

2. Using the available data model, write the following SQL queries and commands:

- o A set of queries to return *all* information on a specific recipe including main details, ingredients, recipe tags, nutrition, comments, food warnings and any available substitutions. Use as few queries as possible and design them to provide the information to a printed report that can use subreports to represent information in related tables. For an extra challenge, remember to use aliases on the field names that are returned so that the raw query results will be more readable.

- o INSERT and UPDATE commands for each of the tables in the data model. Determine which inserts need to be done first to support foreign key relationships in other tables.

- o A SELECT query that would supply enough information to create an index of all recipes in the system with recipe name, category and all tag values. The index should be sorted first by tag value and then by category.

3. The current model enables each recipe to reference *one* other recipe as having inspired it. Cookbooks and recipe databases often use a one-to-many relationship between recipes however, with each recipe citing not only the recipe that inspired it but other similar recipes. How would you change this model to allow for this in the database?

4. Write queries that could be used to identify recipes as "low-sodium" or "low-calorie" based on entries in the *rec_nutrition* table and to insert the necessary tags in the *rec_tag* table for multiple recipes.

Chapter X

User Interfaces

Beyond the Database

In the previous chapters, the focus has been on database design for a new application. At this point, you're probably wondering where the data entry forms and polished reports come in. The view of the database just isn't complete without a look at how these tables and queries can be presented to the end user.

This is where the process starts moving from the area of database design to user interface development. Once the database is ready to be used by more than the original developer, a user interface is required in order to make it easier for all the users to access and update the information as needed. A really effective interface accomplishes the following:

- Provides easy access and visibility for the data
- Simplifies data entry and retrieval with fields that anticipate, where possible, the values to be entered
- Assists in data entry and protects existing data by providing templates and validation rules that enforce rules on the data
- Anticipates user error where possible and prevents or corrects for it
- Offers as much compatibility as possible with current design standards and user expectations in order to minimize the user's learning curve

- Conforms to the user's natural workflow so that data can be easily entered and updated in the relevant order

While this might seem like a lot to ask, it's an ideal to shoot for when deciding on software or developing your own interfaces. While a complete tutorial on interface design is outside the scope of this book, I do want to show you a few tools that will help you to quickly get started building interfaces for MySQL databases.

Website Design Tools

Websites, either on the Internet or on company networks, are the most popular type of interface today. Whether your users are running various versions of Windows, Linux or Mac OS X, they can use the same website without the need to maintain different versions for different users. Website interfaces are also easier and faster to deploy for multiple users than desktop software.

There are many tools available for designing websites, from simple HTML editors to complex graphical development environments. Here are a couple options that you can use to get a website up and running quickly.

WordPress and other Content Management Systems

WordPress is one of the most popular website designers today with over 3 million websites in service. WordPress was originally developed as a blogging tool and has evolved into a *Content Management System (CMS).* It manages web pages, multimedia files, reader comments and users who are authorized to login to the site. The WordPress design interface enables the website designer to focus on the content of a website rather than the code and organization of the files.

WordPress sites are designed through a free and open source online interface that the website designer installs on a local web server or through a hosting account. Many website hosting companies offer to automatically install the WordPress design software on individual hosting accounts. It's a very easy installation that famously takes about five minutes. After that, it's up to the person designing the site to apply the desired themes and graphics and create the site content through the menus and controls that you see in Figure 10.1.

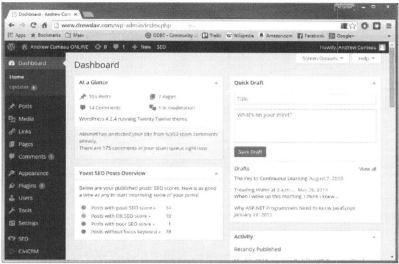

Figure 10.1 - WordPress sites are designed through an online interface which enables the designer to focus on content and appearance rather than coding issues and individual files.

In addition to thousands of free design themes, the WordPress community has made thousands of free WordPress *plug-ins* available. These plug-ins provide specialized functions for the website such as contact forms, photo galleries, search engine optimization, website administration tools and more. There are plug-ins available that will enable users to enter and retrieve job listings and recipes as you've seen in the examples in previous chapters. These can be quickly installed and enable the site to be easily expanded with new functions without a knowledge of programming. The plug-ins are also rated and reviewed by the WordPress user community so that the website designer will have some idea of their quality before installing them.

WordPress is entirely designed in the PHP language and stores all of the data for the website in a MySQL database on the web server. This includes blog posts, page content and data generated by any installed plug-ins. During the initial installation, the website designer creates a MySQL database on the server and makes the necessary changes in the *wp-config.php* file in the root directory of the website.

```
// ** MySQL settings - You can get this info from your web host
** //
/** The name of the database for WordPress */
define('DB_NAME', 'site_DB');

/** MySQL database username */
define('DB_USER', 'siteadmin');

/** MySQL database password */
define('DB_PASSWORD', 'admin_password');

/** MySQL hostname */
define('DB_HOST', 'localhost');
```

Assuming the database user specified in this file has been given the appropriate rights to the database, these few settings enable WordPress to create all the tables and other objects necessary to maintain the website. After this, the website designer might never have to work with the database again as WordPress completely manages its own data. It's still a good idea to understand the basics of how MySQL works in case something goes wrong. It's also good to know how user permissions work in MySQL and to create a separate database user for WordPress to use for accessing the database.

You can learn more about WordPress and download the software from the official site at WordPress.org. If you created an AMP environment (Apache - MySQL - PHP) as shown in earlier chapters, you can even install and run WordPress locally to evaluate it. While WordPress is the most popular content management system, it's not the only one. Joomla (Joomla.org) and Drupal (Drupal.org) are also free and open source content management systems that use MySQL to store their data. While WordPress might be the easiest to learn and use, Joomla and Drupal also have a dedicated following.

CiviCRM

CiviCRM is a web-based Customer Relationship Management software that can be heavily customized to meet the needs of many companies and organizations. The word 'customer' is used in a very general sense here as the software includes modules to manage many types of relationships including:

- Clients
- Contributors
- Event Attendees
- Grant and Charity Recipients
- Volunteers

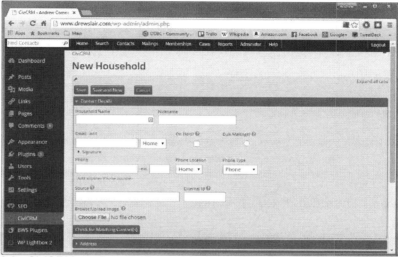

Figure 10.2 - CiviCRM can be used in combination with a content management system such as WordPress (shown here) to create custom data entry systems for managing various types of contacts.

CiviCRM is actually installed as a plug-in for WordPress, Joomla or Drupal, the content management systems mentioned in the last section. It is also designed with PHP and uses MySQL to store the data entered. Even though it's integrated into these systems, it's worth mentioning on its own because of the degree to which it can be customized by individual users. The default installation includes a wide range of standard fields for gathering contact information. The user can easily add additional fields to store information specific to an organization. Existing data entry screens can be customized in order to gather the necessary information and accommodate the order in which information is obtained.

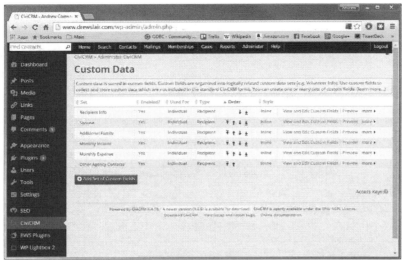

Figure 10.3 - Custom data fields can be easily created with CiviCRM to allow for organization-specific data to be maintained.

CiviCRM can use the existing MySQL database for the content management system or it can maintain its own. A separate database is preferred as stated by the documentation. Regardless of which option is used, the integration of CiviCRM with the website enables data to be entered through forms on the website itself as well as through the CiviCRM interface presented to users who are logged into the system. Users who are willing to learn PHP programming can also design their own features that will hook into the program's data.

If you would like to know more about CiviCRM, you can find full information on the official site at CiviCRM.org.

Desktop Interfaces

Connecting to MySQL from the Desktop

While the majority of users will probably access MySQL through a web interface, there are a couple of tools that can be used to create user-friendly forms and reports for the local desktop. These interfaces can be used to supplement whatever website is used to access the data or to administer data behind the scenes.

In previous chapters, you saw how to connect to MySQL with database management tools such as MySQL Workbench and SQL Buddy. These tools are specifically designed to connect directly to a MySQL server instance and access the database objects within it. Many user interface tools, on the other hand, will need to connect to MySQL indirectly through a programming interface known as *ODBC (Open Database Connectivity)*. ODBC is an *application programming interface (API)* that acts as a middleman between an interface designer such as OpenOffice Base or Microsoft Access and the MySQL database. It provides standardized functions that the user interface design software can use to communicate with different types of databases. This API is not visible to the user but operates in the background, passing commands, queries and query results between the user interface and database as needed.

In order to connect through ODBC, you first need to have the ODBC drivers installed on your system. These can be downloaded either from the MySQL website at dev.mysql.com or installed through the Linux command line.

- On the MySQL website, the Connector/ODBC downloads are available from the MySQL Connectors page at http://dev.mysql.com/downloads/connector/. The connectors are available for both 32-bit and 64-bit systems. If you're installing the connector package on a 64-bit system, it's safe and perhaps even necessary to install both versions in order to connect to various data sources.

- From the Linux command line, use the following command to install the connectors:

```
sudo apt-get install libmyodbc
```

After you install the necessary ODBC drivers, you'll need to specify a data source for your programming software to use. Some programming environments such as Microsoft Visual Studio can use connection strings that access their own specific drivers. For others, such as OpenOffice, you'll need to setup an ODBC data source for the specific database that you want to connect to, either on the local machine or on a remote server.

Windows

In the Windows Control Panel, look for the Administrative Tools section and select **Data Sources (ODBC)**. This will open the ODBC Data Sources Administrator where you can define the following types of data sources.

- **User DSN** - This data source is defined only for the user who is currently logged into the machine.

- **System DSN** - System data sources are available to all users but you must have Administrator access in order to create them.

- **File DSN** - File DSNs are saved to a text file and can be copied to other machines that have the appropriate drivers installed although not all applications can use them.

Starting with either the **System DSN** or **User DSN** tab in the ODBC Data Source Administrator:

1. Click the **Add** button to add a new data source.
2. You will need to select a driver to use for the data source and you might see two MySQL ODBC sources on your system, one for ANSI and one for Unicode. The Unicode driver will function regardless of the character set used by your database although it might sacrifice a little bit of speed to do this. Choose the one you prefer based on your data.
3. At this point, the MySQL Connector screen will appear and you can fill in the information for the connection.

After you click the **OK** button, the data source will show up under the User or System DSN list and will be available to applications on the system.

Figure 10.4 - Setting up an ODBC data source for a MySQL database.

Linux

Linux maintains the list of data sources in a text file under the /etc directory. After you ensure that the MySQL ODBC drivers are installed as directed above, you will need to edit or create the /etc/odbc.ini file to provide the details for each MySQL data source that you want to be available on the system. Here's the entire text of a sample file from a Linux Mint system.

```
[ODBC Data Sources]
odbcname      = MyODBC 3.51 Driver DSN

[JobSearchPlus]
Driver        = /usr/lib/i386-linux-gnu/libmyodbc.so
Description   = MyODBC 3.51 Driver DSN
SERVER        = localhost
PORT          = 3306
USER          = ODBCUser
Password      =
Database      = jobsearch_plus
OPTION        = 3
SOCKET        =

[Default]
Driver        = /usr/lib/i386-linux-gnu/libmyodbc.so
Description   = MyODBC 3.51 Driver DSN
SERVER        = localhost
PORT          = 3306
USER          = root
Password      =
Database      =
```

```
OPTION       =
SOCKET       =
```

It's not necessary to provide the password if you would prefer to have the user login through the application, so long as the application will prompt for it. Once you save the file, the data sources will be available under the name provided in the square brackets at the top of each listing as shown above.

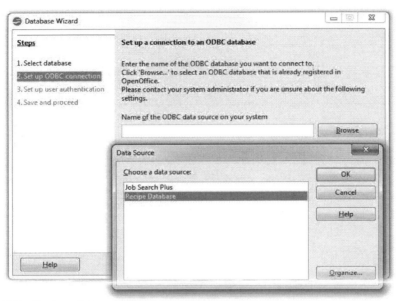

Figure 10.5 - System data sources can be used to connect interface design programs such as OpenOffice Base (shown here) to a MySQL database.

Mac OS X

The official ODBC Administrator utility has been removed from the later releases of OS X but, as of this writing, you can still download it from Apple's support site at https://support.apple.com/db/DL895 and it still installs and works with the El Capitan release. ODBC Manager from ODBCManager.net is an alternative that's advertised as a replacement for the old administrator program.

Both programs will be installed under the **Utilities** folder in OS X and, with either one, you can setup User and System DSNs using the ODBC drivers installed from MySQL.com. You can do this by clicking the **Add** button on the main screen and filling in the details including a

Data Source Name and a description if desired. Then click **Add** on this screen to add a keyword for each attribute of the connection including the database name and login information. See Figure 10.6 for an example.

Figure 10.5 shows part of the Database Wizard from OpenOffice Base. When you start Base in either Linux or Windows, it asks if you want to open an existing database or connect to an external database. It also enables connections to a variety of database types, including MySQL. The ODBC connection portion of the wizard accesses the list of data sources that are defined on the system in either Windows or Linux.

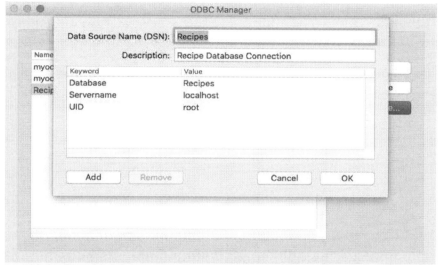

Figure 10.6 - The ODBC Manager is a free download which you can use to create data source entries in Mac OS X.

OpenOffice / LibreOffice

OpenOffice is a free office suite from Oracle that's similar to Microsoft Office. It contains all the standard applications including word processing, spreadsheet and presentation software. Because it's open source software, other software developers are able to make changes to it and distribute their own versions. LibreOffice is the result of one of those development efforts from a company known as The Document Foundation and it's now distributed as an alternative version of OpenOffice. Both titles are available for multiple operating systems including Linux, Windows and OS X.

Base is the database portion of both office suites and can connect to many types of data including MySQL, Microsoft Access, spreadsheets and other types through ODBC. Whether you're connecting to another data source or to Base's native format, Base creates a new database file with the "*.ODB" extension. If you're using it to connect to a database on a MySQL server, it will ask for a user name and password and then create links to all of the tables and views within that database to which the user name you supply has permissions. MySQL continues to manage the database itself, including relationships between tables, while Base simply acts as the user interface and reports back any messages from the server. Base also gives you the option to register the new database file for use as a data source within other OpenOffice / LibreOffice applications. This means you can access the data through spreadsheets in the *Calc* application or for mailing lists in word processing documents.

Once you've connected to MySQL data with Base, you can use the application to create and save queries to be run as needed. Data entry forms and custom reports can also be created using the available tables and fields. Base can also be used to make changes to the table structures or even create entirely new tables on the server although it does not have the wealth of options available through MySQL Workbench or the other dedicated database design programs. Also, stored procedures and functions are not displayed through the interface and cannot be easily accessed through OpenOffice, if at all. If you plan on using OpenOffice or LibreOffice as your interface designer, this is something to take into account when designing the database.

Microsoft Access

For many years, Microsoft Access has been the leading desktop database management system on the market. Like OpenOffice, it's a software that can be used to access a variety of data from different sources, even within the same database application. One database file can contain native Access tables along with links to MySQL or

Microsoft SQL Server tables, spreadsheets and remote databases. Data can be read from and written to these sources interchangeably. Access can link to MySQL data through the same ODBC data sources that OpenOffice uses.

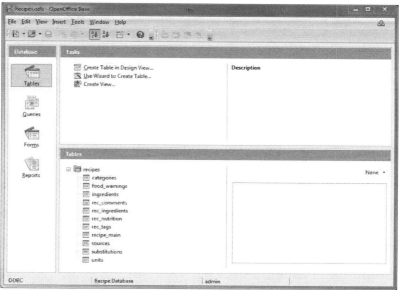

Figure 10.7 - The Base application in OpenOffice and LibreOffice can be used to access MySQL databases through ODBC and create forms and reports for users to work with the data.

Figure 10.8 shows the main job lead screen from the Microsoft Access version of Job Search Plus. This is a great example of how one form can pull together information from many tables so that the user can easily edit it as needed. Access also has the Visual Basic for Applications (VBA) language which advanced users can use to carry out sophisticated operations on the data and to manage the forms, reports and menus within the user interface. While Microsoft is a much more sophisticated database program than OpenOffice Base, it has the drawback of being limited to the Windows platform.

While OpenOffice connects to a single external data source when creating the database file, Microsoft Access can connect to multiple sources as needed. It still leaves the management of the data and the application of rules such as foreign key constraints and indexes to the server. Access has the option of either linking to the external data or importing data into its native file. This provides the flexibility to work locally with reference data that doesn't change often or to link to data that's being managed and updated elsewhere.

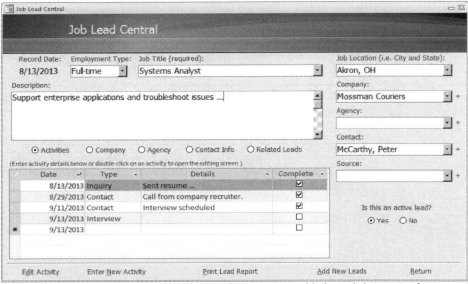

Figure 10.8 - Microsoft Access can be used to create sophisticated data entry forms and reports from MySQL and many other data sources.

Both Microsoft Access and OpenOffice / LibreOffice are desktop database systems so they require an installation of the software on each machine that will be accessing the data. Access does have a free runtime edition that can open an Access database file without the ability to change the design of forms, reports and other parts of the interface. It's a substantial installation, however, and requires the database program interface to be designed so that it can run without any of the Access design features available.

Designing From Scratch

If none of the solutions above meet the needs of your application, you can always program the application yourself. The big question is which language you should use and this strongly depends on what kind of application that you want to design. While there is some overlap, different languages often focus on different environments.

Learning a new language and learning to use it well also takes time and doing so while building a critical application is not a course I usually recommend. Still, I do encourage anyone who is interested to learn at least one language even if they just want exposure to programming. Here are a few to consider when working with MySQL.

PHP

As mentioned earlier, many tools for the web are programmed in PHP. This includes WordPress and other content management systems. Because it's so popular, it's important to at least know the basics of this scripting language if you want to do serious web design. PHP code is integrated with many web pages and you can sometimes spot its presence in a page by the ".php" extension in the address. PHP is a server-side language which means that all of its instructions are interpreted on the server which then generates code that the local browser can understand. This allows PHP to easily access MySQL and other database software with a couple of commands.

```
function connect_local($user, $password)
{
        $connected = mysql_connect('localhost', $user, $password);

        if ($connected)
                return 'Success';
        else
                return 'Could not connect: '.mysql_error();
}
```

PHP has a number of commands like the ones in the function shown above that are meant specifically for working with MySQL. Other commands select the default database and direct queries and commands to the server. PHP can directly access the local MySQL installation.

Because PHP is so popular, there are plenty of resources for learning the language, including the main reference at PHP.net and many other online forums. Because it's a text-based language, it can be written in any HTML editor or even a simple text editor. It is necessary to have the interpreter installed in order to generate PHP web pages. Therefore, you will either need to upload your pages to a web server in order to test them or install PHP on your own system along with Apache or another web server software. This can be done by creating an AMP environment as detailed in Chapter II.

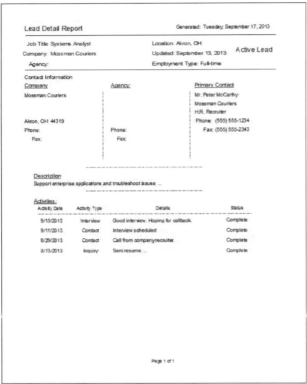

Figure 10.9 - Microsoft Access is also known for its reports designer which can quickly produce informative printable reports.

ASP.NET (C# / Visual Basic)

Microsoft's .NET languages are also very prominent influences on both the Web and the Windows Desktop. ASP.NET, which is a combination of HTML and .NET code, is the second most popular server-side language as of August 2015 although it's a *distant* second to PHP. Despite powering just over 16% of the current websites, ASP.NET still has plenty of support and documentation available from Microsoft and community forums.

ASP.NET has a couple of advantages over PHP. Microsoft Visual Studio, which is the primary development environment for the .NET languages, offers a very sophisticated graphical programming environment with a wide selection of drag-and-drop web components that can be quickly configured and deployed. The coding environment itself offers Intellisense and auto-completion of commands which is helpful to both beginning and seasoned programmers. The files involved in a .NET application are a good deal more structured than in PHP but the Visual Studio environment also takes care of a lot of code and file management which makes things easier on the programmer.

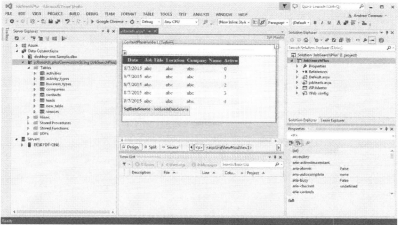

Figure 10.10 - Visual Studio is a powerful graphical IDE for developing .NET applications for the Web or the Windows Desktop.

MySQL has connection drivers that are used specifically for .NET and they're available as a free download from the Downloads section on dev.mysql.com. As shown in Figure 10.10, the Visual Studio IDE is able to connect to the server through these drivers and access all of the database objects available to the user account supplied. The Visual Studio Community 2013 edition is now available as a free download from Microsoft and contains all the functionality previously available through the Visual Studio Professional edition.

When you create a new ASP.NET application with Visual Studio, it offers a choice of using C# (pronounced 'C Sharp') or Visual Basic as the .NET language for the project. While Visual Basic is well known as a beginner's language and is certainly easy to learn, I strongly recommend C# as the choice for all new programmers. Its syntax is derived from the C / C++ programming languages which are also the inspiration for other popular languages including PHP and JavaScript. C# is not difficult to learn, especially with all the resources currently available. Being proficient in this language will help you to learn additional languages if you choose and to benefit from programming resources that use C syntax as the default for algorithm examples.

Visual Studio enables you to create a variety of other applications including Windows Desktop apps, command line applications and Windows services. These apps can also access your MySQL database if you choose.

Java

Java is a cross-platform language used to create applications run in many environments, from web servers to smartphones. While it's only used on approximately 3% of websites, the fact that its applications can be run on many platforms without being rewritten is part of what makes it popular. As with other languages, its syntax also resembles the C++ language which makes it easier for those familiar with that syntax to learn.

While PHP uses an interpreter and ASP.NET uses the .NET libraries, Java uses the Java Virtual Machine in order to run in various environments. This is a piece of software that you might have seen installed on your own computer, maybe under the name Java Runtime Environment.

The Java programming language is currently maintained by Oracle, the same company that owns MySQL. Oracle also offers NetBeans, a free, cross-platform development software that supports software development with Java, PHP, HTML5 and other languages. Eclipse is another development tool that can be used to develop with Java, PHP, C++ and many other languages. Java has its own set of *Java Database Connectivity drivers (JDBC)* for MySQL and other databases. These can also be downloaded from the Downloads page on MySQL.com.

For more information on getting started with Java programming, check out the following links:

- New to Java Programming Center - http://www.oracle.com/technetwork/topics/newtojava
- NetBeans Development Software - http://www.netbeans.org
- Eclipse Foundation - http://www.eclipse.org

Supplemental Languages

While any of the languages mentioned above will get you off to a good start, development of a web or desktop application requires knowledge of multiple technologies . Even if you're working with other developers, it's important to have a good foundation of knowledge so that you can understand how all the parts work and effectively communicate with the team. If you're really interested in being a programmer, then picking up new languages is an important part of the job. While languages do change and evolve, obsolescence isn't really an issue. This is because once a language becomes accepted and widely-used, there will be a large amount of code developed in that language which will need to be supported and maintained for a long time to come. Also, the programming skills that you learn in one language will assist you in the languages you learn later.

Here are a few languages and technologies that you should be familiar with if you want to be active in software development. To get started with any of these technologies, you can check out W3Schools.com which offers free lessons or any one of many other online tutorials.

- **HTML** - HyperText Markup Language, the primary language behind most web pages, is an essential skill for anyone wanting to develop software for the web. Since it's primarily a formatting language that uses specific tags to format plain text, it's relatively easy to learn. You can start with a few basic tags for creating a web page and applying some formatting and then learn more as you go.

- **CSS** - Cascading Style Sheets are used by web pages to separate the formatting instructions from the actual content. This reduces the size of the files to be delivered over the web which helps web pages load faster and improves the user experience. CSS also enables the web developer to specify a specific format for different types of information such as section headers and glossary terms. If that format needs to be changed across an entire site, it can be done by changing one line in the CSS file rather than having to hunt down all references. CSS can be used to create very sophisticated designs for websites. When used properly, the entire appearance of a site can be changed while maintaining the content simply by switching out the CSS file for a new one.

- **JavaScript** - JavaScript is the client-side scripting language that is supported by many of the web browsers that you use every day. The language enables calculations and formatting to be applied within the browser on the local machine or device without going back to the remote web server or refreshing the page. This provides a better user experience overall.

- **SQL** - As mentioned many times in previous chapters, Structured Query Language is the primary language that you will use for communicating with databases from your application. The basic commands are simple enough to learn and, as with HTML, once you've acquired the basics, you can build upon them to become proficient at your leisure.

Chapter Summary

Most databases have some kind of software interface that sits between the data and the user. The main purpose of this interface is to provide the necessary access to the data and to promote the speed and accuracy with which users can enter new data into the system. An efficient interface serves both the end user and the data owners as it ensures that the data in the system is accurate and reliable. Software can use a variety of methods and tools to assist in data entry but ultimately, it's up to the designers to be familiar with the process for which the software is being designed, to take the extra time to talk to the end users and do the necessary testing to ensure that the user is able to understand and work with the software. This effort on the part of software designers is what determines the success of the application.

There are many software tools available which programmers and designers at all levels of experience can use to create database applications. Regardless of the pace at which the technology is changing, each of these products and technologies represents an opportunity to learn more about software design. Each new product and programming language carries forward many of the existing principles with which those who have taken the time to master the current technology will be familiar. The more tools and technologies an individual is familiar with, the better positioned he or she is to be able to deliver the necessary software solutions when called upon.

For Further Study

Review Questions

1. What is the main purpose of writing an interface for a database application?

2. What are two goals that are accomplished by an effective user interface?

3. What is one advantage of a website application over a Windows desktop application.

4. Where does WordPress find the information it needs to connect to a MySQL database.

5. What is the relationship between CiviCRM and WordPress?

6. What is the difference between a User DSN and System DSN in Windows?

7. Where does Linux store the information on system data sources?

8. If you wanted to display PHP files in your computer's browser, what steps would you need to take?

9. What do you need in order to connect a Microsoft Visual Studio application to a MySQL database.

10. What are two development packages that you can use to program with Java?

11. What is the relation of Cascading Style Sheets (CSS) to HTML web pages?

12. What is the main difference in the way PHP and JavaScript operate?

Terms to Remember

Application Programming Interface (API) - A software that functions as an intermediary between a programming language or design software and another part of the system. An API provides a standardized set of commands and functions that can be used by different user interfaces to communicate in the background with databases, operating systems and other resources.

Auto-completion - The ability of a software to predict the words or commands that a user is typing and to offer options for completing the input. In a database environment, this can assist the user in data entry and help to eliminate errors by automatically supplying the needed values.

Content Management System - A software that manages online or other electronic content such as articles, web pages and multimedia. The system provides an interface through which content managers can easily edit existing content and make new content available to an audience.

Customer Relationship Management (CRM) software - A software that enables an organization to manage contacts and all information related to the relationship between the organization and those contacts.

Integrated Development Environment (IDE) - A set of software tools that enables a programmer to write code and compile and deploy applications. These tools are often combined within a single interface from which the programmer can access them.

Intellisense - The ability of a software development interface to analyze code as it's being entered by a programmer and to suggest appropriate commands, options and keywords that the programmer might need to complete the current statement.

Java Database Connectivity (JDBC) - A set of drivers that specifically enable the Java programming language to communicate with various types of databases.

Open Database Connectivity (ODBC) - An application programming interface that enables desktop databases, spreadsheets and other software to communicate with a variety of data sources. ODBC is sometimes used as a generic solution when a software does not have its own method for importing a specific type of data.

Plug-in - A modular software package that is installed as part of a larger software, adding functions that are required to perform specific tasks.

Rapid Application Development (RAD) - Programming tools and methods that allow for the quick development of software with a small amount of planning and documentation. When used in reference to programming tools, it refers to software that enables the designer to quickly create forms, reports and other objects with a minimum of effort.

Software Platform - The environment in which specific software was developed or is designed to run, often referring to some combination of the programming tools with which it was designed and the operating system and hardware used to run it.

User Interface - A group of controls that serves as an intermediary between a program's functions and the user. Interfaces are typically used to provide a less complex form of access to those functions and make them easier to use. In database terms, the interface is whatever software enables the user to enter and retrieve data and which often includes data entry forms and a reporting system.

About the Author

Andrew Comeau is a software programmer and consultant based in Ocala, Florida. Since the 1990s, he has been designing database solutions both independently and for various companies. Since 2000, he has operated the websites Drewslair.com and AndrewComeau.com in order to share programming and design knowledge with others. His previous book, "Microsoft Access for Beginners" started as a successful online series of articles on Drewslair.com. Having achieved modest success as a software programmer, he is now combining his technical and writing talents to pursue a career as an independent consultant and writer.

Made in the USA
Columbia, SC
25 April 2017